PERGAMON INTERNATIONAL LIBRARY
of Science, Technology, Engineering and Social Studies

*The 1000-volume original paperback library in aid of education,
industrial training and the enjoyment of leisure*

Publisher: Robert Maxwell, M.C.

J. BRADSHAW

P9-BXW-868

The Early Window
(PGPS-34)

THE PERGAMON TEXTBOOK
INSPECTION COPY SERVICE

An inspection copy of any book published in the Pergamon International Library
will gladly be sent to academic staff without obligation for their consideration for
course adoption or recommendation. Copies may be retained for a period of 60 days
from receipt and returned if not suitable. When a particular title is adopted or
recommended for adoption for class use and the recommendation results in a sale
of 12 or more copies the inspection copy may be retained with our compliments.
The Publishers will be pleased to receive suggestions for revised editions and new
titles to be published in this important international Library.

Pergamon Titles of Related Interest

Apter TROUBLED CHILDREN/TROUBLED SYSTEMS
Diamond COMPARATIVE TELEVISION NEWS
Furnham/Argyle THE PSYCHOLOGY OF SOCIAL SITUATIONS
Howitt MASS MEDIA AND SOCIAL PROBLEMS
Lorac/Weiss COMMUNICATION AND SOCIAL SKILLS
Rice REPORTING U.S.-EUROPEAN RELATIONS:
Four Nations, Four Newspapers

Related Journals*

CHILD ABUSE AND NEGLECT
CHILDREN AND YOUTH SERVICES REVIEW
JOURNAL OF CHILD PSYCHOLOGY AND PSYCHIATRY

*Free specimen copies available upon request.

PERGAMON GENERAL PSYCHOLOGY SERIES
EDITORS
Arnold P. Goldstein, *Syracuse University*
Leonard Krasner, *SUNY at Stony Brook*

The Early Window
Effects of Television on Children and Youth
Second Edition

Robert M. Liebert
State University of New York at Stony Brook

Joyce N. Sprafkin
Long Island Research Institute,
State University of New York at Stony Brook

Emily S. Davidson
Texas A&M University

PERGAMON PRESS
New York   Oxford   Toronto   Sydney   Paris   Frankfurt

Pergamon Press Offices:

U.S.A.   Pergamon Press Inc., Maxwell House, Fairview Park,
Elmsford, New York 10523, U.S.A.

U.K.   Pergamon Press Ltd., Headington Hill Hall,
Oxford OX3 OBW, England

CANADA   Pergamon Press Canada Ltd., Suite 104, 150 Consumers Road,
Willowdale, Ontario M2J 1P9, Canada

AUSTRALIA   Pergamon Press (Aust.) Pty. Ltd., P.O. Box 544,
Potts Point, NSW 2011, Australia

FRANCE   Pergamon Press SARL, 24 rue des Ecoles,
75240 Paris, Cedex 05, France

FEDERAL REPUBLIC Pergamon Press GmbH, Hammerweg 6
OF GERMANY   6242 Kronberg/Taunus, Federal Republic of Germany

Library of Congress Cataloging in Publication Data

Liebert, Robert M., 1942-
  The early window.

  (Pergamon general psychology series ; 34)
  Includes bibliographical references and index.
  1. Television and children. I. Sprafkin, Joyce N.,
1949- . II. Davidson, Emily S., 1948- . III. Title.
IV. Series.
HQ784.T4L48 1982   305.2′3   82-5327
ISBN 0-08-027548-6   AACR2
ISBN 0-08-027547-8 (pbk.)

Printed in the United States of America

To Eric and Kathy Liebert and Jay Kahn

Contents

Preface

It has been estimated that by the age of 18 a child born today will have spent more time watching television than in any other single activity besides sleep. What are, and will be, the effects of this cumulative exposure?

The question is not a new one. It has been posed repeatedly since the advent of television sets as a common home fixture over three decades ago. Suggested answers, based both on simple opinion and research, have ranged from confident statements that the medium's influence is uniformly undesirable to equally glib assertions that merely watching television entertainment fare can do little to shape children's attitudes and behavior.

By the turn of this decade literally thousands of studies had been done on various aspects of children's exposure to, comprehension of, and reactions to television. Moreover, the issue of television's effects on children has raised significant social questions about possible censorship, and as a result, found its way into several important courtroom battles. After an initial focus on the possible effects of TV violence, investigators turned their attention to using television in more constructive ways, but this effort also turned out to have its tricky side and subtle issues.

The purpose of this book is to provide an account of the theory and research which now bears on television and children's attitudes, development, and behavior, and to explore the social, political, and economic factors that surround these issues. We have tried to write for those most likely to be concerned with television and its role in the future of our society: students, parents, professionals concerned with children's welfare, and men and women in the broadcasting industry or in public office who influence broadcasting policies and practices. Where methodologically complex issues seem to deserve mention, we have tried to explain them in relatively simple, nontechnical terms. We have also provided an appendix to explain briefly the essence of the correlational and experimental methods of social science research as they have been applied to the question of children and television.

The interplay of social science and social policy is both complex and difficult on many counts; we have tried to explain rather than ignore these complexities so as to provide a more complete understanding of our present state of knowledge and of the difficult road that must be followed by anyone who would influence television.

In preparing this volume we received invaluable help from many sources. We are especially grateful to Jerry Frank of Pergamon Press for his wise counsel in the development of this edition, Suzanne Arink for her assistance with the cover design, Dr. Eli A. Rubinstein for his editorial input, Gretchen Daly for her assistance in the preparation of the manuscript, Elizabeth Gable for her technical assistance, and Paula Rohrlick (of Action for Children's Television), Leslie Slocum (of the Television Information Office) and Dr. Carol Keegan (of the Corporation for Public Broadcasting) for providing us with valuable resource materials.

Chapter 1

Background and Issues

OVERVIEW

Television, virtually unknown 40 years ago, is now present in almost every home in the United States and has rapidly spread all over the world. The average child today spends more time in the first 15 years of life watching television than going to school. As a result, it is understandable that thoughtful people everywhere have asked about the effects of all this television viewing on children. In trying to understand and deal with television's effects on children, five issues continue to be raised:

1. Does TV violence instigate aggressive or antisocial behavior or "toughen" children in their acceptance of such behavior in others?
2. Do TV portrayals of minorities and women cultivate social attitudes and stereotypes?
3. Do television commercials take unfair advantage of children?
4. Does commercial broadcast television fulfill its responsibility to "serve the public interest," which it assumes by accepting a license to use the public airwaves?
5. In what ways and under what circumstances (if any) should the TV programming or advertising content that children see be subjected to censorship by government or private groups?

The purpose of this book is to shed light on each of these issues by describing and analyzing the social science research, politics, and legal considerations surrounding them.

Television has changed our daily lives more than any other technological innovation of the twentieth century. To a remarkable degree, people plan their personal schedules to accommodate television. Meals and many social activities are scheduled around television programming. Virtually everyone has a television. The average set in the United States is on more than six hours a day. Television is so commonplace and taken for granted that it is startling to recall that it made its public appearance only recently.

THE SPECTACULAR RISE OF TELEVISION

Imagine that we could curl ourselves back in time to 1945, stop an average seven-year-old child on the street and ask: "What's an *airplane*?" The youngster would surely know what an airplane is and would probably be puzzled by our easy question. But suppose we had asked instead: "What's a *television*?" We can be almost certain that our young subject would *not* have been able to answer this question in 1945 even though virtually every seven year old in the United States could answer it today. It is easy to forget that at the end of World War II airplanes, telephones, and movie theaters were all commonplace, but most children had never seen or heard of television. Figure 1.1 shows the percentage of U.S. households with television sets for every five-year-period from 1940 to 1980.

When television was first introduced, it was little more than a luxury for the wealthy. But it was a luxury with great appeal, especially for children. Children whose families had a television set quickly became popular; groups of neighborhood youngsters swarmed to the nearest TV-equipped home to soak up early cartoon and adventure offerings. Given this response, it is not surprising that within two decades virtually every American home had a TV and many had two or more. (Despite inflation, the cost of TV sets has decreased over the years. While the average cost of a black and white receiver was $279 in 1947, by 1976 the cost had dropped to $89!) Today the overwhelming majority of households have a color receiver.

Television use

Television use in the United States quickly stabilized, cutting out its own substantial niche of time in our daily lives. When television entertainment is constantly available through the day, evening and night (as it has been in the United States for many years), the average household television set is on between five and six hours a day (Steinberg, 1980), a figure that has been remarkably constant for two decades. (See Table 1.1.) Of course, the average person does not watch this much television. Sometimes the set is watched only by the adults or only by the children in a household—occasionally it is on but not being watched by anyone at all.

Still, there is a good deal of actual television viewing. The typical adult watches television between two and three hours per day. Most children are now exposed to television by the time they have had their first birthday and have become purposeful viewers with favorite shows by the time they are three. Viewing time increases and peaks at about two and one-half hours per day just before elementary school. At first, the onset of school seems to diminish available TV time slightly. However, from about age eight viewing increases steadily to an average of almost four hours per day during early adolescence. Viewing then levels off in the later teens at two to three hours a

Fig. 1.1. Percentage of U.S. Households with Television, 1940–1980.

Source: From data reported in Sterling and Haight (1978) and the Television Information Office (1981).

3

**Table 1.1. Average Amount of Time a Television was *ON*
in U.S. Households, 1960–1980.**

Year	Average Amount of Time
1960	5 hrs. + 6 min.
1962	5 hrs. + 6 min.
1964	5 hrs. + 13 min.
1966	5 hrs. + 32 min.
1968	5 hrs. + 46 min.
1971	5 hrs. + 59 min.
1972	6 hrs. + 2 min.
1974	6 hrs. + 12 min.
1976	6 hrs. + 7 min.
1978	6 hrs. + 10 min.
1980	6 hrs. + 13 min.

Source: Adapted from Steinberg (1980) and Broadcasting Yearbook (1980).

day. This same basic pattern, found in several studies over the past 20 years,
is shown in Figure 1.2.*

A similar pattern holds outside the United States. In a review of international TV use, Murray (1980) shows that while the average number of
hours viewed varied somewhat, the same basic developmental pattern — increasing viewing time to a peak in early adolescence followed by a decline —
held across a number of European countries, Canada, and Australia. What
accounted for variations in actual TV use between countries was, to a great
extent, the amount of programming available and the hours of broadcast.
Averaged over all ages, children in countries with large amounts of television available (e.g., Australia, Canada, Japan, United Kingdom, and
United States) watch about two to three hours per day, whereas those in
countries with more limited broadcasts (e.g., Germany, Austria, Italy,
Sweden, Norway) watch about one to two hours daily.

---

*It should be noted that estimates of "average" use do not reflect the tremendous variations in
usage. For example, in one study (Lyle and Hoffman, 1972), 25% of the sixth and tenth graders participating watched eight and one-half hours on Sunday and five and one-half hours on
school days! More than one-third of the first graders in the same study watched four or more
hours on a typical school day, while 10% reported no viewing at all. Some (but by no means
all) of this variability is related to family background. Children from the lower social class and
minority backgrounds watch more television than middle and upper middle class white children, brighter children tend to watch less than other children, and a child's viewing habits are
quite similar to those of the child's parents.

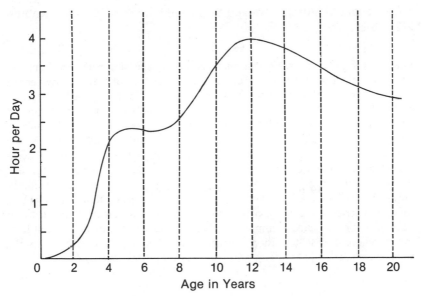

Fig. 1.2. Average Hours of TV Viewing by Age.

Source: Comstock et al. (1978), p. 178. [Reprinted with permission by The Rand Corporation and Columbia University Press.]

How television has changed family life

The appearance of television and its meteoric rise in the 1950s had a significant impact on the structuring of family life. Johnson (1967) reported that 60% of families changed their sleeping patterns because of TV, 55% altered meal times, and 78% used TV as an "electronic babysitter." He also documented that engineers in some large metropolitan areas had to redesign city water systems to accommodate the drop in pressure caused by heavy lavatory use during prime time commercials.

Robinson (1972) investigated the impact of television by comparing daily activities of set owners and nonowners in 15 locations in 11 countries.* Noting that previous research had not adequately considered all the activities which might have been affected by television, he employed the technique of *time budgets*; he asked people to fill out diaries concerning all of their activities throughout a full 24-hour day. Activities that decreased were sleep, social gatherings away from home, other leisure activities (e.g., corre-

---

*Belgium, Bulgaria, Czechoslovakia, East Germany, France, Hungary, Peru, Poland, United States, West Germany, and Yugoslavia.

spondence and knitting), conversation, and household care. Robinson (1972) observed:

> Finally, it is of considerable interest to compare television with other innovations of the twentieth century. Comparing the amount of travel by owners of automobiles with that of nonowners, we were especially surprised that cross-nationally automobile owners on the average spent only six percent more time in transit than nonowners. While automobile owners were undoubtedly able to cover far more territory in the time they spent traveling, the overall shift is pale indeed compared with the 58 percent increase in media usage apparently occasioned by the influence of television. Cross-national data also indicate that time spent on housework is not grossly affected by the acquisition of home appliances like washing machines and dryers. Rather, it appears that time saved on these basic chores as a result of labor-saving devices is quickly channeled into other activities designed to improve the appearance of the home. Thus, at least in the temporal sense, television appears to have had a greater influence on the structure of daily life than any other innovation in this century [p. 428].

TELEVISION'S SOCIAL EFFECTS ON CHILDREN

We can see that television made a spectacular appearance and now has a permanent place in our lives. What effect does all this viewing have on us? It is hard to know how to even begin to answer this question, except to state the well-established fact that we have spent our time very differently since TV's arrival.

Is exposure to television entertainment making us think or act differently? Does it change our attitudes and shape our feelings and reactions? Most adults believe television entertainment does not have an important social influence on them (see Steiner, 1963). It is, after all, only entertainment. But children are seen as more susceptible than adults, and concerns about the effects of other media on children's social and personality development were voiced long before the appearance of television. In fact, sex and brutal violence were taken out of comic books and movies by the forces of censorship groups, created by those concerned about children's social and moral development (Cowan, 1978).

Today's children are getting a far heavier dose of television entertainment than their grandparents got out of comic books, movies, and phonograph records combined. A certain amount of what children see on television is considered to be "children's programming" (or kidvid), mostly Saturday and Sunday morning shows. However, *most* of the programs children watch are designed for adult or family audiences.

RECURRING ISSUES

Because television is so widespread and children watch it so much, many people have been concerned about what television is "doing" to children. There are five basic recurring issues, each with its parallel concern in movies, comic books, and popular music.

Instigation of violent, aggressive, or antisocial behavior

The possibility that certain television content stimulates unwanted or disapproved attitudes or behavior has received more attention than any other issue.

Dramatic instances. The first major study done in the United States, Schramm, Lyle and Parker's *Television in the Lives of Our Children* (1961), presented a collection of documented instances in which TV was implicated in the aggressive or antisocial behavior of otherwise innocent youth. Here are four instances reported by Schramm and his associates:

> In a Boston suburb, a nine-year-old boy reluctantly showed his father a report card heavily decorated with red marks, then proposed one way of getting at the heart of the matter; they could give the teacher a box of poisoned chocolates for Christmas. "It's easy, Dad, they did it on television last week. A man wanted to kill his wife, so he gave her candy with poison in it and she didn't know who did it" [p. 161].

> In Brooklyn, New York, a six-year-old son of a policeman asked his father for real bullets because his little sister "doesn't die for real when I shoot her like they do when Hopalong Cassidy kills 'em" [p. 161].

> In Los Angeles, a housemaid caught a seven-year-old boy in the act of sprinkling ground glass into the family's lamb stew. There was no malice behind the act. It was purely experimental, having been inspired by curiosity to learn whether it would really work as well as it did on television [p. 161].

> A 13-year-old Oakville [California] boy, who said he received his inspiration from a television program, admitted to police . . . that he sent threatening notes to a . . . school teacher. His inspiration for the first letter came while he was helping the pastor of his church write some letters. When the minister left the office for an hour, the boy wrote his first poison pen letter. "I got the idea when I saw it happen on TV," he told Juvenile Sgt. George Rathouser. "I saw it on the 'Lineup' program" [p. 164].

Equally compelling instances were reported at about the same time in testimony before the United States Senate Subcommittee to investigate juvenile delinquency. Below is a sample of the documented instances provided to the Subcommittee (U.S. Senate, 1961).

On July 9, 1959, the *New York Journal-American* reported that four young boys desiring a human skull for their club activities, broke into a Jersey City mausoleum, pried open a coffin and took one. They brought the skull to their clubroom where they desecrated it by sticking a lighted candle in it. Astonished police said the club members — seven boys, whose ages ranged 11 to 14 — got the idea from a television horror show.

The Chicago Tribune reported on November 22, 1959, that two Chicago boys had been arrested for attempting to extort $500 from a firm through a bomb threat. They threatened the owners and members of their families if police were notified. The boys . . . stated they got their idea from television.

According to the *Reading Eagle*, Reading, Pa., of March 2, 1960, a 16-year-old boy was arrested after neighbors spotted him entering the cellar of a home. He was wearing gloves and said he learned the trick of wearing gloves so that he did not leave fingerprints from television shows which he had watched.

A college athlete was arrested in Grand Junction, Colo., in April, 1960, after he had mailed letters threatening to kill the wife of a bank president unless he was paid $5,000. At the time of his arrest, he stated he got his idea from television shows.

The *New York Journal-American* reported on December 22, 1960, that police arrested an 11-year-old who admitted having burglarized Long Island homes for more than $1,000 in cash and valuables. His accomplice was identified as a 7-year-old friend. The boy said he learned the technique of burglary by seeing how it was done on television [pp. 1923–1924].

As a result of the foregoing reports, entertainment television came to be seen by social scientists in the early 1960s as potentially exerting a great influence on the young. Inspired by his own studies confirming that even young children can learn specific novel aggressive behaviors from television, Stanford psychologist Albert Bandura published an article in *Look* magazine in 1963 entitled, "What TV Violence Can Do To Your Child." The first paragraph of the article read:

If parents could buy packaged psychological influences to administer in regular doses to their children, I doubt that many would deliberately select Western gun slingers, hopped-up psychopaths, deranged sadists, slap-stick buffoons and the like, unless they entertained rather peculiar ambitions for their growing offspring. Yet such examples of behavior are delivered in quantity, with no direct charge, to millions of households daily. Harried parents can easily turn off demanding children by turning on a television set; as a result, today's youth is being raised on a heavy dosage of televised aggression and violence [p. 46].

Bandura's article popularized the term *TV violence*. As can be seen from the foregoing extract, he equated TV violence with almost all objectionable behavior.

These concerns, expressed from academia, were paralleled by Congressional hearings. Senator Thomas Dodd, who between 1961 and 1964 headed a Senate subcommittee on children's television, said:

> Glued to the TV set from the time they can walk, our children are getting an intensive training in all phases of crime from the ever-increasing array of Westerns and crime-detective programs available to them. The past decade has seen TV come of age. However, the same decade has witnessed the violence content in programs skyrocket and delinquency in real life grow almost two hundred percent [cited in Merriam, 1968, p. 43].

TV violence and the "toughening" of values. Instigation to violent and antisocial acts is only one of the concerns raised by TV violence. An equally important question is whether exposure to such entertainment thickens children's skins to real-life violence and aggression committed by others. Eve Merriam captured the essence of this concern as early as 1964, in an article in *Ladies Home Journal*:

> The violent entertainment forms affect children in other ways. If they are not becoming actively delinquent — our "good" middle-class children, yours and mine — they are becoming passively jaded. As a kind of self-protection, they develop thick skins to avoid being upset by the gougings, smashings and stompings they see on TV. As the voice of reason is shown to be a swift uppercut to the chin, child viewers cannot afford to get involved, for if they did, their emotions would be shredded. So they keep "cool," distantly unaffected. Boredom sets in, and the whole cycle starts over again. Bring on another show with even more bone-crushing and teeth-smashing so the viewers will react [p. 45].

Stereotyping and the cultivation of attitudes

The concept that television is a teacher reaches far beyond the issue of TV violence. If television can teach by providing examples, then children and perhaps adults may be influenced in a host of ways by the roles, relationships, and values that are implicit in the TV entertainment they see.

Racial stereotyping. On these grounds, the National Association for the Advancement of Colored People (NAACP) demanded in 1951 that CBS stop broadcasting its only series featuring black characters, *Amos and Andy*. The NAACP described the deleterious effect they felt the series was having and provided a "content analysis" of the series as justification for their concern:

> [*Amos and Andy*] tends to strengthen the conclusion among uninformed and prejudiced people that Negroes are inferior, lazy, dumb and dishonest . . . Negro doctors are shown as quacks and thieves. Negro lawyers are shown as slippery cowards, ignorant of their profession and without ethics. Negro women are shown as cackling, screaming shrews, in big-mouth close-ups, using street slang, just short of vulgarity. All Negroes are shown as dodging work of any kind. Millions of white Americans see this Amos 'n' Andy picture and think the entire race is the same (*News from NAACP*, 1951, pp. 4–5].

Sex stereotyping. Racial stereotypes are only one of several disapproved attitudes that might be transmitted by television. In 1970, Marya Mannes, a feminist spokesperson, charged television with sustaining many cultural stereotypes about women's roles. She especially targeted television commercials which

> reinforce, like an insistent drill, the assumption that a woman's only valid function is that of wife, mother, and servant of men: the inevitable sequel to her earlier function as sex object and swinger.

> [Mannes went on to suggest that only four types of women appear in TV ads]: the gorgeous teen-age swinger with bouncing locks; the young mother teaching her baby girl the right soap for skin care; the middle-aged housewife with a voice like a power saw; and the old lady with dentures and irregularity. . . . Only one woman on a commercial . . . has a job; a comic plumber pushing *Comet* [pp. 66–67].

Commercialism

As we will explain in Chapter 2, because U.S. commercial television is corporate, it is responsible to stockholders. Its profit derives from advertising revenues, and this ultimately creates pressure to show advertisements that sell as effectively as possible. Moreover, advertisements directed to children use a variety of sophisticated techniques to appeal to young viewers. Parents claim that children are unable to understand the commercials and that advertising to children over television is unfair. In the words of Peggy Charren (1974), President and founder of Action for Children's Television:

> The ultimate goal of the thirty seconds worth of information contained in the message must be to manipulate the child to desire, want and need the product.

No industry will invest forty million to convince these two- to eleven-year-olds that they do *not* need a lot of these products to be happy, healthy, wealthy and wise. . . .

Ads for the Lone Ranger show that famous Mr. Fix-it with his sidekick Tonto, with the Bad Guy, and with adventure kits. Each of them is "sold separately" and priced separately, but they are all shown in the same commercial, because it's no fun to play with one part without the others. The prices of these and other combined sets (G.I. Joe and his accoutrements, Kung Fu and his friends) is enough to make even an affluent parent shudder [p. 4].

In addition, there are concerns about *what* is advertised on television. Because of pricing and other considerations it makes more sense to advertise manufactured treats than fresh farm items. As a result,

A child watching television programs for children sees ads for sugared cereals, candy, snack foods and sugared drinks in an unceasing barrage and learns nothing of the essentials for a balanced diet. On a typical Saturday morning a child will see no ads for fruit, vegetables, cheese, eggs or other valuable nutritional foods but instead will be cajoled to buy a new sugared cereal with a toy premium or to put syrup into his milk to make it "fun" [ACT, 1972, pp. 2–3].

Serving the public interest

Traditionally, two forms of mass media have been distinguished. *Print media* are those providing access to information by producing and distributing copies. Thus books, newspapers, magazines, phonograph records, stereo tapes, photographs, and movies are all print media. Printing invites competition. Anyone can, for example, go into the newspaper business without interfering with anyone else. By contrast, the *broadcast media*, radio and television, must use specific public airwaves to transmit their signals to individual receivers. Regulation, which is rare for print media because of the concept of freedom of the press (guaranteed in the United States by the First Amendment), is necessary at least up to a point in broadcasting. This is because similar or identical broadcast signals interfere with one another. (Consider, for example, how television reception is sometimes interfered with by operating an electrical appliance on the same circuit.) To avoid chaos, the "right to broadcast" is restricted to those with licenses and, of course, only one licensee is given the right to broadcast on a partiuclar station or channel in a particular area. The government must assign public air waves, raising the question of what the public can expect from the license holder. As we will see in the next chapter, this is a very complicated issue. The licensee has a responsibility to "serve the public interest," monitored by the Federal Communications Commission (FCC), but the scope and nature of this responsibility has proven difficult to define.

Nonetheless, television's critics have long complained that TV broadcasters are delinquent in meeting their responsibility to the public. The most famous expression of this indictment was advanced in 1964 in the first public address of newly appointed FCC Commissioner Newton Minow to the National Association of Broadcasters. Minow (1964) admonished the broadcasters:

> Your license lets you use the public's airwaves as trustees for 180 million Americans. The public is your beneficiary. If you want to stay on as trustees, you must deliver a decent return to the public—not only to your stockholders. So, as a representative of the public, your health and your product are among my chief concerns. As to your health: let's talk only of television today. In 1960 gross broadcast revenues of the television industry were over $1,268,000,000; profit before taxes was $243,900,000—an average return on revenue of 19.2 percent . . . I have confidence in your health. But not in your product . . . when television is bad, nothing is worse. I invite you to sit down in front of your television set when your station goes on the air and stay there without a book, magazine, newspaper, profit-and-loss sheet or rating book to distract you—and keep your eyes glued to that set until the station signs off. I can assure you that you will observe a vast wasteland. . . . Gentlemen, your trust accounting with your beneficiaries is overdue. Never have so few owed so much to so many [pp. 49–53].

Censorship

The First Amendment to the U.S. Constitution guarantees freedom of speech and of the press. This freedom has never been absolute, however. It is unlawful to speak or write so as to incite others to illegal acts, and communities may censor communications that are obscene or profane by their own standards. Those concerned about the effects of television on children have often threatened to use legal means (such as withholding a TV license renewal) to censor what they consider to be unacceptable content. Boycotting of advertisers, which has also been suggested at one time or another, may also be considered a form of censorship. Others, however, have expressed grave concern about placing *any* censoring function in the hands of a government agency or ideological group. These individuals say that the idea of generating lists of "approved" television programming for children frightens them more than anything they have seen so far on entertainment television.

Such questions have a legal as well as a moral component. As we will see, both TV violence and advertising have been involved in fascinating and important courtroom battles that dealt with both psychological and Constitutional issues and raised the question of whether or not any part of children's television should be "controlled" by government restraint.

THE ROLE OF SOCIAL SCIENCE

Social science, especially psychology, began to make its first major impact on society after World War II. Theory and research in the natural sciences had paid off handsomely in terms of technical innovation and accomplishment, and people began to turn to the social sciences for answers to questions concerning the forces that shape their personal and social lives. By the late 1950s research teams and groups in technologically advanced countries everywhere were beginning to study the role of various factors in children's social and personality development. At the same time, several highly influential theories of children's psychological development were being promulgated. These theories allowed conceptual links to be formed between basic socialization processes (of prime interest to academic psychologists) and the specific effects that television viewing might have on the young.

Research

The demand for research appears repeatedly throughout disputes on every aspect of children's television. A major purpose of this book is to summarize and explain the considerable body of research now available on television's effects on the young.

We must make clear at the outset that questions raised about the effects of television have proven tricky for social science researchers. Many issues are phrased in global or ambiguous language, as when terms such as "TV violence" and "aggression" are used to cover a broad but unspecified array of possible instances. There is also the problem of research design. Often research apparently supports one conclusion, but on closer examination admits of alternative explanations.

Questions about *effects* are always questions about *causes*. In the real flow of events, possible causes are intermingled into a subtle and complex fabric. Trying to unravel this complexity and find the specific effects of television is an enormously difficult undertaking, and many of the studies we shall discuss turn out to be quite ambiguous when it comes to answering questions of practical concerns to society.*

Then, too, there is the matter of what questions to ask. The first major studies of the effects of television tried to determine the effects of introducing the television medium (Himmelweit, Oppenheim, & Vince 1958; Schramm, Lyle, & Parker 1961). Later it became apparent that the important social questions revolved around television's specific content since vir-

---

*Readers unfamiliar with the basic methods and terminology used in social science research should consult Appendix A.

tually everyone had a television, and television was here to stay (recall Figure 1.1).

PLAN OF THIS BOOK

We have seen in this chapter that in a few decades television has become a central fixture in the lives of children. Whereas in 1945 television viewing did not occupy any of children's time and the average child spent no more time than a couple of hours a week at movies, by 1970 children were spending more time watching television than going to school. In fact, today the only thing children between 2 and 15 do more than watch television is sleep. This is a profound change in children's experience, and means that for the first time in human history children are exposed to more fictional characters than real people during their formative years. It is understandable that various concerns about all of this television viewing have been raised.

The purpose of this book is to review the question of what effects television has on children and youth from the point of view of both social science and social policy. Despite all the changes that have transpired in the television industry and in the social/political climate and all the objective evidence that has amassed over the years, the issues of concern about television remain largely the same. In this book, we discuss the history of each of these continuing concerns about the medium and the relevant scientific evidence and social issues surrounding each concern. As the reader will see, the research evidence is complex and so are the social issues. Each issue ultimately involves a myriad of forces and ideas coming from child psychology, economics, law, and politics.

Commercial television intends to be a business rather than a social force — indeed "American" television has become one of the most profitable and significant industries in the country and has successfully spread itself all over the world. How, then, does television operate as a business and how are decisions about TV program content actually made? These are the questions we begin with in Chapter 2.

Chapter 2
Television as a Business

OVERVIEW

Most television in the United States is a commercial enterprise, generating operating costs and profits by selling advertising time within and between its entertainment offerings. Decisions about production and program content are made for the most part by the three major networks, which distribute the programs to local affiliated stations. The prime-time and children's programming developed by the networks are both highly profitable, but the profitability of any particular offering is dependent upon the ratings it receives. The overall situation conspires to produce high-action, simple, formularized entertainment.

Because the medium uses public airwaves, it is subject to regulation by the Federal Communications Commission (FCC). Television advertising, like other advertising, is also subject to control by the Federal Trade Commission (FTC). The First Amendment to the United States Constitution prohibits either of these regulatory agencies from censoring content, but each agency has some control and can issue appropriate guidelines within its mandate. A variety of public interest organizations, most notably Action for Children's Television (ACT), make an effort to influence broadcasters and advertisers in the interests of children, both directly and through prodding government agencies. To reduce control pressures and forestall government action, the National Association of Broadcasters (NAB) engages in a degree of self-regulation, primarily through its Television Code. The industry also engages in numerous legal and public relations efforts to protect itself from unwanted pressure to change its broadcasting practices. Some other countries are dominated by a commercial system similar to the one found in the United States, but many others rely on public television to a far greater degree.

The programs shown on TV must be paid for by someone. Someone must decide what to broadcast. And the fact that television uses the open airwaves — a scarce and valuable public resource — means that the right to broadcast must be allocated through licensing and then monitored. Understanding the way in which television is operated, financed, and controlled as a business is essential to understanding the medium and its messages.

BROADCASTING AND THE THREE
U.S. COMMERCIAL NETWORKS

The major television broadcasters in the United States are the three commercial networks: American Broadcasting Company (ABC), Columbia Broadcasting System (CBS), and the National Broadcasting Company (NBC). Simply, a television network is an organization that supplies programs to local stations which broadcast them to the homes in their area. Each of the three networks directly own five licensed stations (the maximum number they are permitted by U.S. federal law) and these are in the largest cities, so that the three networks reach 25–30% of all TV homes through their own stations. In addition, each network has about 200 affiliated stations, so that of the 717 commercial television stations in the United States, 90% are affiliated with one of the three networks. Every day these affiliated stations broadcast 12 to 14 hours of programming and advertisements provided by the networks, including three hours during the lucrative prime time period (from 8:00 P.M. to 11:00 P.M. on the east and west coasts and from 7:00 P.M. to 10:00 P.M. in the Rocky Mountain and midwest states) and nine hours at other times. Another way of looking at the reach of the networks is that a full two-thirds of the programming shown by network affiliated stations are supplied by the networks who buy the programming from production companies. Later in this chapter, we will discuss how the networks decide what programs to air.

The networks make their profits by selling air time to advertisers who are interested in securing audiences for their advertisements. The network affiliates receive one-third of the network's advertising revenues earned in the affiliate's market, plus they have two minutes each hour to sell advertising time on their own.

SELLING TIME

Television is commercial when the costs of production and broadcasting as well as all profits are derived from advertising revenue. Manufacturers of products and providers of services wish to persuade the consuming public to use their goods and services or support their causes. To do so, they create messages cast as television commercials. Obviously, most people would not buy television sets simply to watch commercials. Therefore, interesting or entertaining programs are also created and made available "free," so that the commercials will be seen by those drawn to the set by the entertainment. Thus, as William Melody (1973) astutely observed, the programs are the bait used to lure the viewers into a position where they can be exposed to persuasive messages.

Commercial television is designed to make money and has succeeded admirably well. In 1980 the networks and stations enjoyed revenues of $8.8 billion and profits of $1.6 billion through advertising (*Broadcasting*, 1981). Television's success as a business mirrors its success as an entertainment medium (recall Figure 1.1). For example, in 1948 NBC was losing $13,000 a day on its TV operation. But within two years its revenues more than tripled, and by 1951 it was in the black, where it has remained ever since. In fact, NBC, like the other networks, enjoyed an enviable growth pattern in TV advertising revenues during its formative years. (See Figure 2.1.) On an individual company basis, the expenditures on TV advertising are also impressive. In 1980 the top ten advertisers spent well over 1 billion dollars on TV spot advertising. (See Table 2.1.)

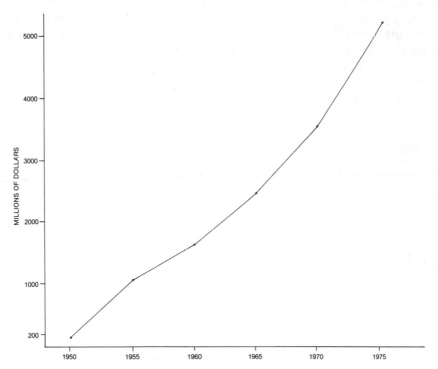

Fig. 2.1. Total Advertiser Expenditures on U.S. Television*.
*Includes network, spot, and local advertisements.
Source: From data reported in Sterling and Haight (1978).

How the transaction works

The transaction underlying the TV business involves selling time—"minutes" in the industry jargon—to advertising agencies or directly to potential

Table 2.1. TV's Top Ten Advertisers in 1980, and the
Amounts They Spent.

1.	Procter & Gamble	$486,310,200
2.	General Foods	278,406,400
3.	American Home Products	157,281,500
4.	Ford	153,848,000
5.	PepsiCo	144,462,600
6.	General Motors	140,380,500
7.	General Mills	136,855,300
8.	Bristol Myers	124,868,900
9.	McDonalds	120,213,100
10.	Philip Morris	118,971,500

Source: TV Bureau of Advertising (1980).

sponsors. Television stations, following the National Association of Broadcasters (NAB) guidelines (1981), offer 9.5 minutes per hour during prime time and 16 minutes per hour during other times. For children's programming (designed for viewers under 12 years of age), the guideline limits are 9.5 minutes per hour on Saturday and Sunday and 12 minutes per hour during such programming aired on weekdays.*

When the networks sell, they do not simply offer a spot to a prospective buyer. Rather, a package of time is sold, with minutes on shows of varying quality and attractiveness and at a package price which is negotiated according to time, network and, of course, the acumen of bargainers. But even if they fluctuate, prices are not wholly arbitrary. The Nielsen ratings are used to determine the number of homes in which a particular show ostensibly is seen. Then advertisers compute their cost for reaching each thousand homes. By this logic, a show that reaches 10 million families with spots at $40,000 per minute and one that reaches 8 million families at $32,000 per minute are equal in cost: $4 per thousand homes. In 1980, the cost of a 30-second spot on a prime time network TV program averaged $75,000, ranging from $45,000 for low-rated series to $150,000 for top-rated series. Still more expensive are spots within special programming. For example, 100 million people watched the 1980 Super Bowl telecast during which a 30-second ad cost $234,000 (*Broadcasting Yearbook*, 1980).

Advertising revenues from children's programming

Advertising on children's programs accounts for between 6 and 9% of all advertising revenue or about $500 million yearly. The biggest spenders are

---

*The reader may be surprised to learn that the industry itself has guidelines, given our earlier emphasis on the dominance of the profit motive. In fact, as will be apparent later in this chapter, such self-imposed restraint by the industry serves a self protective counter-control function.

toy manufacturers ($40 million yearly), followed by cereal companies ($35 million), and candy companies ($20 million). The average price per minute to advertise on a children's program is $20,000 (*Broadcasting*, 1979). Because programming costs and risks are far lower than with prime time shows, children's programming, on a percentage basis, is one of the more profitable segments of commercial television. (The news is the least profitable.)

Advertisers, of course, are interested in selling their products. Thus, they want to reach the largest possible number of people with their commercial messages and are willing to pay more money for spots on programs with large audiences. As Les Brown (1971) succinctly stated, "advertisers buy audiences, not programs" (p. 58). The ratings, to which we turn next, are supposed to provide them with the information necessary for making decisions about where to invest their advertising dollars.

The ratings

The value of any particular commercial minute depends upon the popularity, or presumed popularity, of the show on which it appears. Ratings thus play a vital role in the commercial enterprise of television.

The rating system virtually came in with the television set; a group of advertisers formed an organization to telephone people to ask them what they had watched the night before. The technique was a questionable one, so the phone call was soon supplanted by the diary, which then became the preferred mode of obtaining a family's self-report of viewing patterns. Then came Nielsen.

The Nielsen Ratings. Among inveterate TV viewers, Nielsen is almost a household word. For network shows, it is these evaluations that determine which offerings will be dropped and which will continue.

The Nielsen evaluations come from machines—the patented Audimeters of the A.C. Nielsen Company. About 1,170 households selected to represent a cross section of American homes are reimbursed for half their TV repair bills (averaging $1 monthly per TV set) so that the company's device can record the activity of their television sets. The Audimeter, which was improved in 1971 and called the Storage Instantaneous Audimeter, records the minute-by-minute impulses of channel changes and stores them in an electronic memory. The unit, which is connected to both the television set and a special phone line, relays the stored information at least twice daily to a central office computer.

Nielsen provides two important figures to those who buy the service. First is the "rating" which is the percentage of the total possible audience that a program attracts. A rating of 20 means that 20% of the homes with television are tuned to the program. The second is the "share" which reflects how a program is doing opposite other programs aired at the same time; it is a competitive rating, indicating percentage of viewership out of the actual number of sets in use. In a three network system, a program needs a one-third share to be maintained.

The Nielsen system and a similar one used by Britain's commercial network, the Independent Television Authority, can only indicate whether the set is on or off and the location of the channel selector. Whether anyone is in the room (much less watching the show or commercial message) is ignored. The real question of interest to advertisers, "How much watching actually occurs?" is not really measured by the Nielsen ratings. This was dramatically shown in a 1972 study by Robert Bechtel and his associates in which videotape cameras were placed in the homes of 20 families, so that as the family watched television, the television watched the family. This permitted careful, complete, and reliable comparisons of diary reports and simple measures of when the set was on (the Nielsen method) with what and how much was actually viewed. The results were startling. Both the Nielsen and the diary techniques consistently overestimated by a factor of 30 to 50% the actual viewing of television. Second, the amount of viewing that occurred when the set was on varied substantially with type of program: movies, for example, were watched 76% of the time while on, sporting events less than 60%, and commercials, literally at the bottom of Bechtel's list of eleven types of program events, 54.8% of the time. (See Table 2.2.)

Nielsen supplements its Audimeter service with information obtained from diaries to provide the broadcasters with some information about the

Table 2.2. Program Categories Ranked by Percentage of Time Watched while Program Was on in Bechtel et al.'s Study

Percentage of time watched while program was on	
Program type	%
Movies	76.0
Children's	71.4
Suspense	68.1
Religious	66.7
Family	66.4
Game show	65.9
Talk show	63.7
Melodrama	59.3
Sports events	58.7
News	55.2
Commercial	54.8

Source: Bechtel et al. (1972), p. 294.

age and sex of the viewers, information critical to advertisers. A total of 2,200 families, each paid about 50¢ per week, keep viewing diaries for one week out of every month, rotating so that 550 families report on their TV viewing each week. Each quarter hour, these families record the program watched, channel, the number of persons viewing, and the age and sex of each viewer. Thus, 1,170 Audimeter families and 2,200 diary families determine the TV offerings for 200 million American viewers.

Nielsen dominates the national ratings market. However, for local TV audiences, the American Research Bureau's rating service, Arbitron, has been estimating TV audiences since 1949. Arbitron is a diary method much like Nielsen's, with participants mailing in weekly diaries of programs viewed and viewers' age and sex breakdowns. To supplement the diary, Arbitron also uses telephone surveys and personal interviews.

The diary method has proven to be fallible. For example, the respondent is supposed to fill them out daily but according to Mayer (1972):

> One suspicious investigator distributed a hundred diaries, telling recipients he would be back to pick them up in seven days—and then returned in five days instead. He found a number of diaries still blank, the householder having put off till tomorrow what he forgot to do today—and an almost equally large number already complete for all seven days, the helpful respondent having gone through *TV Guide* at once and written in the shows the family "always" sees [p. 37].

Nevertheless, the ratings figures collected by Nielsen and Arbitron determine the TV advertising rates. When are these rates derived? Three times a year, Nielsen and Arbitron conduct their ratings over four-week "sweeps" of 200 individual TV markets, and most stations use only the ratings during the sweeps to calculate their seasonal national advertising rates. Many stations substitute specials and audience-drawing movies over the four-week sweep periods during October–November, February–March, and April–May to inflate the audience size figures which would in turn increase their revenues. (This explains much of the variability in the quality of program offerings throughout the year.)

PRODUCTION AND CONTENT

Television production is a complex business, dependent on artistic, political, and economic factors. The process of producing a series is lengthy and risky, as the increasingly rapid turnover indicates. Most important, it is expensive. In 1979–80 the cost of a single episode of an hour prime-time network series averaged more than $400,000, and a half-hour situation comedy averaged $210,000. Even more expensive are special events such as the ABC production of *Masada*, which cost $18 million for the eight-hour mini series (Steinberg, 1980). Because TV programs are so expensive to produce, a very large audience is required to obtain the advertising revenue to cover the costs. Locally produced programs could not draw sufficient advertising revenue to offset production costs for most types of programs. It is for this reason that only three networks in the United States system supply most of the TV fare (more than three-fourths of all evening prime-time programming and about two-thirds of all of their affiliates' programming). The independent stations (not network affiliated) do not produce much of their own programming and rely instead on syndicated shows, often old network series and old movies. This type of fare is also shown by the network affiliates when they are not showing network programming.

With the exception of daytime soap operas and game shows, the programs seen on U.S. commercial television were almost all developed either as prime-time series and specials or as children's programming. Prime-time series and specials are designed to be seen by audiences of all ages and backgrounds and are "targeted" at those between 18 and 49. Children's programming is targeted at those under 12 and usually enjoys its first run on either Saturday or Sunday morning. These same program types are rerun by independent stations and at non-prime times. The pattern of production and revenue expectations differ for the two types in a number of interesting ways, as we shall see.

Development of prime-time programming

The networks' annual expenditures for prime-time programming now exceed one billion dollars a year (*Broadcasting*, 1980). Successful programming decisions can propel a TV executive to the top level of management in the industry and to international fame, as was the case with Fred Silverman (who also exemplifies the fall from glory when programming decisions turn sour). Decisions about program concepts and treatments are made at the highest level of management and with the utmost seriousness.

A variety of ideas and even scripts are bandied around during early phases of a program's development, but the critical test comes when network executives decide whether to foot the bill for a pilot. According to Steinberg (1980) an average one-hour pilot costs a million dollars to produce. If the pilot is judged successful on the basis of its ratings and the reactions of network decision-makers, the series goes into full-scale production. The producer handles the day-to-day work necessary to get a program on the air every week and determines the content of the series under the network's supervision. The producer selects the writers and often provides the story line. Once the script is written, rarely anyone but the producer changes it.

Directors are under too much time pressure to interfere with content decisions, and actors rarely exert their potential power.

Each network has a programming department that supervises the entire production process with an eye toward securing the largest possible audience of 18 to 49 year olds—the group that spends the most money and, therefore, is most likely to appeal to potential advertisers. Network censors work through the programming department and try to protect the network from public outcry and government regulation.

Underlying assumptions about the prime-time audience. The networks make certain assumptions that influence what gets on the air. First, although 98% of the households in the United States have TV sets, one-third of that potential audience does two-thirds of the daily viewing. It is on this group of steady TV viewers that the programming decisions are based. These viewers watch television, not programs, and they tend to watch during certain hours regardless of what is offered. Given this audience's predominance, the ratings are heavily weighted by their "votes," and it is the ratings that virtually determine what is aired.

In terms of programming decisions, the motivation to avoid flops is more pronounced than that of selecting winners. Based on the ratings and on the network executives' conception of the steady TV viewer, certain informal rules have evolved for the development of new programs. New programs should: (1) be visually pleasing, (2) have a formula, so endless scripts can be written, (3) have appealing elements that carry over from show to show, (4) draw 30% of the audience, preferably a young audience, (5) win an audience early, (6) contain likeable characters, (7) not be so complex that viewers go elsewhere for light entertainment, (8) have a hint of newness without being alien to the viewer, because totally novel ideas would make viewers insecure, and (9) avoid controversy, because advertisers don't want negative feelings associated with their products (Brown, 1971). Thus:

> The character of television programs is determined by the three networks' notions of what will appeal to large numbers of people, sell products or services for advertisers, and not jeopardize the valuable licenses or the good will of affiliates by creating a negative audience response [Baldwin & Lewis, 1972, p. 294].

The fear of controversy and preference for sticking to familiar themes and tried and true methods has kept much of television programming predictable and formularized. Another factor restricting the diversity of programs is the limited number of professionals who actually create them. There are only a handful of studios in Hollywood and a few independent production companies that provide all the network programming.

Children's series

The procedure for acquiring a children's series is somewhat different. Unlike prime-time shows, there are no pilots for children's series. The animation format which represents the bulk of chidren's programming is far too expensive to produce for pilot purposes. The idea for the series including its characters is spelled out in an outline, and artwork is drawn up that presents the main characters in several poses and situations. If it is a live program, a casting tape of suggested actors for the roles replaces the artwork. Then children may be interviewed about these visual displays to determine the potential appeal of the program. A script may be ordered. On the basis of these materials, the network decides whether it wants to buy the series (Morgenstern, 1979; Rushnell, 1981).

In adult fare, the producer sells 13 episodes for half a season, and then another 13 for the second half if the series is retained. These episodes may be rerun, but usually not more than once during the summer. (A few highly successful series may be syndicated and shown again.) In contrast, when a network buys a children's series from a producer it signs a contract including provision for reruns and guarantees that each episode will be shown *at least four times*. This incredible rerun practice, which would draw cries of outrage from adult viewers, is feasible because the audiences for children's shows change quickly. This year's audience is replaced by younger brothers and sisters next year. Although the profit margin on children's programming is smaller than on adult series, once the series is sold it will almost never fail, and the programs become more profitable with repeated airings. Children's programs are also more likely to be syndicated; after being used by the network, they may be shown for years (Cantor, 1972). Also if a series is popular, the characters will be used in merchandising and the music may be made into a record—both practices which make more money. So the overall profits that can result from children's programming are considerable.

The network must approve every show before it goes on the air. Therefore, producers must always consider the network and work closely with its programming department from the outset, remembering that although children will watch the show, only adults can buy it. Once the network buys the series, the producer remains responsive to network requests; their aim is to please the buying customer—the network. Those who cannot accept the system quit. Based on her extensive confidential interviews with producers, Muriel Cantor (1972) wrote:

> Those producers who are committed to particular artistic and ethical values
> have trouble remaining in the commercial field. One well-known producer of a
> series presently on the air left the field of children's programming because he

could not reconcile what he considered the networks' lack of social conscience with his own ideas of good craftsmanship and content [p. 266].

Assumptions about the child audience. Just as with adult and family programming, producers of children's series have some ideas about the nature of their audience. For example, they feel that a child's attention span is limited, so that quick movement and loud noises are necessary. Further, because the ultimate goal of the programming is to attract the largest possible child audience, the programming is geared to appeal to the target age range of two to eleven year olds. Obviously, it is not judged to be financially sound to tailor the programming to the needs of any specific age group. Accordingly, formats and themes are selected that have the widest appeal.* In an analysis of children's programs, Barcus (1978a) found that the most widely used format was animation (particularly cartoon comedy), and the most frequently used themes invovled crime, domestic affairs, love and romance, and science and technology.

REGULATION AND CONTROL OF TELEVISION

No individual, organization, or business can operate without some constraints. The exact nature and extent of external regulation required, however, depends on the nature of the entity being considered. The print media are subject to relatively few constraints because they can operate in a highly competitive market and without the use of any public resources. By contrast, both the telephone company and airlines are subject to greater government regulation. The telephone company needs government approval to change its rates, because it enjoys a virtual monopoly over certain direct, "on-line," two-way communication. The airlines are also controlled by government regulation, backed by actual inspections, in the design and maintenance of aircraft and in their use of public air lanes. Assuring public safety and the fair use of public property is the justification.

The regulation of television turns out to be a good deal more complex and subtle than the regulation of either telephone or airline service. Television is a communication medium using a public resource and is thus subject to technical controls (e.g., determining the strength and nature of signals which may be broadcast), business and economic controls (e.g., prohibitions against clearly deceptive or inaccurate advertising claims), and social

---

*Producing programs for more restricted age ranges becomes possible with cable technology. For example, *Nickelodeon*, a cable channel featuring only children's programs, offers age-specific programs such as *Pinwheel* (for pre-schoolers), *Dusty's Treehouse* (for 4-to-7 year olds), *Hocus Focus* (for 6-to-10 year olds), and *Livewire* (for teenagers).

controls (e.g., it is unlawful to be "obscene" in public or incite others to il-legal acts, and this prohibition is applied to television content).

In the United States, there are two federal agencies responsible for regu-lating television, the Federal Communications Commission (FCC) and the Federal Trade Commission (FTC). Television is also subject to extra-legal control. Public interest groups may apply pressure on advertisers and broadcasters to edit and censor certain content, and they may do so either through boycotts and economic sanctions or by advocating and demanding action from one of the regulatory agencies.

Commercial enterprises seem invariably to resist regulation, and the United States broadcasting industry is no exception. Through the National Association of Broadcasters (NAB) and legal and public relations efforts by each network, broadcasters attempt to counter the controlling power of the government and public interest groups. "Self-regulation" plays an impor-tant role in the overall countercontrol effort. As we will see both in this chapter and throughout the remainder of the book, the complex and often dramatic interplay of these forces has left some classic battle stories in its wake. But first it is necessary to further identify each of the players in the regulation game.

The FCC

Broadcast regulation in the United States has its roots in the Radio Act of 1927 in which Congress created the Federal Radio Commission (FRC) to assign radio broadcast wavelengths and to determine the power and location of transmitters. The FRC granted three-year licenses, and broadcasters had to prove that they would serve the "public interest, convenience, and neces-sity." In 1934, by an act of Congress, the FRC became the Federal Com-munications Commission (FCC) which extended its authority over telecom-munications as well.

The FCC is composed of seven commissioners who serve seven-year terms. They are nominated by the President and confirmed by the Senate. The Federal Communications Act (1934) enpowered the FCC with licensing responsibilities:

> the Commission shall determine that public interest, convenience, and necessity would be served by the granting of a license to a broadcast . . . any station license may be revoked because of conditions . . . which would warrant the Commission in refusing to grant a license on an original application [Public Law No. 416. The Communications Act of 1934].

Unfortunately, there are no clear standards for what constitutes "serving the public interest." More important, perhaps, is that the Federal Communications Act of 1934 also specifically denies the FCC the authority to "interfere with the right of free speech" or to intervene in program content. Written originally for radio but extending to telecommunications, the Act states:

> Nothing in this Act shall be understood or construed to give the Commission the power of censorship over the radio communications or signals transmitted by any radio station, and no regulation or condition shall be promulgated or fixed by the Commission which shall interfere with the right of free speech by means of radio communication [The Communication Act of 1934, sec. 326].

The effect of the FCC's imbalanced authority is captured by Les Brown (1977):

> The FCC's contradictory mandates—that of looking after the public interest and that of refraining from any involvement with programming which might constitute censorship—have kept the agency under constant criticism from Congress and citizens for failing to exert stricter program controls and for in effect "rubber stamping" license renewals. It has been called weak, bureaucratic and overly protective of the industry it regulates [p. 146].

Some members of the FCC express frustration with the agency's inability to act on objectionable content, but support strict adherence to the First Amendment. Margita White (1978), an FCC Commissioner, criticizes the medium for sexual exploitation of women, but opposes any censorship measures by government:

> I'm not sure whether I'm more outraged because the medium has missed the message of the antiviolence campaign, or more offended because women are to be battered through a new low in sexploitation. . . . But please, please don't turn to the Commission, which is precluded by the First Amendment and statute from censorship of program content. Even if it were not, it would make no sense to have seven government officials in Washington set standards of morals, taste, and creativity. This simply would shift influence from one powerful elite to another, with frightening implications for the future of free expression.

Other factors also conspire to limit the FCC's interest in program content. One is that the commissioners typically come from and return to the communications industry or the law firms that service it. Then, too, licensing TV stations is certainly not the only function of the FCC, whose members have a staggering array of other responsibilities. Cole and Oettinger (1978) point out:

> On the face of it, a commissioner's job is overwhelming. He is called upon to

decide questions involving radio and television programming and technical matters, telephone and telegraph rates, international communications by satellite and undersea cable, emission standards for microwave ovens and garage-door openers, citizens band radio, amateur radio, maritime communications, police and fire department communications, cable television, pay-television on air or by cable, data transmission services, educational broadcasting, antitrust considerations, and consumer electronics standards [pp. 4–5].

Also, the FCC has a long precedent of *not* denying renewal applications, and such precedents turn out, practically speaking, to be almost unshakable.*

Some content control is openly enjoyed by the FCC. The Commission "recommends" *categories* of programming to broadcasters (e.g., local and national news, children's shows) and creates a balance of content that might shift if either (1) the recommended category list was changed, or (2) the practice of recommending categories was abandoned. More important, though, is the FCC's power to shape television content through its license granting function.

What the Commission is explicitly concerned about is diversification in the media and the avoidance of any concentration of control. It is out of this concern that the Commission prohibits the same individual or group from operating (1) more than one station in the same service (AM, FM, or TV) in the same geographic market, or (2) more than five VHF stations in the nation.

A sample of brief case studies reveals much about the FCC in action.

The WLBT case. In the context of the civil rights movement of the early 1960s, the local United Church of Christ charged that the TV station in Jackson, Mississippi (WLBT) had been presenting biased news coverage of the civil rights movement. Everett Parker, director of the United Church of Christ's National Office of Communications, tried to influence the station to change its coverage and failed. He then tried to get the FCC to conduct a hearing on the station's renewal application and failed again. Up to this point, the public was denied entry into the FCC license renewal proceedings. Parker then brought the case before the U.S. Court of Appeals. In 1966, Judge Warren Burger ruled that the FCC had to hold a hearing on the WLBT license and permit public participation.† The FCC hearing was held but the FCC ruled in favor of granting a license renewal to WLBT. Parker

---

*The practice of virtual automatic license renewals goes back to the early days of television in the 1940s–1950s when the government wanted the new broadcast industry to succeed. Investments in TV stations had to be substantial, and it was quite risky; so to encourage investments, the FCC didn't require high performance (Brown, 1971).

†It is out of this case that the public was granted entry into the licensing proceeding.

appealed the decision to the U.S. Court of Appeals, and the court ruled against WLBT. This was a hard slap in the Commission's face, inasmuch as the Court of Appeals may only overturn an FCC decision if judged to be "arbitrary, capricious or unreasonable."

The great cigarette war. The demise of cigarette advertising on television is a clear instance of the FCC's involvement in restricting content (censorship) in the public interest, though with advertising rather than programming content. Thomas Whiteside (1970) writing for *The New Yorker*, provides a brief history of a long debate.

Television had been enormously effective for the cigarette advertiser. Sales of Benson & Hedges 100's rose from less than 2 billion cigarettes in 1966 to over 14 billion in 1970, following an amusing and sophisticated television campaign. The television industry was pleased with its highly lucrative arrangement with cigarette manufacturers. It took in over 200 million dollars each year in revenue, accounting for 8–10% of the commercials (*Newsweek*, 1971). Not surprisingly, neither the advertisers nor the networks were particularly interested in any move that might damage the relationship.

The first blow against cigarette advertising on TV was struck in June 1967, when the FCC ruled that the "Fairness Doctrine" (that both sides of a controversial issue be given equal time) applied to cigarette advertising. The FCC suggested that a ratio of three cigarette commercials to every one anti-smoking commercial was fair. During the summer, about a dozen petitions were filed with the Commission on behalf of ABC, NBC, CBS, the National Association of Broadcasters, over 100 individual radio and television stations, six major tobacco companies, the Tobacco Institute, and Federal Communications Bar Association, each asking for revocation of the regulation. Activist John Banzhaf III, who had originally requested that anti-smoking commercials be aired, asked various health organizations to assist in preparing a reply to these petitions. According to Banzhaf, one official remarked, "Let me tell you the economic facts of life. My organization depends on free broadcasting time for our fund-raising drives. We are not going to jeopardize that time by getting involved in this move" (Whiteside, 1970, p. 48). So Banzhaf prepared the brief personally, and was successful. The FCC upheld its ruling in September 1967.

But enforcement was another matter. The FCC had a staff of only four persons to monitor about 1,000 TV and 7,000 radio stations. Since the Commission clearly could not handle the load, Banzhaf again decided to do it himself. With the help of friends, he watched prime-time television for two weeks on one large station, WNBC-TV in New York. His monitoring revealed a ratio of cigarette commercials to anti-smoking commercials of 10 to 1; the station said the ratio was 3 or 4 to 1. The discrepancy was due to the fact that WNBC counted two cigarette commercials, one right after another, as one, and did not count simple announcements ("This show is brought to you by Marlboro") at all. Also, the anti-smoking ads were aired at what might be considered by most standards rather odd hours – 2:30 A.M., 6:30 A.M. (WNBC-TV defended the 6:30 A.M. ads, explaining that it wanted to reach the kids before they left for school.) Banzhaf's work resulted in the FCC requiring more anti-smoking ads.

Then in 1969, the FCC signaled its intention to call for a total ban on cigarette ads, which required an Act of Congress. Congress opened special hearings to consider such a bill. Testimony revealed contradictions in the NAB Television Code and its practices. (The TV code called for cigarette ads that do not present smoking as an activity to be imitated, but a private study by the NAB indicated that many commercials did just that, making smoking appear attractive and socially desirable.) In 1968, the Director of NAB said, "Network [affiliates] . . . see in the area of cigarette copy nothing to be achieved by Code Authority involvement and in fact [see] potential injury to cigarette-advertising revenue if the Code Authority pursues such a course" (Whiteside, 1970, p. 70). In the end, after vigorous lobbying by both the tobacco and the broadcasting industries, the House passed a bill that would prevent federal and state intervention for six years.

Chances for the bill's passage in the Senate did not appear favorable, so both the networks and the tobacco industry began to offer compromise plans. The networks offered to gradually fade out advertising of brands with the highest tar and nicotine content; this plan was rejected. The broadcasters then suggested that they would phase out advertising over a three and one-half year period, beginning in January 1970. The tobacco industry offered another plan: a promise to end all radio and television advertising by September 1970. In return, it hoped to win legislation that would prevent the Federal Trade Commission from requiring health warnings in all ads. This plan rather annoyed the broadcasters (who would lose an additional three years of advertising revenue), and one commented:

> The thing that irks us is that the tobacco people couldn't have got the bill through the House without our help. We really lobbied for that. It would never have passed the House without us, because we have more muscle than the tobacco people have. . . . In every congressman's district, there is at least one broadcaster. These congressmen all get exposure on the local TV and radio stations. . . . I know how hard we worked through our local broadcasters on this bill, pointing out to congressmen how unfair it was to bar advertising for a product legally sold [Whiteside, 1970, p. 78].

The tobacco industry had advertising contracts with the stations; they asked that the contracts be broken. The networks refused. Finally, a bill was proposed to ban cigarette ads on TV after January 1, 1971, giving the networks the ad revenues from the lucrative football season. The Public Health Cigarette Smoking Act was passed by both the House and Senate and signed into law by President Nixon on April 1, 1970. The last cigarette commercial was shown on January 1, 1971.

This incident in the history of broadcasting points out clearly the array of political influences that underlies regulation of television programming. More specifically, it demonstrates that while the FCC is capable of initiating censorship, it requires great impetus from the outside (e.g., Banzhaf's group).

The Prime Time Access Rule. Another way in which the FCC felt it could legitimately respond to the public interest regarding content was through the Prime Time Access Rule of 1970, which limited stations to showing network fare for no more than three hours per night (8 to 11 P.M.), which meant that the period between 7:30 and 8:00 P M was left for local station use. The intent of this ruling was to encourage the stations to serve local community needs in this half-hour with public service programming, to break the network monopoly in prime time, to provide independent producers with a new market outside of the three networks, and to encourage the production and airing of new program formats (Brown, 1977). In retrospect it seems that these were idealistic rather than realistic expectations. The stations themselves responded with characteristic practical business sense. Rather than producing their own local public service programming, they aired game shows and syndicated films which limited expenditures and maximized profit while honoring the letter but hardly the spirit of the Prime Time Access Rule.

The FTC

The Federal Trade Commission (FTC) is the government agency that regulates interstate commerce. In 1938 it was given the power to protect both consumer interest and private competition by prohibiting "false advertisements" and "unfair or deceptive acts or practices." It has the power to act on individual commercials and to issue broad trade rules and regulations which restrict or require specific advertising practices. The FTC can take into account not only what is presented in an advertisement but also what is not revealed, especially in the case of information about the possible consequences of using the product. Thus, within not entirely clear guidelines, the FTC has the power to censor content that appears on television as commercial advertisements. According to the Commission's own most recent statement:

> The Federal Trade Commission is primarily a law enforcement agency charged by Congress with protecting the general public—consumers and business people

alike — against anticompetitive behavior and unfair and deceptive business practices [FTC, 1981a, p. 3].

The FTC is composed of five commissioners who serve staggered terms of seven years each. The commissioners may not engage in any other business during their term of office. They are nominated by the President and confirmed by the Senate. No more than three commissioners may be from the same political party. The President chooses the chairman, who has management responsibilities. The most recent chairman is James C. Miller III, appointed by President Reagan in 1981.

If a company is thought to be violating an FTC regulation, the Commission can:

- investigate the alleged violation.
- then, if appropriate, take legal action against the company by filing a formal charge known as a complaint and sometimes by asking the court to forbid immediately the alleged activity by issuing an injunction.
- then, either negotiate a consent order, in which the company agrees to stop the disputed practice but usually does not admit to having violated the law.
- or hold formal hearings called adjudicative proceedings, the result of which is, if the company is found to have violated the law:
- to issue a cease-and-desist order.
- or to seek civil penalties, which are like fines, and/or an injunction against a violator by suing the company in federal court [FTC, 1981a, p. 5].

Based upon letters it receives from individuals, organizations, or businesses about allegedly unfair or deceptive practices, the FTC decides whether it should investigate a particular company, industry, or business practice. The Commission staff gathers information about the company or practice in question. If the FTC staff member and the company agree that the company would end the disputed practice without a formal FTC hearing and without an admission that the company has done anything wrong, they draw up a "consent agreement" specifying that the FTC prohibits the practice in question and that the company will take certain actions. This agreement is then submitted to the FTC for approval. If it is approved, the complaint and proposed order are put on public record in the Federal Register and in the FTC headquarters. The public is given 60 days to comment on the agreement, after which time the FTC either issues the order, modifies it with the cooperation of the company, or rejects it. If the company violates its agreement to stop a practice, the FTC can fine the company $10,000 per day for each violation.

If the FTC staff member and the company cannot come to an agreement, the staff member submits a report including its recommendations to the Commission. The FTC reviews the evidence and if it appears the law has been violated, it issues a formal complaint and a hearing is held. The administrative judge presiding over the proceedings (which resemble a court trial) issues a decision. If either of the parties disagrees with it, that party can appeal to the full FTC, which then functions as an appeal court. If the FTC decision is contested, the case can be brought before the U.S. Court of Appeals and then to the U.S. Supreme Court.

During fiscal 1980, the FTC issued 21 final consent orders; 12 more consent orders were accepted and published for public comment in fiscal 1980 and then issued in fiscal 1981; and five more consent orders were issued which were settled in litigation (FTC, 1981c). An example of a recent FTC consent agreement issued in final form is the case of AMF. The complaint alleged that two AMF TV commercials portrayed children following unsafe bicycle/tricycle riding habits which child viewers could imitate. AMF agreed to stop broadcasting these commercials and to produce two public service announcements on safe bicycle riding and submit them to TV stations that reach substantial child audiences.

The FTC usually holds hearings in response to complaints about deceptive ads. These investigations have revealed some interesting information about the deception prevalent in many advertisements. One ad for a major shaving cream demonstrated that its product gives a cleaner shave; the commercial showed the shaving cream being spread on sandpaper, and then being whisked off perfectly. The FTC claimed that this could not be accomplished unless the sandpaper was soaked for an hour; in fact, it was done even more neatly, by "shaving" sand off a pane of glass! Other examples include the case of an advertiser who substituted oil for coffee to make the coffee product look richer and darker, and the one who put marbles in a bowl of vegetable soup to force the vegetables to rise to the top and make the contents look more appealing (Brown, 1977).

Rule-making. In addition to its power to act on individual commercials, the Magnuson-Moss Act (passed by Congress in 1975) gave the FTC the power to set industry-wide standards in the form of trade-regulation rules which specify what are "unfair or deceptive acts or practices" in particular industries. These rules have the force of law. Table 2.3 presents the step-by-step procedures the FTC follows to establish trade-regulation rules. As we will see in Chapter 6, special rules for advertising directed at children triggered one of the most impassioned legal and political battles in FTC history.

Public interest organizations

A major force that has influenced the actions of both the FCC and FTC in recent years has been public interest or advocacy groups.

Table 2.3. The FTC Rulemaking Proceeding.

Step 1. A proposal for a trade-regulation rule is published in the *Federal Register*.
2. A presiding officer is chosen to conduct the proceeding.
3. The Commission accepts written comments on the proposed regulation and the issues involved (until 45 days before the start of hearings).
4. The Commission accepts written proposals of issues for possible cross-examination during public hearings (up to 60 days after publication of the initial notice).
5. A "final notice of proposed rulemaking" is published in the *Federal Register*.
6. Persons who want to cross-examine witnesses during the hearings notify the presiding officer (within 20 days after publication of the final notice).
7. Informal hearings are held (approximately 90 days after the final notice is published).
8. The Commission accepts written rebuttals of issues raised during the hearings.
9. The FTC staff prepares its own report making its own recommendations.
10. The presiding officer prepares a report summarizing the record and listing his or her findings.
11. The public is given a chance to comment on both the presiding officer's report and the staff report (up to 60 days after Step 10).
12. The Commission reviews the rulemaking record and takes final action.

Source: FTC, 1981a, p. 17.

Action for Children's Television (ACT). Founded in 1968 by a group of mothers in Boston, ACT has developed into a national nonprofit consumer organization devoted to improving broadcasting practices related to children. ACT's efforts include filing petitions to the FCC and FTC and testifying before the U.S. Congress. Unsuccessful at obtaining cooperation from the networks directly, ACT turned to the FCC in 1970 with a petition proposing rulemaking that would:

1. Abolish commercials on children's programs.
2. Abolish the practice of having performers on children's programs promote products or services.
3. Require TV stations to provide age-specific programming for children totalling at least 14 hours weekly.

In response to the ACT petition and growing concerns over TV violence, the FCC initiated proceedings in 1971 to examine children's programming and advertising practices and created a permanent children's unit within the FCC. In 1974 the FCC issued the Children's Television Report and Policy Statement, which emphasized that broadcasters have a "special obligation" to serve children as a "substantial and important" audience but allowed the industry to meet these obligations through self-regulation.

In 1978 ACT petitioned the FCC to conduct an inquiry to determine the degree to which the broadcasting industry complied with the 1974 Policy Statement and to adopt rules where self-regulation proved ineffective. The

FCC then established a task force which in 1979 reported that the broadcasters had failed to meet their obligations to improve children's programming and recommended that the FCC take regulatory action to achieve the goal of sufficient age-specific programming for children. The FCC responded by having panel hearings about children's television programming. However, in December 1980 FCC Chairman Charles D. Ferris announced that the agency would be unable to consider the controversial proposal to require more children's television programs before Ronald Reagan took office and appointed another chairman* (*Los Angeles Times*, 1980).

In an effort to reintroduce the issue to the FCC, in September 1981 ACT released to the FCC the results of a study it commissioned (Barcus, 1981) which examined the license renewal applications of 588 commercial television stations to determine the amount of regularly scheduled children's programming between 6 A.M. and 6 P.M. weekdays. The study revealed that 29% of the stations reported *no* regularly scheduled children's programs between these hours, 45% reported none between 6 A.M. and 2 P.M., and 62% reported none between 2 P.M. and 6 P.M.

The NABB. The first public interest media group in the United States was the National Association for Better Broadcasting (NABB) which was founded in 1949. The NABB's objectives are primarily educational, making the public aware of the broadcasters' responsibility to serve the public interest. It has published newsletters and other printed materials for use by the public. Initially, their activities had been limited because until 1966 the FCC did not admit such groups (or any public representatives) into broadcast licensing proceedings. In recent years, the NABB has been more active, testifying before the FCC and Senate and House committees in Washington, but it is still considered by most reformers to have a cozy relationship with the industry and to have accomplished little of substance.

Small activist organizations. A host of other, less well-known activist groups have come into being (and occasionally disappeared) over the past 10 or 15 years. For example, the Media Action Research Center (MARC) was incorporated in the mid-1970s with funds from the United Methodist Church and other Protestant denominations to undertake research on children and television. More recently, MARC has redirected its efforts toward stirring consumer action about television by means of a training program it developed called Television Awareness Training (TAT). Making use of prepared workbooks and films, the series of workshops has been used through-

---

*Mark Fowler was appointed as the new FCC Chairman. Formerly a Washington broadcasting lawyer who represented radio stations, he has not been an advocate of government regulation of broadcasting.

out the United States and Canada to sensitize people to how television influences them (Logan & Moody, 1979).

An entirely different type of organization, more or less a one man show, is the Council on Children, Media and Merchandising (CCMM), which is founded, headed, and personally financed to a large degree by children's advocate Robert Choate. His earliest efforts were directed at TV ads that encouraged poor nutritional habits. In 1970. Choate appeared before a Senate Commerce Subcommittee and showed that the cereals promoted to children were less nutritious than those promoted to adults. Choate describes the influence process of the CCMM as involving behind-the-scenes political pressures. In Choate's (1980) own words:

> The Council was in an excellent position to stimulate political interest in children's rights in the marketplace. Its personnel were experienced with Washington scene bureaucracies; its leaders were names familiar to the press; its ability to communicate with both Republicans and Democrats gave it an ear in both houses of Congress. Communication with the business community had always seemed natural to CCMM and thus the Council had contacts in various trade organizations and individual companies.

> The Council pattern and strategy was to interact regularly with the Food and Drug Administration (FDA), the Federal Communications Commission (FCC), and the Federal Trade Commission (FTC). Their staffs were exhorted; their Commissioners were solicited. More to the point, the Council maintained pressure on Republicans and Democrats on both sides of Capitol Hill, and they in turn kept the regulatory agencies aware that children did interest the Congress [p. 324].

Other media reform groups that have emerged in recent years represent the interests of minority and women's groups that are poorly served by television: Gray Panther Media Task Force (representing the elderly), National Organization for Women Media Committee, National Black Media Coalition, and Chinese for Affirmative Action (Branscomb & Savage, 1978).

The most controversial recent media reform group is the Coalition for Better TV (CBTV) which is backed by the Moral Majority and headed by the Rev. Donald Wildmon, a Methodist preacher from Mississippi. Wildmon has also been the leader of the National Federation for Decency which has monitored the amount of TV sex since 1977 and has published lists of the sexiest programs and their sponsors. Corporate executives from targeted companies have met with Wildmon in an attempt to be deleted from "the list," promising policy changes in sponsorship practices. For example, Proctor and Gamble, TV's largest advertiser, announced that it had and would continue to withdraw advertising support from several of the listed programs. Dissatisfied with the overall response of the industry, however, the CBTV threatened a boycott of products sold by the guilty sponsors early in July 1981 that was later cancelled, presumably to give the sponsors a chance to execute their promises for change (*Newsweek*, 1981; *Time*, 1981a,b).

Although the media reform groups have been somewhat effective in stimulating changes in broadcasting practices — either directly on the television/advertising industry (e.g., CBTV) or indirectly through actions of the FCC or FTC (e.g., ACT) — there are strong forces within the system that oppose such efforts to regulate broadcasting. These *counter*-control influences, each with its own ideological, legal, and economic roots, will be discussed next.

COUNTER-CONTROLS ON THE TV BUSINESS

As we saw in the last section, the FCC and FTC regulate some aspects of the TV business. The FCC grants and renews licenses to television stations. However, the FCC generally has not interfered with the content of television. Likewise, the FTC has intervened in TV advertising which has been unfair or deceptive, but has otherwise stayed clear of regulating the content of commercials.

First Amendment

The factor limiting these government agencies from regulating television content is the First Amendment of the United States Constitution which is explicitly upheld in the Federal Communications Act of 1934. The First Amendment states that "Congress shall make no law . . . abridging the freedom of speech or of the press."

While the First Amendment has been used as the automatic attack on almost any broadcast regulation, it is important to keep in mind the many situations outlined by Victor Cline (1974) in which free speech is limited in the interest of society:

1. False advertising. . . .
2. Speaking a prayer, reading from the Bible, or giving instruction in religious matters . . . in public schools. . . .
3. Libel, slander, defamation of character. . . .
4. Saying words which amount to a conspiracy or an obstruction of justice.
5. Sedition . . . plan for the violent overthrow of our government. . . .
6. Words that tend to create a "clear and present danger."
7. Using words that constitute offering a bribe. . . .
8. Words that threaten social harm because they advocate illegal acts.
9. Words (from a loudspeaker) at 3:00 A.M. in a residential neighborhood, disturbing the peace.

10. A public address in the middle of Main Street at high noon, which as a consequence interferes with the orderly movement of traffic.
11. Being in contempt of court. The judge may send you to jail if either your behavior or your speech is inappropriate.
12. Committing perjury under oath.
13. Television cigarette advertisements.
14. Saying words or giving information which have been classified (e.g., secret) by the government.
15. *Obscenity. While the Supreme Court has repeatedly affirmed that obscenity is not a protected form of speech, it has permitted local communities to form their own criteria of what is and is not permitted as long as these criteria include appeal to prurient interest and lack of redeeming artistic, scientific or literary value.*
16. Copyright violations.
17. Pretrial publicity which might interfere with a defendant's opportunity to secure a fair trial by his peers.
18. U.S. Government employees engaging in political speech or activity [pp. 7–9, emphasis in original].

Clearly, restricting certain types of content on television, whether it be violence or sex, is in a gray area. Some people would argue that such content threatens the health and safety of society. But others argue that it is more important to uphold the First Amendment principle.

Self-regulation

Up to a point, at least, the industry regulates itself by anticipating or responding to the pressures of public interest groups and government officials. Part of self-regulation is public relations, though, as illustrated by the NAB Code.

The NAB Code. The industry itself, embodied in the National Association of Broadcasters, has a television code pertinent to a number of aspects of television programming. All three major networks and about two-thirds of the nation's stations subscribe to it. However, as we shall see, the NAB has absolutely no enforcement power. The code (1981) states in part:

> Television is seen and heard in nearly every American home. These homes include children and adults of all ages, embrace all races and all varieties of philosophic or religious conviction and reach those of every educational background. Television broadcasters must take this pluralistic audience into account in programming their stations. They are obligated to bring their positive responsibility for professionalism and reasoned judgment to bear upon all those involved in the development, production and selection of programs.

It is the interest of television as a vital medium to encourage programs that are innovative, reflect a high degree of creative skill, deal with significant moral and social issues and present challenging concepts and other subject matter that relate to the world in which the viewer lives.

To achieve these goals, television broadcasters should be conversant with the general and specific needs, interests and aspirations of all the segments of the communities they serve. They should affirmatively seek out responsible representatives of all parts of their communities so that they may structure a broad range of programs that will inform, enlighten, and entertain the total audience.

Broadcasters should also develop programs directed toward advancing the cultural and educational aspects of their communities.

. . . in selecting program subjects and themes, great care must be exercised to be sure that treatment and presentation are made in good faith and not for the purpose of sensationalism or to shock or exploit the audience or appeal to prurient interests or morbid curiosity.

Broadcasters have a special responsibility to children. Programs designed primarily for children should take into account the range of interests and needs of children from instructional and cultural material to a wide variety of entertainment material. In their totality, programs should contribute to the sound, balanced development of children to help them achieve a sense of the world at large and informed adjustments to their society.

In the course of a child's development, numerous social factors and forces, including television, affect the ability of the child to make the transition to adult society.

The child's training and experience during the formative years should include positive sets of values which will allow the child to become a responsible adult, capable of coping with the challenges of maturity.

Children should also be exposed, at the appropriate times, to a reasonable range of the realities which exist in the world sufficient to help them make the transition to adulthood.

Because children are allowed to watch programs designed primarily for adults, broadcasters should take this practice into account in the presentation of material in such programs when children may constitute a substantial segment of the audience.

Violence, physical or psychological, may only be projected in responsibly handled contexts, not used exploitatively. Programs involving violence should present the consequences of it to its victims and perpetrators.

Presentation of the details of violence should avoid the excessive, the gratuitous and the instructional.

The use of violence for its own sake and the detailed dwelling upon brutality or physical agony, by sight or by sound, are not permissible.

The presentation of techniques of crime in such detail as to be instructional or invite imitation shall be avoided.

The presentation of marriage, the family and similarly important human relationships, and material with sexual connotations, shall not be treated exploitatively or irresponsibly, but with sensitivity. Costuming and movements of all performers shall be handled in a similar fashion.

Special sensitivity is necessary in the use of material relating to sex, race, color, age, creed, religious functionaries or rites, or national or ethnic derivation.

There shall be no graphic portrayal of sexual acts by sight or sound. The portrayal of implied sexual acts must be essential to the plot and presented in a responsible and tasteful manner.

The broadcaster and the advertiser should exercise special caution with the content and presentation of television commercials placed in or near programs designed for children. Exploitation of children should be avoided. Commercials directed to children should in no way mislead as to the product's performance and usefulness.

One of the most dramatic displays of the NAB's resistance to enforce its own code came in 1963. Newton Minow, then FCC Commissioner, proposed that public hearings be held on the problem of over-commercialism. The FCC debated between regulating on a case by case basis or formulating a general rule. It finally decided to take the latter course, and announced that stations would have to adhere to rules stated in the Television Code of the National Association of Broadcasters. This seemed like a reasonable procedure, since the government would thereby impose only those standards formulated by the industry itself. But the NAB opposed the plan of using its own code and actually organized committees in each state to lobby against it. Such a move, the broadcasters felt, would have set a dangerous precedent leading perhaps to further enforcement of a public relations document never intended to guide actual practices.

Before the FCC could hold hearings on the NAB's system, the Subcommittee on Communications and Power of the House Committee on Interstate and Foreign Commerce approved a bill prohibiting FCC control. By that time (February 1964), the FCC had gained a new member who also opposed the plan and cast the deciding vote against it. In the absence of an FCC ruling to abide by the NAB guidelines, the NAB has virtually no power and no wish for it. (Details of the proposed adoption of the NAB Code by the FCC may be found in Longley, 1967; Mayer, 1972; and Baker, 1969.)

It is no surprise that the NAB would resist effective enforcement of any code that would restrict the broadcaster's freedom. The NAB was born in 1923 out of the need for a trade organization to represent and protect the interests of the radio broadcasters. An in-depth study of the workings of the NAB by Stookey and Waz (1980) reveals that the most important function of the organization has been to represent the broadcasters' interests before various government agencies, a task it performs well.

> The organization's power in influencing legislation and regulation stems from its sizeable financial and human resources, its access and accessibility to government decision-makers, and its network of members who can be mobilized for support.

> NAB's professional and support staff numbers well over one hundred people. Its battery of lawyers, located mainly in the legal and government relations departments, is well-paid and well-seasoned. The association's lobbyists are regarded as among the best in Washington — in any field. And nearly one-sixth of the NAB budget for fiscal year 1979 was set aside for participation in the regulatory arena [p. 1].

The study also revealed that the NAB's annual budget is close to $7 million.

Broadcast standards and practices — network self-regulation. In practice, regulation of television content is carried out by employees of each network. Each network has a *standards and practices* department with several standards editors (or "censors") and a director who reports to a vice president for broadcast standards, who in turn reports to the network president.

Baldwin and Lewis (1972) interviewed 48 producers, writers, directors, and network censors involved in the production of network television series. They learned that the censor sees himself as an agent of the licensee who makes sure that the programs fed to him conform to the National Association of Broadcasters Code and meet uniform network standards. On the other hand, the producers and writers described the censor as serving as "a buffer between the public, the FCC, and Congress on the one hand and the network and corporate executives on the other . . . to protect the executives from troublesome and costly criticism" (p. 324).

The censors become involved in the production process from the earliest stages, approving or suggesting changes in presentation at each stage — from the story outline, to script drafts, rough cuts, and final film cuts. According to Baldwin and Lewis, censors tend to cover themselves by issuing warnings about every conceivable aspect of programming that could be objectionable in the final film. Not all censor recommendations are followed, however. Suggestions that require reshooting are extremely costly. The ultimate decisions for changes are made by the standards and practices director whose decisions often involve compromising with producers. One producer said of the network censors:

> We fight them as hard as we can in regard to their absolutely asinine decisions. You can get away from the rules by going to the top . . . I call the boss and say, "Would you like to hear what your people are doing? Isn't that asinine?" And he's likely to agree [p. 325].

No one envies the censors. Baldwin and Lewis described the network censors' plight:

> They're trying to pacify federal agencies, religious groups, educational groups, moral critics of all kinds who are coming at them—and still put together entertainment which people will enjoy enough to keep them in business [p. 330].

How do the network censors make their decisions? In terms of formal codes, all three networks refer to the NAB Television Code as a general guide. Both NBC and ABC have created their own manuals, but these too are loaded with public relations talk and could rarely be used in making actual specific decisions. More likely, both of these networks follow the strategy that is openly used at CBS, namely an "oral tradition" in which the old timers in the department recount the history of the decisions made about various types of content in the past. Factors such as broadcast year, season, day, hour, type of show, and character are essential descriptors that influence decisions. Aside from considering these cues, the editor has to be sensitive to a much larger context:

> In the absence of a rigid code, the editor's personal sensitivity becomes the essential litmus. There are a number of things they are trying to be sensitive to, including the image of CBS, the libel and slander laws, the concerns of pressure groups, congressmen, CBS's affiliated stations, Hollywood writers and producers, and the ethical, cultural milieu of the American living room [Levin, 1980, p. 326].

TELEVISION OUTSIDE THE UNITED STATES

Is there any other way than that used in the United States to run the business of television? Murray (1980; Murray & Kippax, 1979) compared the broadcasting structure of 16 countries and found numerous variations. Table 2.4 presents each country with the date television was introduced, the number of channels and type of ownership, the number of broadcast hours, frequency of advertising messages, and the amount of imported programming.

The broadcast systems most similar to the United States are those of Australia and Canada. Both have a predominantly commercial system, a public broadcast station,* many hours of daily broadcasting, and generous advertising time allowed. In addition, both countries import many U.S. programs, causing the specific TV content to be similar and often identical to that of the United States. England has a similar system to that of the United States in that the broadcasting hours are quite ample, and there are both commercial and publicly owned stations. However, the commercial station (Independent Broadcasting Authority) came onto the scene after 18 years of an exclusively public system (British Broadcasting Corporation). This history has largely shaped current programming practices in that the commercial station in England offers more educational and special audience programming (e.g., children's programs) than those of the United States or Australia (Murray, 1980).

The Japanese system resembles both the American and British systems. Initially, Japan relied on public broadcasting, largely modeled on the BBC. Nippon Television Network (NTV), a conglomerate of commercial stations, started broadcasting shortly after and operates much like the American commercial network system including the availability of many hours of programming and the use of advertising to generate revenue. However, all commercials must pass government approval.

Israel, which has only one publicly owned station (Israel Broadcasting Authority), offers the least amount of programming (four hours daily). The IBA relies on government funds and license fees for its revenue, because there is no advertising at all. About half of its programming is imported, and much of it is from the United States.

The Scandinavian countries (Denmark, Norway, and Sweden) also rely on a government-controlled broadcasting system without advertising and offer rather restricted broadcast hours. These hours, however, are filled with programs emphasizing the arts, education, and children's programming. The programming in Finland is of the same type, although the broadcasting system is slightly different from that of its neighbors. There is only one station, 92% of which is owned by the government, and it is largely controlled by the government. Some advertising is allowed.

The Western European countries, Austria, France, Italy, and West Germany, have government-funded and controlled broadcast systems with little, if any, advertising. The Swiss government licenses one broadcasting company which operates three channels and generates its revenue through ad-

---

*We will explain public broadcasting in the United States in Chapter 8.

Table 2.4. The Structure of Television Broadcasting in Sixteen Countries.

Country	Date of onset	Number of channels or networks and ownership	Broadcast hours	Advertising[a]	Control of violence		Imported content (allowed/ actual, %)
					Formal	Informal	
Australia	1956	1 public 3 commercial	100 hr/week 140 hr/week	None 11 min/hr, P 13 min/hr, O	X		50
Austria	1957	1 public 1 public	12 hr/day 4 hr/day	None 20 min/day		X	
Canada	1952	1 public 1 commercial	18 hr/day 18 hr/day	12 min/hr		X	40
Denmark	1954	1 public	4 hr/day	None		X	52
Finland	1957	2 govt./private	16 hr/day	15%	X		35
France	1945	2 public 1 public		Minimal None		X	60
Germany	1945	1 public 2 public	3 hr/day 8 hr/day	20 min/day		X	40
Israel	1968	1 public	4 hr/day	None		X	50
Italy	1948	1 public	7 hr/day 4 hr/day	5% 5%		X	Minimal

Country	Year	Channels	Hours	Advertising[a]			
Japan	1953	1 public	18 hr/day	None	X		
		1 commercial	18 hr/day	18%		X	10
Norway	1960	1 public	50 hr/week	None		X	50
Poland	1954	1 public	9 hr/day	Minimal	X	X	18
Sweden	1956	1 public	22 hr/week	None		X	40
		1 public	100 hr/week				
Switzerland		3 govt./private	100 hr/week	20 min/day	X		
United Kingdom	1936	1 public	82 hr/week				
		1 public	42 hr/week	6 min/hr		X	14
		1 commercial	105 hr/week				
United States	1939	1 public	16 hr/day	None		X	Minimal
		3 commercial	24 hr/day	9.5 min/day, P; 13 min/hr, O*			

[a]P, prime time, usually 5 to 9 PM; O, other times.

*Changed to 16 min/hr. in 1981.

Source: Murray and Kippax (1979), pp. 258–259.

vertising and license fees. Despite the economic structure, Switzerland's broadcasting system is largely controlled by the government to the extent that bans are issued prohibiting certain content, including violence.

Poland has a government-owned broadcasting system comprised of two channels, one of which airs educational and general entertainment programming, and the other science and arts programming. A full 82% of the programming is produced within the system, and the government bans content that criticizes the government in any way or threatens the maintenance of law and order.

In Communist China, there are three TV stations operating in Peking and 37 other stations in the country. All stations are owned by the government, and limited advertising brings in some revenue. Most of the stations broadcast several hours nightly, and 25% of the programs are instructional; however, some movies are shown including those produced domestically and by Western and Soviet countries. Television ownership has expanded dramatically in China—in 1971, there was one set for each 16,400 people, and by 1981 there was one set for each 280 people. A black and white set costs between $120–$240 (U.S. dollars), and there is usually a waiting list (Gertner, 1981).

Chapter 3
TV Violence: Early Politics, Theories and Research

OVERVIEW

The effect of TV violence on children has been hotly debated for more than three decades. Senate hearings in 1954 and 1961, a Senate report in 1964, and the report of the National Commission on the Causes and Prevention of Violence in 1968, all concluded that there was a great deal of violence on television and that such content *probably* had an adverse effect on the young. At the same time it was recognized that the then available laboratory studies bore only indirectly on the question of the relationship between viewing of actual TV content and real acts of aggression.

As public concern about TV violence mounted, academic psychologists developed theories of how such material might influence young viewers. Bandura and Walters' social learning theory emphasized that TV provided instructional models for behavior (as suggested by the famous Bobo doll studies). Berkowitz, Tannenbaum, and others emphasized the immediate arousing and instigating effects of viewing TV violence. Finally, Feshbach and Singer, financed by CBS, published a unique experimental field study which seemed to support their catharsis hypothesis. Youngsters exposed to a steady diet of TV violence were found to be *less* aggressive than those exposed to a nonaggressive television diet.

The clear implication was that more definitive research on the nature and effects of TV violence was needed, and this recognition paved the way for the Surgeon General's Report.

We mentioned in Chapter 1 that there are many parallels between concerns expressed about television and concerns expressed about movies in an earlier period. One difference between the two media is that while violent content was one of many issues for the movies, it was for TV *the* issue for over a decade. In this chapter we will tell the story of early investigations into the effects of TV violence and describe the response these investigations provoked in the first government hearings on the subject. Looking backward, many of the early investigations into TV violence seem quite naive, and, indeed, we will see later that much more sophisticated research methods have been devised. Nonetheless, the early inquiries are important because they laid the foundation for the later work by defining the impor-

47

tant issues and setting forth the basic theories of exactly how TV violence might work its effects. Equally important are the early government hearings into TV violence, which set the tone for politicizing the possible effects of television on children and for threatening possible censorship.

EARLY GOVERNMENT HEARINGS
AND INDUSTRY RESEARCH

As we will see in Chapter 4, a variety of political, social, and scientific developments converged to instigate a major inquiry into the effects of TV violence on the young, the Surgeon General's Report. In this section we will examine the political and commercial backdrop out of which the Surgeon General's Report grew. The next section is devoted to scientific and academic developments that also played an important role in instigating and defining this report.

1954—The Kefauver Committee on Juvenile Delinquency

As early as 1954, Senator Estes Kefauver, then Chairman of the Senate Subcommittee on Juvenile Delinquency, questioned the need for violent content on television entertainment. Network representatives claimed at that time that research on the effects of violence viewing upon children was inconclusive, although they admitted that some risk existed (United States Senate, 1956). In addition, Harold E. Fellows, President and Chairman of the Board of the National Association of Broadcasters, promised that the NAB would undertake research on the impact of television programming on children.

1961—The Dodd Hearings

In 1961 Senator Thomas Dodd, then chairman of the same subcommittee, inquired about violence on children's television. Testimony during hearings revealed that violence had remained a staple in the networks' TV diet.
   Industry spokesmen again promised more research:

> We are moving significantly in this area [of research on effects of television on children] now. At a meeting of our joint radio and television board of directors last week approval was given to proceed with the initial planning of an NAB research and training center in association with one of the leading universities in the nation [cited in Baker, 1969, p. 594].

Testimony at the same hearings also revealed that the previously promised research had yet to be carried out. Leroy Collins, the new president of the NAB explained:

Soon [after Mr. Fellows' testimony] the television code review board undertook a pilot study of "viewer attitudes" to determine the feasibility of a broader study, but about that time the Columbia Broadcasting System announced that it was engaged in sponsoring a survey which, while broader, would cover essentially the same ground. In view of this overlapping inquiry, NAB deferred to CBS in order that the larger survey could go ahead in preference to the narrower inquiry which the NAB had initiated. It is anticipated that the CBS project will be completed by the end of this summer [1961] and that a final report will be published before the end of this year [cited in Baker, 1969, pp. 593–594].

Industry research in the 1960s

In 1962, the industry, along with the United States Department of Health, Education and Welfare, co-sponsored the Joint Committee for Research on Television and Children. This committee, which consisted almost entirely of network personnel, solicited research proposals from various members of the scientific community. Unfortunately, it became clear in 1964 that few of these proposals were being carried out. In fact, only three papers were even begun as a result of the work of the joint committee. The first, by Ruth Hartley (1964), constituted a criticism and analysis of the inadequacies of research which was detrimental to the industry, not an investigation of the actual effects. The second was conducted by Seymour Feshbach, a psychologist who believed that TV violence was not harmful and might in some cases even help to drain off aggressive impulses (Feshbach & Singer, 1971). The third study was not even completed.

In 1963, the long awaited CBS report (which had superseded the research promised by the Kefauver Commission in 1954) was published by Gary Steiner. The title, *The People Look at Television*, indicates clearly the subject matter of the volume: the attitudes and beliefs of parents and other viewers about the effects of television on children, not the actual effects as determined by scientific investigation.

But the earlier hearings did have an impact, which one observer described this way:

[The subcommittee staff for the 1961 Dodd hearings] noted that many network series mentioned in early testimony as especially violent were being syndicated, and shown on independent stations throughout the country. One committee aide observed: "It's as if they used our 1961 hearings as a shopping list!" Many of the programs were scheduled at earlier hours than before, and were reaching younger audiences [cited in Barnouw, 1972, p. 203].

In 1964, as Senator Dodd's hearings continued, network executives again promised to do more research. By this time the excuses had become rather pathetic. When asked by Dodd what had been done, NBC Executive Vice President Walter D. Scott replied this way:

I have asked the same question, Senator, because I have wondered why there has not been more in the way of results up to this point. I have been reminded by our people who are working very actively and closely with the Committee that it is appropriate to bear in mind that the work of scholars frequently sets its own pace and that time may be the price we must pay for meaningful results. As I understand it, they have had work done by a very large number of competent scholars in the field of social sciences. I understand that there have been something like one hundred separate projects that have been studied, that these have been narrowed down, that they are now at the stage of being ready to go ahead with, I believe, either five or six specific projects out of which they hope to get some meaningful answers [cited in Baker, 1969, p. 595].

No new research was ever published or reported by the Committee. Scott went on to become NBC's board chairman.

1964 — The Report of the Senate Subcommittee on Juvenile Delinquency

On October 27, 1964 the Senate Subcommittee on Juvenile Delinquency issued a report that was very critical of the networks.

The extent to which violence and crime are currently portrayed on the nation's television screens is clearly excessive. And in the face of repeated warnings from officials directly concerned with coping with juvenile delinquency and from competent researchers that this kind of television fare can be harmful to the young viewer, the television industry generally has shown little disposition to substantially reduce the degree of violence to which it exposes the American public [*U.S. News & World Report*, 1964, p. 210].

With regard to the effects of this type of content, the report indicated:

It is clear that television, whose impact on the public mind is equal to or greater than that of any other medium is a factor in molding the character, attitudes and behavior patterns of America's young people [p. 211].

The report went on to say that industry self-regulation through the NAB Code has been largely ineffective:

The industry's claim that this Code is an effective vehicle cannot be substantiated in light of the evidence of chronic violation. Network programming policies which deliberately call for the insertion of violence, crime and brutality are hardly conducive to building respect for any central authority within the industry [p. 211].

Finally, in the absence of an effective self-regulatory system, the report hinted at government intervention:

Effective self-policing is the desirable approach to this problem which poses so clear a threat to our present and our future.

But the patience of Congress, though considerable, is not endless. The public's demand for concrete results grows more intense, and indeed it should [p. 213].

1968 — The National Commission on the Causes and Prevention of Violence

In 1968, the National Commission on the Causes and Prevention of Violence held hearings on the role of the mass media. Once again, network executives were questioned about the promised research; once again, it was not forthcoming. By this time, the networks were arguing that *they* should not be doing research anyway. One ABC executive stated:

Research should be done from an objective standpoint and one that the public would be satisfied with as being done objectively, rather than that which is directly financed by our particular company [Baker, 1969, p. 598].

Network executives also suggested that research was impossible due to the lack of adequate research design. Frank Stanton, then president of CBS and himself a Ph.D. psychologist, remarked:

It isn't unwillingness on the part of the industry to underwrite the research. It is that no one in the thirty-odd years I have been in the business has come up with a technique or methodology that would let you get a fix on this impact. . . . These people from the outside [of the industry] have been given every encouragement, every funding they have asked for to come up with methodology, and this is the field that is very illusive [sic] and it doesn't do any good to spend a lot of money and come up with facts somebody can punch his fingers through [Baker, 1969, p. 598].

However, the Commission staff report did not concur, stating that:

there is sufficient evidence that mass media presentations, especially portrayals of violence, have negative effects upon audiences . . . [and] that the burden of research and proof should be placed squarely on the mass media, especially commercial television, to carry out meaningful research on the psychological and social effects of mass media portrayals of violence [Baker and Ball, 1969, p. 381].

In all, the Commission concluded:

We believe it is reasonable to conclude that a constant diet of violent behavior on television has an adverse effect on human character and attitudes. Violence on television encourages violent forms of behavior, and fosters moral and social

values about violence in daily life which are unacceptable in a civilized society
. . . it is a matter for grave concern that at a time when the values and the influence of traditional institutions such as family, church, and school are in question, television is emphasizing violent, antisocial styles of life [National Commission on the Causes and Prevention of Violence, 1969, p. 199].

It is interesting to note that the National Commission on the Causes and
Prevention of Violence based its hearings on a series of review articles. With
the exception of an analysis of how much violence is presented on television
(by George Gerbner, details to be discussed in the next chapter), no new research was commissioned. It was not until the end of these hearings in 1968
that Congress appropriated the funds for new studies to be conducted. This
was the Surgeon General's Report which is the focus of the next chapter.

EARLY THEORIES AND ACADEMIC RESEARCH

Three basic theories were brought to bear on the issue of TV violence in
the 1960s by academic psychologists. These were social learning theory, instigation theory, and catharsis theory. Each of these viewpoints was still in a
relatively early stage of development in the 1960s and, as we shall see, each
theory matured concurrently with further developments in our understanding of the effects of television on children.

Social learning theory

In Chapter 1 we mentioned Stanford psychologist Albert Bandura, whose
1963 *Look* magazine article, "What TV Violence Can Do to Your Child,"
made the TV violence issue vivid for a popular audience. Bandura has become eminent in academic psychology for his development of *social learning theory*. In fact, the history of social learning theory is intertwined with
the history of exploring the effects of television on children. A closer look at
the nature of social learning theory reveals the reason for the partnership.
The principles of social learning theory were first stated in Bandura's
monograph with his student Richard Walters, *Social Learning and Personality Development* (1963). This small book, addressed to an academic audience (mainly psychologists), took issue with the prevailing psychoanalytic
view of the child's personality development as a result of sexually tinged
conflicts with parents. Bandura and Walters suggested instead that children
learn their personalities from experiences and interactions with culture, sub-
culture, family and peers. Acknowledging the role of rewards and punish-
ments in shaping children's development, Bandura and Walters nonetheless
insisted that *modeling* played a uniquely important role in the child's social

development. The best and most effective way to teach children novel ways of acting and their consequences is to show them the behavior you wish them to learn and display. Declaring that "models are utilized in all cultures to promote the acquisiton of socially sanctioned behavior patterns," Bandura and Walters provided simple but compelling examples to make their point:

> The manner in which complex adult-role behavior may sometimes be acquired almost entirely through imitation is illustrated in an account given by Nash (1958) of the social training of children in a Cantelense subculture of Guatemala. The young Cantelense girl is provided with a water jar, a broom, and a grinding stone, which are miniature versions of those used by her mother. Through constantly observing and imitating the domestic activities of the mother, who provides little or no direct tuition, the child readily acquires a repertory of sex-appropriate responses. Similarly, small Cantalense boys accompany their fathers while the latter are engaged in occupational activities and reproduce their fathers' actions with the aid of smaller versions of adult implements.
>
> North American parents do not provide female children with miniature functioning replicas of the complex appliances that are customarily found in their households, since these would be prohibitively costly, readily damaged, and dangerous for children to operate. They frequently, however, supply their young daughters with a varied array of play materials—toy kitchen ensembles, dolls with complete nursery equipment and wardrobes, cooking utensils, and other junior-size homemaker kits—which foster imitative adult-role behavior. Play materials for male children in our culture are, generally speaking, less likely to be of direct relevance for the acquisition of sex-appropriate, everyday adult-role activities (partly, perhaps, a result, in middle-class families, of the relatively abstract nature of the occupational activities of the adult male), but they nevertheless frequently include building and other construction kits and mechanical gadgets that are associated with male occupational roles. While playing with toys that stimulate imitation of adults, children frequently reproduce not only the appropriate adult-role behavior patterns but also characteristic or idiosyncratic parental patterns of response, including attitudes, mannerisms, gestures, and even voice inflections, which the parents have certainly never attempted directly to teach. As the example taken from the Cantelense society most clearly indicates, children frequently acquire, in the course of imitative role-playing, numerous classes of interrelated responses *in toto*, apparently without proceeding through a gradual and laborious process of response differentiation and extinction or requiring a lengthy period of discrimination training [pp. 47–48].

Bandura and Walters were in the tradition of post-World War II, academic psychologists who tried to extend theories of learning which had been developed in the 1930s based on research with laboratory animals into useful tools for social application with human beings. At the same time, they wanted their claims to stand on a research base that was reputable in the eyes of their academic colleagues. (Psychoanalysis was not considered reputable because it was not built on a base of objective research.) In order to demonstrate the importance of modeling objectively and vividly, Bandura and Walters had conducted a series of controlled laboratory experiments on the modeling of play aggression. The most famous and important of these were the Bobo doll studies of the early 1960's. (Appendix A provides an explanation of the experimental method.)

Direct imitation of play aggression: The Bobo doll studies. A major purpose of the Bobo doll studies was to demonstrate that there are two distinct effects of exposing young children to aggressive models: a teaching effect and a motivating effect. The series of studies was also designed to explore variations in each of these effects.

Although in principle there would be an enormous number of ways of displaying and measuring aggression, in practice the range of choices was sharply limited by ethical and practical considerations. The Bobo doll studies were designed to probe whether and under what circumstances novel aggressive acts will be learned and copied by young children. This question was clearly related to the concerns raised by politicians and parents that children might copy what they saw on TV, as mentioned in our earlier discussion.

Bandura selected a plastic Bobo doll as the "target" for aggression in his experiments. Though the individual Bobo doll studies differed in many particulars, all shared the feature that a child was shown another individual displaying a series of novel and distinctive assaults against an inflated plastic clown designed as a young child's punching bag (with a sand base so that it bounced back when punched and a nose that squeeked when struck with sufficient force). After exposure to such a display of behavior, the child was watched at play with the Bobo doll and other toys while his or her acts of imitative aggression were counted by trained observers. (See Figure 3.1.) Within this framework Bandura and his colleagues demonstrated several principles of their social learning theory as applied to aggression.

Vicarious consequences and the acquisition-performance distinction. Bandura and Walters (1963) declared that to understand modeling it was critical to distinguish between the child's *acquisition* of novel responses and the actual *performance* of these responses. The clearest demonstration of this fact was in a classic Bobo doll experiment, described by Bandura and Walters (1963) and subsequently published by Bandura (1965).

The children who participated as subjects were nursery school boys and girls, and the modeling sequence they saw was filmed and then projected on

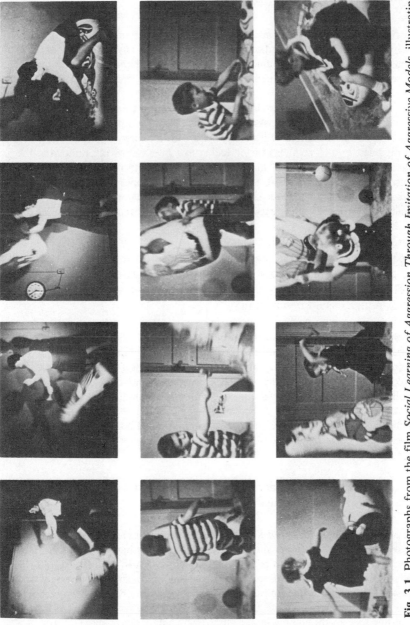

Fig. 3.1. Photographs from the film *Social Learning of Aggression Through Imitation of Aggressive Models*, illustrating children's acquisition of aggressive responses through observational learning.

Source: Courtesy of Dr. Albert Bandura.

a simulated television set referred to when speaking to the children as a "TV show."* As Bandura (1965) described it:

> The film began with a scene in which [an adult male] model walked up to an adult-size plastic Bobo doll and ordered him to clear the way. After glaring for a moment at the noncompliant antagonist the model exhibited four novel aggressive responses each accompanied by a distinctive verbalization.

> First, the model laid the Bobo doll on its side, sat on it, and punched it in the nose while remarking, "Pow, right in the nose, boom, boom." The model then raised the doll and pommeled it on the head with a mallet. Each response was accompanied by the verbalization, "Sockeroo . . . stay down." Following the mallet aggression, the model kicked the doll about the room, and these responses were interspersed with the comment, "Fly away." Finally, the model threw rubber balls at the Bobo doll, each strike punctuated with "Bang." This sequence of physically and verbally aggressive behavior was repeated twice [pp. 590–591].

One group of the children in this experiment saw a sequence which ended at this point. Children in two other groups saw the same sequence, but with an additional scene showing consequences to the aggressive model. Returning to Bandura's vivid description:

> For children in the *model-rewarded* condition, a second adult appeared with an abundant supply of candies and soft drinks. He informed the model that he was a "strong champion" and that his superb aggressive performance clearly deserved a generous treat. He then poured him a large glass of 7-Up, and readily supplied additional energy-building nourishment including chocolate bars, Cracker Jack popcorn, and an assortment of candies. While the model was rapidly consuming the delectable treats, his admirer symbolically reinstated the modeled aggressive responses and engaged in considerable positive social reinforcement [p. 591; italics added].

The final group saw the model receive a quite different kind of consequence for his assaults against the clown:

> For children in the *model-punished* condition the reinforcing agent appeared on the scene shaking his finger menacingly and commenting reprovingly, "Hey there, you big bully. You quit picking on that clown. I won't tolerate it." As the model drew back he tripped and fell, the other adult sat on the model and spanked him with a rolled-up magazine while reminding him of his aggressive behavior. As the model ran off cowering, the agent forewarned him, "If I catch you doing that again, you big bully, I'll give you a hard spanking. You quit acting that way" [p. 591; italics added].

---

*Videotaping equipment was not yet widely available.

So much for the modeling. Next came the tests of its effects. First was a test of *performance*, designed to see how much spontaneous copying occurred under each of the three conditions. Thus, after viewing the film to which they had been assigned, children were brought individually into an experimental room which contained a plastic Bobo doll just like the one in the film, three balls, a mallet, a pegboard, plastic farm animals, and a doll house which was equipped with furniture and a miniature doll family. This array of toys permitted the child to engage either in imitative aggressive responses (i.e., the model's responses) or in alternative nonaggressive and nonimitative forms of behavior. The child was subsequently left alone with this assortment of equipment for ten minutes, while judges made periodic observations from behind a one-way vision screen. The results of this test showed quite a bit of spontaneous imitation for children who had seen the model either rewarded or receive no consequences, but the children showed little tendency to spontaneously imitate the acts of the model whom they had seen punished. Boys also displayed considerably more imitative aggression than girls in this situation.

Social learning theory predicted that although the children in the model-punished condition had not spontaneously performed the novel aggressive acts of the model, they had nonetheless learned or *acquired* these responses and could perform them if the circumstances were made inviting. The purpose of the second test in Bandura's experiment was to see whether such acquisition had in fact occurred. The experimenter now reentered the room well supplied with sticker pictures and an attractive juice dispenser. The experimenter gave the child a small treat of fruit juice and told the child that, for each imitative response he or she could now reproduce, an additional treat would be given. These incentives for reproducing the model's behavior led to very high rates of reproduction of the model's responses in all groups, including those who had seen the model punished. In the language of social learning theory, consequences to a model (such as those in Bandura's experiment described above) are referred to as *vicarious consequences*.

Other Bobo doll studies. Other Bobo doll studies demonstrated additional propositions that related social learning theory to what children commonly see on television. For example, in one study (Bandura, Ross, & Ross, 1963) some children saw the sort of aggressive display we have already described perpetrated by an adult while other children saw the same display perpetrated by a cartoon-like figure, Herman the cat. The results showed that learning occurred almost as readily when the model was Herman the cat than when it was an adult, and thus seemed to implicate cartoon as well as live formats as potential means by which children could learn aggressive responses from television.

Later in the decade, additional Bobo doll studies were conducted by other investigators. Hicks (1965, 1968), for example, showed that many children exposed to films such as those used by Bandura (1965) could still reproduce the novel aggressive responses on request 6 to 8 months later.* In a series of studies, Hanratty and others (Hanratty, Liebert, Morris, & Fernandez, 1969; Hanratty, O'Neal, & Sulzer, 1972; Savitsky, Rogers, Izard, & Liebert, 1971) showed that preschool children would spontaneously imitate aggression against a human adult dressed as a clown, which took the results out of the realm of completely harmless play. They found direct copying of aggressive acts even when the model did not receive vicarious rewards and the children were not frustrated or provoked in any way.

Studies of disinhibitory effects. Bandura and Walters' (1963) theory recognized that direct learning and copying were only two of the many effects that could result from exposure to models. Equally important were disinhibitory effects, in which the observation of a response of a particular class (for example, an aggressive response) leads to an increased likelihood of displaying other, different responses that also belong to the same class.

The earliest demonstrations of the disinhibitory effects of observing aggression, like the earliest Bobo doll studies, involved aggressive play as their critical measure.

Lovaas (1961) showed that nursery school children's aggressive play increased after viewing an aggressive film. Half the children saw one cartoon figure aggress against another by hitting, biting, and so on, for virtually the entire duration of the film. The remaining children saw a film of a mother bear and three baby bears playing together. Each child was then presented with two toys, and his play was observed. Pushing a lever on one toy caused one doll to turn and hit another doll over the head with a stick. Depressing the lever on the other toy caused a wooden ball, enclosed in a cage, to jump through obstacles. The toys were presented side by side; the child could operate either or both at once if he wished. Children who were exposed to the aggressive film used the hitting doll toy more often than those who watched the nonaggressive film. Thus, at least at the level of play, disinhibition occurred.

In view of the fact that most television programs appeared to depict aggression as a potent technique for power and achievement, investigations which focused upon the inhibiting and disinhibiting effects of consequences accruing to a model for aggression are of particular importance. In one such study, Bandura, Ross, and Ross (1961) exposed one group of nursery school boys and girls to a simulated television program in which one character,

---

*It should be noted, though, that the children in Hicks' studies had been asked to give a demonstration of the modeled violence immediately after seeing it, and this experience might well have riveted their attention to the situation by signaling its importance.

Johnny, refused another, Rocky, the opportunity to play with some toys. The program goes on to show a series of aggressive responses by Rocky, including hitting Johnny with a rubber ball, shooting darts at Johnny's cars, hitting Johnny with a baton, lassoing him with a hula-hoop, and so on. At the end of this sequence, Rocky, the aggressor, is playing with all of Johnny's toys, treating himself to sweet beverages and cookies, and finally departs with Johnny's hobby horse under his arm and a sack of Johnny's toys over his shoulder. At this point, a commentator announces that Rocky was victorious. In a second group, the program was rearranged so that after Rocky's initial aggression, Johnny retaliated in kind by administering a sound thrashing to the aggressor.

Two other groups served as controls; in one, a nonaggressive but highly expressive television program was observed, and in the second no television program was seen. Children's subsequent aggressive responses while playing for 20 minutes in a special test room constituted the primary dependent measure. The results clearly showed that those who observed a rewarded aggressor showed far more aggression themselves than children in the other groups. Moreover, at the conclusion of the experiment the children were asked to state which of the characters, Rocky or Johnny, they would prefer to emulate. Sixty percent of those who observed Rocky rewarded for his behavior indicated that they would select him as a model; only 20% of those who saw him punished indicated that they would choose to emulate him. Additionally, the authors noted a classic example of how socially reprehensible but successful modeled aggressive acts may influence children. One of the girls, who had expressed marked disapproval of Rocky's aggressive behavior as it occurred, later exhibited many of his aggressive responses. Finally, in an apparent effort to make her emulation of the ruthless but successful Rocky complete, she turned to the experimenter and inquired, "Do you have a sack here?"

A number of other studies by other investigators in the 1960s also used aggressive play as a measure of aggression; all found that subjects who viewed an aggressive film model engaged in more aggressive play than children who were not so exposed (Hartmann & Gelfand, 1969; Nelson, Gelfand, & Hartmann, 1969; Rosenkrans & Hartup, 1967; Walters & Willows, 1968).

The important limitation of all these studies, of course, is that they are measuring *play*. Beating on plastic dolls which are designed to be punched and kicked around does not seem shocking or antisocial behavior, and critics of these studies were quick to note that very few parents would be upset to learn that their children had punched a Bobo doll which was designed for the purpose.

What about "real" aggression? The question is obviously an important one, but it has proven difficult to design studies that can pass as both ethically responsible and scientifically compelling.

The aggression machine. A number of early studies employed a method that measured how much a person was willing to inflict pain on others. Originally devised by psychologist Arnold Buss and referred to as "the aggression machine," the method involved giving participants a pretext for giving another person electric shocks. For example, in one version participants are told that the effects of punishment on learning are being tested and that they are to serve in the role of "teacher." The participant is free to choose the intensity of the shock given for each wrong answer by the other person (the "learner"), and thus shock intensity becomes the measure of interest. (The learner is always a confederate of the experimenter in these studies, and does not really receive any electric shock.)

In one early study using the aggression machine (Walters & Thomas, 1963), hospital attendants, high school boys, and young women viewed either the knife-fight scene from *Rebel Without a Cause* or a film of adolescents engaging in constructive activities. Both before and after viewing the film, everyone participated in an experiment which ostensibly required shocking another person for making errors on a learning test. The critical measure was the difference in the intensity of shocks given during the two sessions. In all three groups, those who saw the aggressive film gave stronger shocks in the second session than did those who saw the constructive film.

The aggression machine was subsequently used in many other investigations which demonstrate both that viewing violence increases aggression and that laboratory shock is related to real-life violence (Berkowitz & Geen, 1966, 1967; Geen & Berkowitz, 1966, 1967). In one study (Hartmann, 1969), delinquent adolescent boys were either angered or treated neutrally and then shown one of three films, two of which were aggressive in content. Regardless of whether they were angered or not, seeing an aggressive film produced more subsequent aggression (ostensible electric shocks to another person) than the neutral film. At the same time, boys with a past history of aggressive behavior were more aggressive than other boys.

Clearly by the end of the 1960s there was a great deal of theoretical rationale and laboratory evidence showing that televised aggression can disinhibit young viewers, at least in some contrived circumstances, so that they become more likely to behave aggressively. But the TV programs seen were often either simulated or taken out of context, which greatly limits the conclusions that can be drawn. Nor was there agreement as to precisely *how* TV violence worked its influence.

Thus, although social learning theory has played an unusually important role in analyzing TV's possible effects on children, other theoretical viewpoints also played important parts in early discussions of TV violence.

Instigation theories

There is an alternative to the social learning analysis of the effects of TV violence. One could take the view that exposure to the violent content in these studies somehow *instigated* an immediate aggressive response (Berko-witz, 1962, 1969; Tannenbaum, 1971). In addition to various properties of the modeling sequence, the emotional state of the subject would presumably influence the likelihood that instigation to increased aggression would ac-tually occur.

Tannenbaum and Zillmann advanced an arousal model of how TV vio-lence instigates aggression. The theory contends that many comunication messages can evoke varying degrees of generalized emotional arousal and that this arousal can influence any behavior an individual is engaged in while the arousal persists. Increased aggression following exposure to TV violence would be viewed as the result of the level of arousal elicited by con-tent, rather than merely because the content was aggressive. One of the pro-positions of the theory is that nonaggressive but arousing TV content can instigate increased aggressive behavior. This proposition has been sup-ported by experiments showing that an erotic film which was more arousing than an aggressive film produced more aggressive responses in viewers (Tannenbaum, 1971; Zillmann, 1969).

Justification as a factor. Another significant empirical contribution of the instigation theories in the 1960s was that they demonstrated the importance of whether or not the observed aggression was justified in determining the instigating effect of an aggressive TV or movie sequence. The reason for thinking that justification would be an important factor is straightforward. In real life it is considered more appropriate to act aggressively when one is justified than when one is not. Thus, observing justified aggression is more closely associated with actual aggression, and when justified aggression is observed, it therefore tends to instigate (i.e., "trigger") aggression in ob-servers.

An experiment by Berkowitz (1965) is typical of the research. In this ex-periment male college students were individually exposed to an experi-mental confederate secretly following a script. The confederate insulted half of the subjects during the course of his interaction with them. Then half of the insulted and half of the noninsulted subjects viewed a film showing jus-tified aggression, while the other half saw a film showing unjustified aggres-sion. Finally, they had an opportunity to shock the experimental confed-erate—the very one who had insulted them. The young men who were most likely to give a large number of longer duration shocks were those who had been angered and then seen entertainment in which justified aggression was depicted.

A later investigation within the same theoretical framework (Hoyt, 1970) examined some of the factors that influence justification. College men were angered, not by insulting them but by having an experimental confederate give them a large number of electric shocks in a learning experiment. The young men next saw a film clip of a fight scene. In one condition, the justification was based on vengeance; the victor was seen as avenging an unfair beating which he had previously received. In a second condition, justification was based on self-defense. In a third situation, the introduction to the film combined both vengeance and self-defense motives. In the fourth condition, there was no introduction and thus no justification was provided at all. Then the roles were reversed: the students had the opportunity to shock the experimental confederate. In terms of number and duration of shocks given to the confederate, those in the fourth (no justification) condition were lowest in level of aggression; students in the third (vengeance and self-defense) condition were the highest.

Other studies involved trying to show the importance of a link between the film and cues in the observer's actual situation in order for a sequence to trigger aggression. A description of one of these studies (Berkowitz & Geen, 1966), entitled "Film Violence and the Cue Properties of Available Targets," will serve to illustrate the nature of the research. Berkowitz and Geen predicted that a violent film would be most likely to trigger aggression when the observers were angry and the available target for their own aggression was in some way related to the violent film. In their actual experiment there were eight different groups, based on all possible combinations of seeing the vicious fight scene from the film *Champion* or an exciting but nonviolent track meet, being angered or not by an experimental confederate, and whether or not there was a link between the person beaten up in the movie (a character played by actor *Kirk* Douglas) and their own potential victim.

The experiment was introduced as a study of problem solving, conducted by a research assistant introduced as either Bob Anderson or as *Kirk* Anderson. The research assistant could apparently choose the number of shocks to give the subject as "feedback" in the first part of the problem-solving task. To half of the subjects he gave one shock; to anger the other half, he gave seven. Then the subjects saw the film sequence to which they had been assigned, under the pretext that the effects of such "diversions" were being studied. Finally, the roles were reversed and the subject chose how many shocks to give the research assistant. In addition to the unsurprising fact that those who received more shocks gave more shocks back, the study provided support for the subtler hypothesis it was designed to test. Subjects who saw Kirk Douglas beaten up and were then angered by a man also named Kirk gave more shocks than those in any other group.

The catharsis hypothesis

Many centuries before television aggression became a subject for public concern and controversy, Aristotle speculated about the psychological effects of drama, suggesting that by witnessing dramatic offerings the audience "purges" its feelings of grief, fear, and pity. Since then the same idea has been extended to feelings of aggression and anger. The notion that aggressive impulses can be drained off by exposure to fantasy aggression has its roots in psychoanalytic and drive theories, which assume that mental as well as physical energies can (and must) be released in various ways. The idea is very much what people have in mind when they talk of "letting off steam." The basic assumption is that frustration (for example, not getting one's way), being insulted, and the like, produce an increase in aggressive drive. Increased drive is unpleasant, and the individual seeks to reduce it through aggressive acts. But according to the catharsis hypothesis, the drive may also be reduced by fantasy aggression.

The original catharsis hypothesis simply predicted that viewing violence would reduce aggression in the observer (Feshbach, 1955). Despite some limited support in studies with college students, this hypothesis was rejected in a number of investigations with children.

In a study by Alberta Siegel (1956), for example, pairs of nursery school children were taken to an experimental room where they saw a film. Then the experimenter left the room, and the children played and were observed for a 14-minute period. Play with aggressive toys (e.g., toy daggers) as well as outright assault on each other were recorded. Each pair of children saw both an aggressive film (a Woody Woodpecker cartoon) and a nonaggressive film (about the Little Red Hen) about one week apart. If the catharsis hypothesis were correct, the children should have been *less* aggressive after viewing the violent cartoon; in fact, they were actually somewhat *more* aggressive after viewing it. This has been the usual result, but the catharsis hypothesis was not discarded entirely.

Feshbach and Singer's Television and Aggression. Seymour Feshbach and Robert Singer (1971) presented a modified formulation of the catharsis hypothesis. They suggest that the mass media serve to stimulate fantasy, and that the fantasy thus provided must satisfy some sort of need. In this view, fantasies can be seen as:

> Substitutes for overt behavior which are partly rewarding in themselves and which may reduce arousal, as coping or adaptive mechanisms useful when delays in gratification occur, and as aids to arousal possibly culminating in overt behavior [p. 11].

According to Feshbach and Singer, fantasy may act to reduce aggression in one of several ways. It may, for example, reduce the arousal level of an angry individual. If he can sufficiently punish his nagging mother-in-law or demanding boss in his thoughts, he will feel less desire to punish them in his actions. Or if the individual is rewarded often enough for fantasy aggression (he pushes his boss off a bridge in thought and feels better afterward), he gets into the habit of using fantasy aggression to "cathart" (drain off) his aggressive feelings with the result that he is *less* likely to actually behave aggressively. Television, according to this view, can provide fantasy material usable for catharsis, especially if viewers perceive the circumstances and the characters as similar to themselves and their own circumstances.

According to Feshbach and Singer, televised violence might also reduce aggression through inhibition.

> It may frighten the viewer of violence and its possible consequences; it may create anxiety over aggressive impulses and the eventuality that they may be acted out. The viewer consequently avoids aggressive behavior in order to reduce his fear of what he may do or what may be done to him [p. 15].

In the late 1960s Feshbach and Singer performed an ambitious test of their revised catharsis hypothesis, investigating the effects of television violence on a large number of boys in the natural environment (Feshbach & Singer, 1971). The subjects were approximately 400 adolescent and preadolescent boys in institutional settings in New York and California. Three of the institutions were private schools, drawing on upper middle-class youngsters. The remaining four were homes for boys who lacked adequate home care or were experiencing social and personal adjustment difficulties. These latter youngsters were of predominantly lower-class background; 35% were black and an additional 10% were Chicano or Puerto Rican.

The boys were divided into two groups, according to whether they watched aggressive or nonaggressive television. Each boy was required to watch at least six hours of television per week for six weeks; he could watch more if he wished, but all programs had to be from a designated list. The aggressive diet consisted of about 75 programs, of which 20 were seen most frequently (e.g., *Bonanza*, *I Spy*, *Rifleman*, and *The Untouchables*). The nonaggressive diet consisted of about 150 programs, with about 50 being viewed relatively frequently (e.g., *Andy Williams*, *Gomer Pyle*, *Petticoat Junction*, and *Wide World of Sports*).

A number of measures of aggression were employed, including projective tests and attitude questionnaires. The most important measure concerning the effects of television violence on aggressive behavior was the behavior rating scale. This scale consisted of 26 items, 19 of which pertained to aggression. Five items referred to physical aggression toward others, self, or property. The remainder referred to nonphysical aggression including grumbling, being bossy, sullen, or disobedient, as well as cursing or arguing angrily. Each behavior was rated once a day according to whether it was directed toward authority or toward peers, whether it was provoked or unprovoked, and whether it was mild or moderately strong. The raters were house parents, supervisors, teachers, and proctors.

Feshbach and Singer found that on the behavior rating scale boys in the nonaggressive TV group were more aggressive than boys in the aggressive content group, both in aggression toward peers and in aggression toward authority. When the data were analyzed by institutions, this difference was found to be due solely to three of the seven institutions—all boys' homes. Here, then, aggression was less frequent among those on the aggressive TV diet, as predicted by the catharsis hypothesis. On a week-by-week basis aggression in boys in the nonaggressive TV group increased over the seven weeks in which data were gathered; that of boys in the aggressive TV group declined over the same period.

In the private schools, the reverse pattern appeared; boys in the nonaggressive TV groups declined significantly in aggression, and boys in the aggressive television group tended to increase. This suggested that disinhibition was at work, with violence viewing making some boys more aggressive; but when the two groups were compared, the differences were not significant.

While these findings provide some support for the catharsis hypothesis, the study is subject to a number of technical criticisms (Liebert, Sobol, & Davidson, 1972). A particularly important problem concerns differential liking of the programs viewed by control and experimental subjects. Based on the data presented by Feshbach and Singer, Chaffee and McLeod (1971) showed that boys in the nonaggressive TV group liked their assigned programs significantly *less* than boys in the aggressive television group. Thus, an important alternative explanation—or rival hypothesis—for the fact that some control subjects were more aggressive is that they resented being restricted to nonaggressive programs, and this resentment was expressed in an increase in aggression. [We should point out that in any experiment using TV diets, the data become meaningless if the diets are not equally enjoyed by the viewers. The deKonig, Conradie and Nell (1980) study described in Chapter 5 also encountered this problem.]

Another difficulty relates to the experimental treatments themselves. A crucial requirement of experimental studies is that all groups be treated identically except for the manipulation of the independent variable (in this case, the different TV diets). Unfortunately, the Feshbach and Singer study did not meet this requirement. Boys in the nonaggressive TV group in institutions where the catharsis effect appeared had objected strongly to not being permitted to watch *Batman* (a highly aggressive program); the investigators then permitted them to include *Batman* in their list. This procedure constitutes an important difference in the treatment of the groups. Yielding to "a very strong objection" could have encouraged such related actions as grumbling, complaining, breaking rules, becoming sullen, refusing tasks, or acting bossy in other matters (all of which were scored as aggressive behaviors on the rating scale). Thus, another possibility is that experimental differences may have resulted from subjects having won an unreasonable demand from experimenters in one group and not in the other, rather than from differences in the television diet *per se*.

This does not finish our discussion of the validity of Feshbach and Singer's results, but we can only do so in the light of the Surgeon General's Report.

Chapter 4

The Surgeon General's Report

OVERVIEW

Stimulated by a request from Senator John O. Pastore, the United States Department of Health, Education and Welfare organized and directed the Surgeon General (Chief Government Health Officer in the United States) to undertake an investigation of the effects of TV violence on children and youth. The effort was quickly mired down by "politics," as it was learned that the committee appointed to actually guide the investigation — the Surgeon General's Scientific Advisory Committee on Television and Social Behavior — had been selected in a highly biased way. The industry had been allowed to secretly blackball seven possible committee members (including Bandura, Berkowitz and Tannenbaum), and had also been able to load the twelve person committee with five of its own officers and consultants.

Operating under this cloud, and led by government health official Dr. Eli A. Rubinstein, the committee agreed to let the National Institute of Mental Health (NIMH) solicit and fund one million dollars worth of research. Forty projects were selected in this way, touching on diverse aspects of television and children's social behavior. The project themes pertinent to our inquiry include measuring the level of violent content on TV (which was found to be high), establishing the level of viewing by U.S. children (which was discussed in Chapter 1), and determining the effects of TV violence through both correlational and experimental studies. While each of the projects had its limitations, researchers consistently found some significant relationship between TV violence and aggressive or other objectionable behavior by children and adolescents. The research made it equally obvious that the occurrence of such behavior always involves many factors. In almost all of the studies, viewing TV violence affected some youngsters more than others.

When the projects were completed, the technical reports were sent to the committee which then had to interpret the findings and submit its own report to the Surgeon General. At Dr. Rubinstein's urging, the committee hammered out a unanimous report, but it was so complex, hedged, and ambiguous that one reporter concluded that TV violence was really not a factor in children's aggressiveness at all.

As we have seen, as late as the 1960s surprisingly little of practical importance had been established about the real, practical effects of television violence on children. Meanwhile, the medium was continually being accused of

67

cultivating "undesirable" attitudes and behavior. And the industry, for its part, continually promised research which was either never completed or turned out to be irrelevant to the general question of television's effects on the aggressive or antisocial behavior of children. Finally, everyone thought increased regulation was possible. By the end of the decade, TV violence was ripe to become a public issue. It was against this backdrop that Senator John O. Pastore, Chairman of the Subcommittee on Communications of the Senate Commerce Committee sent a letter to Health, Education, and Welfare Secretary Robert Finch, which said in part (Cisin et al., 1972):

> I am exceedingly troubled by the lack of any definite information which would help resolve the question of whether there is a causal connection between televised crime and violence and antisocial behavior of individuals, especially children. . . . I am respectfully requesting that you direct the Surgeon General to appoint a committee comprised of distinguished men and women from whatever professions and disciplines deemed appropriate to devise techniques and to conduct a study under his supervision using those techniques which will establish scientifically insofar as possible what harmful effects, if any, these programs have on children [p. 1].

Pastore apparently envisioned a definitive report such as the then famous Surgeon General's Report of 1964, *Smoking and Health*, which concluded rather unambiguously that there existed a causal relationship between cigarette smoking and lung cancer and led to the currently required warning on all cigarette packages sold in the United States.

THE SURGEON GENERAL'S SCIENTIFIC ADVISORY COMMITTEE ON TELEVISION AND SOCIAL BEHAVIOR

Secretary Finch directed Surgeon General William H. Stewart to select a committee to authorize and examine evidence relevant to questions about the effects of television on children. The Surgeon General, announcing that he would appoint an advisory panel of scientists respected by the scientific community, the broadcasting industry, and the general public, requested nominations from various academic and professional associations (including the American Sociological Association, the American Anthropological Association, the American Psychiatric Association, and the American Psychological Association), distinguished social scientists, the NAB and the three major networks.

The blackball procedure

From the 200 names suggested, the office of the Surgeon General drew up a list of 40 and sent it to the presidents of the National Association of Broadcasters and of the three national commercial broadcast networks. The broadcasters were asked to indicate "which individuals, if any, you would believe would *not* be appropriate for an impartial scientific investigation of this nature." They responded with a list of seven names,* including three prominent social scientists whose work was mentioned in Chapter 3 — Albert Bandura, Leonard Berkowitz and Percy Tannenbaum. The secretly black-balled seven were:

> Albert Bandura, Professor of Psychology at Stanford University, and an internationally acknowledged expert on children's imitative learning. Bandura had published numerous research articles which suggested that children might learn to be more aggressive from watching TV.

> Leo Bogart, Executive Vice President and General Manager of the Bureau of Advertising of the American Newspaper Publishers Association. Dr. Bogart had previously published a book on television.

> Leonard Berkowitz, Vilas Professor of Psychology at the University of Wisconsin, principal investigator of an extensive series of studies showing that watching aggression can stimulate aggressive behavior, author of two books on aggression and consultant to the 1969 Task Force on Mass Media and Violence.

> Leon Eisenberg, Professor and Chairman of the Department of Psychiatry at Harvard University.

> Ralph Garry, then Professor of Educational Psychology at Boston University, author of a book on children's television, and a principal consultant to the U.S. Senate Subcommittee on Juvenile Delinquency.

> Otto Larsen, Professor of Sociology at the University of Washington and editor of *Violence and the Mass Media*.

> Percy H. Tannenbaum, then Professor of Psychology and Communication at the University of Pennsylvania and prominent for his theoretical analyses of the arousing effects of media entertainment depicting violence and sex.

The names of all these people were thereupon removed from the list of possible committee members in deference to the wishes of the industry whose product was under scrutiny.†

---

*It should be noted that CBS did not eliminate any names from the list.

†There was a somewhat parallel precedent for this blackball procedure — the Surgeon General's Advisory Committee on Smoking and Health — whereby the tobacco industry had been given the opportunity to review the names of proposed Committee members. The reasoning for this practice was that it prevented the tobacco industry from weakening the impact of the Committee report by claiming that the Committee was prejudiced against it.

Another significant fact added insult to injury, and that was that the industry had submitted the names of some of its own officers and permanent consultants as possible committee members. These people were not blackballed by the industry, and no public interest or professional society was ever sent the list of names for comment. So, when the 12-person committee was selected (and given the awesome name, "The Surgeon General's Scientific Advisory Committee on Television and Social Behavior"), five industry executives and consultants were among those appointed. They were:

- Thomas E. Coffin, Ph.D., Vice President of NBC
- Ira H. Cisin, Ph.D., CBS Consultant
- Joseph T. Klapper, Ph.D., Director of CBS Social Research
- Harold Mendelsohn, Ph.D., CBS Consultant
- Gerhart D. Wiebe, Ph.D., former CBS executive

The remaining seven individuals appointed were:

- Irving L. Janis, Ph.D., Professor of Psychology, Yale University.
- Eveline Omwake, M.A., Professor of Child Development, Connecticut College.
- Charles A. Pinderhughes, M.D., Associate Clinical Professor of Psychiatry, Tufts University.
- Ithiel de Sola Pool, Ph.D., Professor of Political Science, Massachusetts Institute of Technology.
- Alberta E. Siegel, Ph.D., Professor of Psychology, Stanford University Medical School.
- Anthony F.C. Wallace, Ph.D., Professor of Anthropology, University of Pennsylvania.
- Andrew S. Watson, M.D., Professor of Psychiatry and Professor of Law, University of Michigan.

Disclosure

This biased selection procedure of systematic inclusion and exclusion was not intended to be a matter of the public record. Even the nonnetwork members of the committee, all of whom are well respected by the scientific community, were not told anything about it. However, on May 22, 1970, six months after the Committee was formed, the blackball procedure was publicized in a *Science* article entitled, "Seven Top Researchers Blackballed from Panel." HEW Secretary Robert Finch tried to explain away the travesty as handily as he could, saying that the selection was designed to assure impartiality. James J. Jenkins, then chairman of the American Psychological Association's board of professional affairs, took a different view. He described the procedure as deplorable and analogized (Boffey & Walsh, 1970):

> It looks like an exemplar of the old story of the "regulatees" running the "regulators" or the fox passing on the adequacy of the eyesight of the man assigned to guard the chicken coop [pp. 951–952].

The committee takes shape

The committee was now under the shadow of a dark cloud. Its composition appeared "rigged," but disbanding the committee would be tantamount to a confession of guilt by the politicians and government officials who had set up the dubious appointment and blackballing procedure. The urgent political need in Washington was to keep the committee "clean" and quiet after that. (As we shall see later, this effort was not entirely successful.)

A new figure now emerged as central on the stage, Eli A. Rubinstein. Rubinstein, a psychologist who had served as Assistant Director of Extramural Programs at the National Institute of Mental Health, was appointed in 1969 as vice-chairman of the Surgeon General's Scientific Advisory Committee on Television and Social Behavior and was given the task of guiding the committee through its work.

Decision to forego a coordinated research approach in favor of individual projects. Many options were theoretically available to the committee, but the built-in antagonism between industry-linked and independent members, together with practical considerations, sharply limited the options that could be seriously considered. The committee rejected the possibility of developing any sort of research plan on its own and purposely decided to support many small, uncoordinated studies by different investigators with different goals. Scientists were simply invited, through the government's usual advertising channels, to submit proposals which might be pertinent to the interests of a "scientific advisory committee on television and social behavior." The proposals were evaluated by small review panels of prominent academic researchers who judged each proposal on its scientific merit. The budget allocation for the research itself, one million dollars, was a fraction of the amount put into research on cigarette smoking and cancer. Nonetheless, the project was described as generously funded by politicians and even by the researchers.

The freedom and independence of the review panels was stressed both to the panels and the press (whose members sensed, quite rightly, that more headline material would come out of the committee). Albert Bandura, though blackballed from the committee, reviewed some proposals, and Percy Tannenbaum, also blackballed, received a substantial piece of the one million dollars for his research. (Remarkably, Tannenbaum was funded for a project that he announced would not be completed until after the committee had submitted its report and been disbanded.)

Altogether about 40 formal proposals were submitted, which is a sizable number given the short notice and the complicated bureaucratic steps involved in applying for a grant or contract from the National Institute of Mental Health to do social science research. Twenty-three projects were selected and funded in this way;* the investigators were free to proceed with their contracted research without interference and to prepare technical research reports of their findings and of any conclusions they deemed appropriate. The committee was, however, to receive interim reports and enjoyed the prerogative of finally writing the official report to the Surgeon General. Individual investigators were asked not to discuss or disclose their findings until the official report had been published.

The role of overview writers

An additional effect of disclosures about the political nature of the committee appointments was to influence the form of the final report. Publication plans were made for (1) an official report of the committee to the Surgeon General and (2) a series of simultaneously published technical volumes written by the principal investigators with little or no editorial interference from the committee or anyone else.

In anticipation of the published volumes, the projects were grouped into five categories, and one of the principal investigators from each category was invited to "overview" the projects in his category as they were conducted. (See Table 4.1.) The overview writers had no authority, but during a period of almost two years they visited each research team and exchanged progress reports of their research. The overview writers' most important task was to write an overview summary of the work done in their category, to be the lead chapter of each of the anticipated technical volumes.

PROJECT THEMES

Despite the lack of coordination or integration, the projects did fall into meaningful groupings. The most frequent questions posed were about the relationship between exposure to TV violence and subsequent aggression by the viewer. But the individual projects differed enormously in their concep-

---

*It should be noted that many of the projects served as umbrellas for several individual studies, and thus sometimes a project had several aims or resulted in several different chapters within one of the technical volumes.

Table 4.1. The Five Categories of Projects Composing the Technical Volumes of the Surgeon General's Report.

Topic	Overviewer
Media Content and Control	George A. Comstock
Television and Social Learning	Robert M. Liebert
Television and Adolescent Aggressiveness	Steven H. Chaffee
Television in Day-to-Day Life: Patterns of Use	Jack Lyle
Television's Effects: Further Explorations	Bradley S. Greenberg

tions, procedures and methods, which were largely chosen on the basis of the independent predilections of each of the principal investigators.*

In addition to studies of TV violence and aggression, there were studies designed to determine the level of exposure to TV among children today and the degree to which TV entertainment was, in fact, violent. There were also studies of advertising, of producers' perceptions of television, and even one on the difference in children's reactions to color and black and white TV. We will describe those studies that seem pertinent to the practical questions about children and television discussed in Chapter 1. (Appendix B briefly describes all the studies done for the Surgeon General's Report.)

Level of violent content

A persistent accusation about television since the 1950s is that it was too violent. To establish this fact, both early academic researchers and public interest groups performed simple content analyses in which the number of aggressive or violent acts were counted. (Other information was also gathered from these content analyses and will be discussed in later chapters.)

Although it may not seem so at first, useful content analyses can only result when careful, systematic, "scientific" procedures are followed. There are three matters that must be considered in evaluating any content analysis.

Problems of definition. Definition is extremely important for content analyses. For example, what is a violent act? Almost everyone would agree that purposeful stabbing and shooting are violent. But what about verbal insults? What about threats of violence? If a sequence is ongoing (a fist fight or a shoot out) would it count as one act of violence or several? Many other problems and issues of this sort can easily be raised.

---

*Government grants and contracts of this sort are awarded to institutions (such as universities) rather than individuals, but the scientist who writes and is responsible for the project is designated the *principal investigator* and enjoys most operational prerogatives and responsibilities.

Sampling. The aim of content analysis is usually to provide a characterization of television content in general (e.g., to answer the question, "How much violence are children actually exposed to on TV?"). This raises the question of which programs to sample. Does one look only at prime time or at other times as well? Should only new network programs be included, or should one also include independent stations and reruns? Again, this is a very brief example of the types of problems that invariably arise and must be addressed.

Reliability. A final issue concerns reliability. This technical term refers to the degree to which a measurement procedure (whether it is a standard psychological test or a procedure for observers to use in noting and recording violent acts on television) produces consistent results. Reliability is often determined by asking two or more people to use a procedure (for example, in counting the number of violent acts on a videotape of a TV show) to see if they come up with the same results.

Early content analyses of TV violence. The first content analyses of television were conducted in the early 1950s. Two researchers, Smythe (1954) and Head (1954), independently analyzed a large sample of television programming. The results of both studies are quite similar and together provide a picture of TV's portrayal of violence during the early days of television. First, crime and violence were prevalent TV themes. During one television week in 1953, there were 3,421 violent acts and threats (Smythe, 1954). More aggression appeared in children's programs (7.6 acts per program) than in general dramas (1.8 acts), situation comedies (.8 acts), or even crime-detection programs (5.1 acts) (Head, 1954). While interesting, however, the results of these early analyses should be regarded cautiously. It is unclear in either study what was used as a definition of violence or aggression. Further, Smythe did not report the reliability of his coding procedure.

Gerbner's work. The person to provide the most systematic method of analyzing television for violent content was George Gerbner, long-time Dean of the Annenberg School of Communications at the University of Pennsylvania. Gerbner proposed a definition of TV violence which raters (college students) could be trained to use through apprenticeship and by following a manual, and he video-recorded a large sample of programs (requiring many videotape recorders and a substantial library of tapes). In 1968 Gerbner conducted a study of violence in television drama for the Mass Media Task Force of the National Commission of the Causes and Prevention of Violence (Lange, Baker, & Ball, 1969). His analysis on the 1967 and 1968 TV seasons formed the basis of his report to the Commission (Gerbner, 1969). This information along with what he collected in 1969 was included in a report that was a critical part of the Surgeon General's Report.

Gerbner (1972) first established the representativeness of programming for one week in October by comparing it to that of other times during the year. Then trained teams of observers watched each dramatic program shown during an October week selected in 1967, 1968, and 1969, recording the number of violent episodes. For the purposes of this study, violence was defined as:

> The overt expression of physical force against others or self, or the compelling of action against one's will on pain of being hurt or killed. The expression of injurious or lethal force had to be credible and real in the symbolic terms of the drama. Humorous and even farcical violence can be credible and real, even if it has a presumable comic effect. But idle threats, verbal abuse, or comic gestures with no real consequences were not to be considered violent [p. 31].

Gerbner used two units of analysis: the play or skit and the program hour. Although in most prime-time programs these units are equivalent, many children's programs present several plays per hour (e.g., as in a half hour cartoon program). Investigating more than the amount of violence, he also examined what types of programs contained the most violence, who acts violently, who is victimized by violence, and what happens to the participants.

Gerbner's report was striking. In 1969 "about eight in ten plays still contained violence, and the frequency of violent episodes was still about five per play and nearly eight per hour" (p. 33). Further, the most violent programs were those designed exclusively for children—cartoons:

> The average cartoon hour in 1967 contained more than three times as many violent episodes as the average adult dramatic hour. The trend toward shorter plays sandwiched between frequent commercials on fast-moving cartoon programs further increased the saturation. By 1969, with a violent episode at least every two minutes in all Saturday morning cartoon programming (including the least violent and including commercial time), and with adult drama becoming less saturated with violence, the average cartoon hour had nearly six times the violence rate of the average adult television drama hour, and nearly 12 times the violence rate of the average movie hour [p. 36].

In fact, according to Gerbner, in 1967 and 1968 only two cartoons were nonviolent, and only one in 1969. The overall situation had not improved since 1954 when Smythe and Head found that children's programming contained about three times as much violence as adult drama.

The conclusion that TV content was highly violent was considered to be scientifically validated by Gerbner's report. As we shall see in the next chapter, Gerbner's work continued under federal funding for many years after the Surgeon General's Report was completed. Also, critics have now identified many potential problems with Gerbner's procedures, using the criteria

of definition, sampling, and reliability that we mentioned above. We shall
return to these issues in the next chapter.

Level of viewing

Advertisers have had estimates of audience size available since they began to
employ television for commercial purposes in the late 1940s. However only
one major public report of TV use by children had been done, as part of
Schramm, Lyle, and Parker's (1961) *Television in the Lives of Our Children* (see Chapter 1). Lyle and Hoffman (1972) were funded to update the
earlier report. Based on interviews, self-administered questionnaires, and
viewing diaries from 274 first graders, 800 sixth graders, and 500 tenth
graders from a town in Los Angeles, the researchers found that television
viewing continued to be a very time consuming activity, surpassing all other
activities except sleep and school. Indeed, over one-quarter of the sixth
graders and only a slightly smaller proportion of the tenth graders watched
at least five and one-half hours on a given school day, and over one-third of
the first graders watched four or more hours daily. Viewing diaries indicated that many of the "most violent" programs (as determined by a study
based on ratings by the public and television critics, Greenberg and Gordon,
1972a) were broadcast when youngsters were viewing, and they often at-
tracted the majority of such viewers.

Perceived reality

One would expect from social learning theory and from much research in
developmental psychology that the impact of TV violence (and other TV
content) would depend on how it is perceived. The presumption is that children, like adults, are more likely to act on what they perceive as real than on
what they consider to be only "make believe."

The issue is somewhat more complicated than it first appears, however,
because TV fare can be real in some ways and make believe in others. Only
the youngest children believe that TV dramas are actual life events occurring
in real time inside the television box. Preschoolers can be usefully told that
animated shows are make believe, and many first graders will agree quickly
that a TV crime drama is only a story. But fictional stories about fictional
characters can portray life as it is and thus be quite realistic in suggesting appropriate ways of solving problems or dealing with others. (One can get the
message of honesty in the story of Pinnochio without believing that wooden
boys can become alive or that anyone's nose literally grows lie by lie.) So,
questions about how real TV seems to children are about the social attitudes
and beliefs portrayed, rather than whether the stories themselves are true.

Two studies done for the Surgeon General's Report pertain directly to how youngsters perceive television. Other studies to be described when we discuss TV violence later in the chapter also bear on children's perceptions of the reality of television.

Lyle and Hoffman (1972) asked the youngsters in their study how realistically TV portrayed life. About half the first graders felt that people on TV were like those they knew. The sixth and tenth graders were more skeptical, but large percentages believed that TV characters and real people were alike most of the time. Lyle and Hoffman also found that Mexican American or black children were less skeptical than Caucasian youngsters.

The perceived reality of television was addressed in a slightly different way by Greenberg and Gordon (1972b). They showed 325 fifth grade boys and 263 eighth grade boys a series of violent and nonviolent (control) scenes from television dramas and then asked them questions about their perceptions. They found that the children from the lower socioeconomic class, both black and white, rated the violent behavior shown as more acceptable, more lifelike, and more enjoyable to watch than those from more economically advantaged families.

Possible effects of TV violence: Correlational studies*

If TV violence stimulates aggressive behavior, then those who watch large amounts of it should be more aggressive than those who do not. Does such a correlation in fact exist? A number of studies funded for the Surgeon General's Report asked this question, and all found the answer to be "yes."

McIntyre and Teevan (1972) examined the relationship between viewing habits and deviant behavior in 2,300 junior and senior high school boys and girls in Maryland. About 300 of the youngsters were black, and the overall sample represented a wide range of socioeconomic backgrounds.

To obtain information, McIntyre and Teevan asked each youngster to list his/her four favorite programs—"the ones you watch every time they are on the air." A violence rating was assigned to each program, and then an average violence score was computed for every subject. These scores were then correlated with a measure of deviance—a self-report checklist with five scales. The first scale measured aggression or violent acts, such as serious fights at school, hurting someone badly enough that he needed a bandage, and participating in gang fights. The other scales were petty delinquency (including trespassing and vandalism), defiance of parents, political activism, and involvement with legal officials (representing the more serious forms of delinquency). Answers on all five scales were scored for frequency. The relationship between the various types of deviance and objective violence ratings of the four favorite programs were small but most were *statis-*

---

*See Appendix A for an explanation of the correlational method.

tically significant.* In general, the greater the deviance on any scale or on the combined scales, the more violent the programs that the youngsters called favorites.

McIntyre and Teevan considered not only the influence of television on deviant behavior per se, but also on attitudes toward deviance, especially aggression. Consistently, those whose favorite programs were violent were significantly more likely to approve of both adult and teenage violence. They concluded that:

> Certainly television can be no more than one among many factors in influencing behavior and attitudes. However, there is consistently a significant relationship between the violence rating of four favorite programs and the five measures of deviance, three of approval of violence and one of beliefs about crime in the society. Furthermore, these relationships remain when variables expected to decrease the likelihood of deviance are introduced. The regularity with which these relationships appear suggests that they should not be overlooked [p. 430].

In another major correlational study, Robinson and Bachman (1972) questioned more than 1,500 older adolescents concerning their television viewing habits. The subjects were asked how many hours of television they watched in an average day and what their four favorite programs were. For those who were able to list favorites, a violence viewing index was computed based on the total amount of rated violence for their favorites. This sample was divided into four groups ranging from none to high preference for violence. The measure of aggression was a self-report checklist that included eight items about serious physical aggression.

When a total score was computed based on all eight items, adolescents in the three groups who reported at least some preference for violent programs were significantly more aggressive than those who did not list violent programs among their favorites. The same pattern was found for individual items; for example, in response to an item about getting into a serious fight at school, 50% more subjects in the high violence viewing group than in the low violence viewing group responded "yes." The tendency for those who preferred violent television to be more aggressive themselves held for most of the eight items; of particular interest is that there was a steady increase in aggression across the four groups. Certain other variables, such as mother's education, race, and previous level of reported aggression also were related to present levels of aggression, but in all subgroups those who reported a preference for (and presumably watched) a high level of violence were always the most aggressive. Robinson and Bachman concluded that television

---

*In social science research a *statistically significant* result is one that has a low likelihood (usually less than one in twenty) of having occurred in a particular sample by chance.

violence probably served a reinforcing or a facilitating function for adolescents who were already high in aggression.

Dominick and Greenberg (1972) determined the amount of exposure to television violence for each of 434 fourth, fifth, and sixth grade boys enrolled in Michigan public schools during the spring of 1970. Exposure to violence was then related to each youngster's approval of violence and willingness to use it himself. Measures were also obtained of the degree to which the boys both perceived violence as effective and suggested it as a solution to conflict situations. Higher exposure to television violence in entertainment was associated with greater approval of violence and greater willingness to use it in real life. The investigators concluded:

> For relatively average children from average environments . . . continued exposure to violence is positively related to acceptance of aggression as a mode of behavior. When the home environment also tends to ignore the child's development of aggressive attitudes, this relationship is even more substantial and perhaps more critical [pp. 332–333].

When Dominick and Greenberg repeated their research with girls, they found a pattern which closely followed that seen for boys, and reported that for girls exposure to TV violence makes a "consistent independent contribution to the child's notions about violence. The greater the level of exposure to television violence, the more the child was willing to use violence, to suggest it as a solution to conflict, and to perceive it as effective" (p. 329).

McLeod, Atkin, and Chaffee (1972a,b) questioned 473 adolescents in Maryland and 151 in Wisconsin about aggressive behavior, television viewing, social characteristics of their families, and reactions to television violence. The subjects were mostly white and middle class, although about 15% of the Maryland sample was black.

Violence viewing was indexed by giving each subject a list of 65 prime-time programs, which had been rated for violent content, and requesting information on frequency of viewing. For each subject, the frequency score of each of the 65 programs was multiplied by its violence rating. These scores were then summed to give a measure of overall violence viewing.

Self-report measures of aggression included an overall aggression score, based on: (1) a 17-item scale in which the respondent was asked to judge how much each statement applied to him (e.g., "When I lose my temper at someone, once in a while I actually hit them"); (2) a behavioral delinquency scale, in which the subject was asked how often he had been in school fights, gang fights, or achieved revenge by physical aggression; (3) a self-report scale of generalized aggression; and (4) a four-item test that presented hypothetical conflict situations and asked the subject to choose his most likely response among several alternatives (e.g., "Suppose someone played a real dirty trick on you, what would you do? Hit, yell, ignore, or laugh at them"). In addition to the overall aggression score, subjects were also asked about how well they control their tempers and the degree to which they approve of aggressive behavior.

Reactions to television violence were assessed, including perceived learning of aggression (e.g., "Some programs give me ideas on how to get away with something without getting caught"), linkage of television violence to real life (e.g., "Action and adventure shows tell about life the way it really is"), and involvement in violent programming (e.g., "I sometimes forget that characters in these shows are just actors"). Additionally, identification with violent characters (each subject picked the TV star he would most like to resemble, and the violence of that person's typical role was then rated), and the perceived efficacy of such characters were measured (e.g., "The guy who gets rough gets his way"). Finally, family environment data were gathered. The various indices included perceptions of parental control over television, parental emphasis on nonaggression, parental interpretation of television violence, parental punishment and affection, and social class. Again, the results from this extensive study showed that violence viewing was significantly related to self-reported aggressive behavior.

For the 151 adolescents in their Wisconsin sample, McLeod, Atkin, and Chaffee (1972b) also reported data gathered from questioning others about the subjects. They queried mothers on a number of items (including a comparison of her own child's fighting to fighting by other children, how often her child did mean things or was aggressive when younger, and how her child would handle an argument). They asked peers for ratings on irritability, physical aggression, and verbal aggression and obtained teacher ratings on a four-point overall aggression scale for the sixth graders. The mothers also estimated viewing habits for themselves and their children, and each filled out a questionnaire on family environment.

As with the self-reports, correlations between others' reports of aggression and violence viewing were significant. Additionally, the correlations between past violence viewing and present aggressive behavior were very similar to those for present violence viewing; past violence viewing was actually somewhat more strongly related to aggression than present viewing. This latter finding suggests that aggressive habits are indeed built over time by exposure to aggressive TV content.

Process-oriented correlational studies

So far we have described what are technically called "synchronous correlational studies." That is, these studies correlated one measure (some index of exposure to TV violence) with another measure (of aggressiveness or willingness to act in a disapproved fashion) with both measures capturing the same slice of time (which is what is meant by "synchronous"). Correlations observed under these conditions are often logically ambiguous with respect to cause and effect. The fact that watching more TV violence goes with being more aggressive does not, by itself, show that viewing TV violence *causes* aggressiveness.

There are two logical problems with interpreting the studies we have discussed, the third-variable problem and the directionality problem. Each of these is explained below in the context of studies done for the Surgeon General's Report.

The third variable problem. The problem is that some "third variable" may be responsible for producing the correlation between TV violence viewing and aggression, although neither is causing the other. For example, parents who emphasize nonaggression may cause their children to be relatively nonaggressive and to watch relatively little violent television. Contrarily, parents who emphasize aggression may cause their children to be aggressive and watch a lot of violent television.

It is possible, however, to assess the influence of a third variable with a procedure called the *partial correlational technique.* Conceptually, we want to "subtract out" the third variable's influence and see what is "left over." If the relationship (previously strong in either direction) is now reduced to insignificance, then the third variable remains a very likely candidate as a plausible cause for the relationship. If, however, the relationship that remains after "partialing" is as strong or nearly as strong as it was before, then the third variable is a poor rival hypothesis for explaining the relationship.

McLeod, Atkin, and Chaffee (1972a) used partialing to analyze their findings. For their first set of data (self-reported aggression and viewing violence) they found that subtracting out the influence of total viewing time, socioeconomic status, and school performance left the relationship unchanged. Similarly, when the effects of various types of parental punishment practices, parental affection, and perceived learning of aggression were removed, the relationship between violence viewing and adolescent aggressiveness continued to be significant.

For the second set of data (others' reported aggression and viewing violence) partialing out the effects of total television viewing time, socioeconomic status, and school performance, again left the relationship essentially unchanged. Partialing other variables, such as parental punishment practices, parental affection, and perceived learning of aggression, reduced the correlation somewhat, but still showed that aggression based on both others' and self-reports was associated with violence viewing (McLeod, Atkin, & Chaffee, 1972b). The researchers concluded:

Our research shows that among both boys and girls at two grade levels [junior high and senior high], the more the child watches violent television fare, the more aggressive he is likely to be as measured by a variety of self-report mea-

sures. . . . Partialing out [total] viewing time slightly reduces the positive correlations of violence viewing and aggressive behavior in most cases, but the basic
result is the same as for the raw correlations. . . . Similarly, the partialing out
of socioeconomic status and school performance does not alter the basic pattern
of raw correlations. . . . We may conclude, then, that adolescents viewing high
levels of violent content on television tend to have high levels of aggressive behavior regardless of television viewing time, socioeconomic status, or school
performance [McLeod et al., 1972a, pp. 187–191].

The directionality problem. The partial correlational technique attempts to
solve one of the problems correlational research is subject to, that of the
possible influence of third variables. An additional problem remains — directionality. If we know that A and B are directly related, we still do not
know whether A causes B or vice versa. Procedures can be employed in an
attempt to solve the directionality problem. One involves examining data on
the various theoretical rationales that underlie each of the competing causal
hypotheses.

Chaffee and McLeod (1971) performed such a process analysis on the
data presented above. The two rival causal hypotheses are that viewing television violence increases aggressive behavior (H_1), and that aggressiveness
increases television violence viewing (H_2). Each of these hypotheses assumes that some process is acting to produce the observed relationship; in
other words that there are secondary hypotheses underlying each of the primary ones. Chaffee and McLeod suggested the process analysis presented in
Table 4.2.

**Table 4.2. Two Hypotheses about Violence Viewing and Adolescent Aggressiveness,
Showing Secondary Hypotheses Involved in a Process Analysis.**

H_1: Viewing television violence increases the likelihood of an adolescent behaving
   aggressively.

    H_{1a}: By viewing television violence, an adolescent learns aggressive forms of
   behavior; this increases the probability that he will behave in this fashion
   in subsequent social interaction.

H_2: Aggressiveness causes adolescents to watch violent television programs.

    H_{2a}: Aggressiveness leads to a preference for violent programs, which in turn
   causes the aggressive adolescent to watch them.

Source: Adapted from Chaffee and McLeod (1971).

The "learning hypothesis" (H_{1a}) derived from laboratory studies is considered to be the process underlying H_1. Support for H_1 can be provided by
demonstrating that subjects do indeed learn from television violence and
realize the potential use of what they learned. McLeod, Atkin, and Chaffee
measured perceived learning of aggression using the following three items.

1. These programs show me how to get back at people who make me
   angry.

2. Sometimes I copy the things I see people do on these shows.
3. Some programs give me ideas on how to get away with something without being caught.

The process underlying H_2 (aggressiveness increases television violence viewing) is presumed to involve a preference for televised violence that exists previous to observing it. Thus, support for H_2 can be provided by showing that subjects who are high on measures of aggressive behavior are more likely than other youngsters to show preference for aggressive television programs. The relevant measure, then, is choice of favorite programs.

Chaffee and McLeod compared the two hypotheses as shown in Figure 4.1. The arrows indicate the time order suggested by the two hypotheses. As can be seen from the figure, viewing violence is related to learning, and learning is related to aggressive behavior. But even though preference is related to viewing,* it is *not* related to aggressive behavior. These data, then,

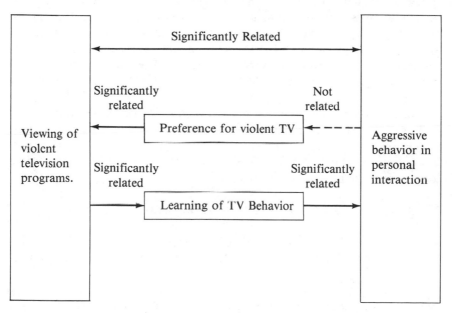

Fig. 4.1. Correlations of violence viewing, aggressiveness, and two intervening processes. Entries indicate hypothesized time order. The overall relationship is clearly accounted for more adequately by the learning path (H_1) than by the preference path (H_{2a}).

Source: Chaffee and McLeod, 1971.

---

*Interestingly, this relationship is perhaps not as strong as might be expected. Evidently, children's violence viewing is only relatively selective and intentional; many may watch violence even though they do not prefer it (e.g., "it may just happen to be on").

offer relatively clear support for the hypothesis that viewing violence causes aggression, rather than the reverse.

Long-term effects. But what about long-term effects? To answer, Lefkowitz, Eron, Walder, and Huesmann (1972) used the so-called *cross-lagged panel technique* to assess the relationship between television violence viewing and aggressive behavior. Earlier, Eron (1963) had determined the amount of violence viewing and aggression of 875 third-grade youngsters. Aggression was measured by peer ratings. Each child rated every other child in his class on a variety of physical and verbal aggressive behaviors. A child's aggression score was determined by the number of peers who said he was aggressive. A measure of television violence viewing was obtained from an interview with each child's mother. Eron found that boys who watched a great many violent programs were more likely to be rated high in aggressive behavior by their peers. This relationship did not hold for girls.

Ten years later when the original participants were 19, Lefkowitz and his associates again obtained information about violence viewing and aggression for 460 of the original 875 subjects. The measure of aggression was again peer ratings based on most recent contact, with the items essentially the same as those used in the third-grade study. The data for boys are presented in Figure 4.2. (The data collected from the girls did not reveal significant differences.)

The relationship between viewing television violence in the third grade and aggression ten years later is significant, while the one between aggression in the third grade and violence viewing when the boys were 19 is not. The pattern supports the hypothesis that viewing television violence is a long-term cause of aggressive behavior.*

Possible effects of TV violence: Experimental studies

However carefully designed, correlational studies always leave the possibility that some unknown additional factor or combination of factors is re-

---

*To understand the logic behind this conclusion more fully, consider the possibility raised in our earlier discussion of correlational studies, that a relationship will appear between overt aggression and preferences for aggressive television simply because persons who are more willing to use aggression themselves are also more likely to enjoy seeing it used by others in television dramas. This is an important "rival hypothesis" to the notion that seeing aggressive television *causes* aggressive behavior. However, if the rival hypothesis was correct, preferences for aggressive television at age 19 in the Lefkowitz study should "go together" with overt aggression in the third grade as closely as preferences for aggressive programs in the third grade go with aggression at age 19. In other words, the relationships, if accounted for by a constant third variable, should go both ways in time. In contrast, if television aggression does cause aggressive behavior later, it would be plausible to find a link between earlier television watching and later aggression but not vice versa. This is exactly what was disclosed by the Lefkowitz data.

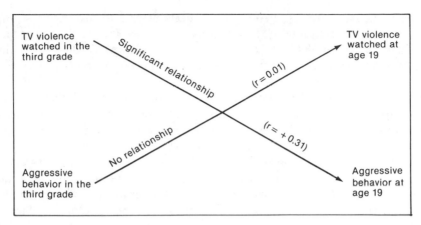

Fig. 4.2. The correlations between television violence and aggression for 211 boys over a 10-year lag.
Source: Lefkowitz, Eron, Walder, and Huesmann, 1972.

sponsible for the observed relationship. In contrast, true experiments (that is, those in which participants are randomly assigned to different experiences or treatments) can lead to fairly unambiguous statements about cause and effect. The limitation of experiments is that they are usually restricted to weak or shallow representations of the circumstances of ultimate practical interest. For example, few parents would be willing to have their child's TV viewing (or their own) drastically altered for the next five years in order to determine for certain what the effects might be. Similarly, investigators cannot ethically create harm or put anyone at risk, which rules out experimental studies of physical aggression except in artificial forms. (Recall the "aggression machine" discussed in Chapter 3.)

On first exposure, many of the experiments done as projects for the Surgeon General's Report seem artificial, but they were earnest and useful attempts to demonstrate a direct causal relationship between viewing of actual violent TV content and many measures of a child's willingness to hurt other children.

Stated willingness to aggress. Leifer and Roberts (1972) investigated the effects of the motivation for and consequences of televised violence on a child's willingness to aggress. Previous justification studies had usually employed college students, not young children. Additionally, earlier justification studies and the response consequences studies used relatively short sequences, in which motivations and/or consequences were closely related, especially in time, to the action. But real television programs usually last a half hour or more, the motivations of the characters are less explicitly stated, and consequences to the aggressor may occur long after the aggressive acts themselves. Leifer and Roberts wished to investigate young children's understanding of these two factors in regular programming and their influence on children's attitudes toward violence. To do so they developed a measure of aggression based on the concept of the *response hierarchy*.

When an individual has a number of responses available, his/her alternatives are arranged in a hierarchy—a steplike progression from most probable to least probable. For example, in a threatening situation a very timid individual may prefer to run away. If unable to do so, the individual's next choice may be to call for assistance. If this, too, is impossible the person may attempt to placate the threatening party. Fighting may only be a last resort. In other words, if our first response is blocked, we will then try the second, and so on, until we have exhausted our repertoire of possible responses.

Leifer and Roberts suggest that the overt behavioral tests used in many studies tap only the first response in the hierarchy, but that the influence of television violence may be to change the relative positions of other responses as well. Televised violence may raise physical aggression from, say, the sixth most probable response to the second most probable response and thus increase the likelihood that aggression will occur.

Based on interviews with youngsters, Leifer and Roberts developed six situations that were likely to anger younger children aged 4–10 and six situations appropriate to older children and adolescents aged 10–16. There were four characteristic types of responses: physical aggression, verbal aggression, escaping the situation, and positive coping (including telling an adult). A situation was presented, and then the alternative responses were shown in such a way that each response was paired with every other response, giving a total of six pairs. These were presented to young children in a booklet; the child marked the picture depicting his or her chosen response. Older children saw the pictures on slides, and marked the letter "a" or "b" on an answer sheet. An example of a complete item, including the situation and the possible responses, is shown in Figure 4.3.

One study employing this measure involved six programs that had been assessed by adults in the community for the amount of violence contained: two children's programs (*Rocket Robin Hood* and *Batman*), two westerns (*Rifleman*, and *Have Gun, Will Travel*), and two crime dramas (*Adam 12*, and *Felony Squad*). They were asked to list the violent episodes, the aggressor and victim in each incident, the victim's response, the justifiability of each act, and the appropriateness of immediate and final consequences. To ensure that the episodes were truly aggressive, the three most frequently listed ones were then used.

Participants were 271 youngsters in kindergarten, third, sixth, ninth, and twelfth grades. Each saw one of the programs, then filled out a multiple choice questionnaire and the response hierarchy instrument. Children who viewed the more aggressive programs were more likely to select physical aggression as a response. Surprisingly, though, motivations, consequences, and the child's understanding of these factors were unrelated to subsequent aggressive responses. As the investigators themselves put it:

> Whatever analysis was performed, the amount of violence in the program affected the amount of aggression subsequently chosen. Nothing else about the program — the context within which violence was presented — seemed to influence subsequent aggression [p. 89].

Increased "hurting" another child via an aggression machine. Liebert and Baron (1972) conducted an experimental laboratory study in which the measure of aggression was an adaptation of the aggression machine described in Chapter 3. The participants, 136 boys and girls between the ages of five and nine, were taken to a room containing a television monitor and told that they could watch television for a few minutes until the experimenter was ready. The sequences they saw came from actual television shows, but had been videotaped earlier. For all the children, the first two minutes of film consisted of commercials selected for their humor and attention-getting characteristics. The following three and one-half minutes constituted the experimental treatment. Half the children viewed a sequence from *The Untouchables*, which contained a chase, two fistfighting scenes, two shootings, and a knifing. The other children saw an exciting sports sequence. For everyone, the final minute seen was another commercial.

Each child was then escorted to another room and seated in front of a large box that had wires leading into the next room. On the box were a green button labeled HELP and a red button labeled HURT. Over the two buttons was a white light. The experimenter explained that the wires were connected to a game that another child in the adjoining room was going to play. The game involved turning a handle, and each time the child started to turn the handle the white light would come on. The experimenter explained that by pushing the buttons the subject could either help the other child by making the handle easier to turn or hurt the other child by making the handle hot. The longer the buttons were pushed, the more the other child was helped or hurt. The child was further told that he or she had to push one of the buttons every time the light came on. After insuring that the child understood which button was which, the experimenter left the room, and the light came on 20 times. After this, each child was taken to a playroom containing aggressive and nonaggressive toys, and aggressive play was assessed.

Using total duration of pushing the HURT button as their measure of aggression, the investigators found that children who viewed the aggressive program were significantly more willing to hurt another child than were

Fig. 4.3. Sample of a complete response hierarchy item.
Source: Leifer and Roberts, 1972.

D. LEAVE THEM OR CALL THEM "STUPID"?

E. HIT THEM OR CALL THEM "STUPID"?

F. TELL A GROWN-UP OR HIT THEM?

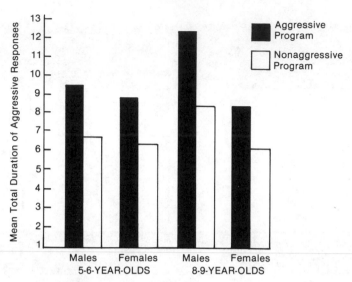

Fig. 4.4. Mean total duration of aggressive responses.
Source: Liebert and Baron, 1972.

those who watched the sports sequence. When average duration was computed (total duration divided by the number of HURT responses), the same results were obtained. As seen in Figure 4.4, the pattern appears for boys and girls of both ages.

It was possible that children who viewed the violent television scene pushed the HURT button longer because they were more excited or aroused. If this line of reasoning is correct, *any* response of this group would be of higher intensity; therefore, they also should have pushed the HELP button longer. They did not. The programs used made no difference in total duration, average duration, or number of HELP responses. Consistent with previous research, children in the aggressive film condition also were more aggressive in the play situation, with the effects much stronger for younger boys than for any of the other groups. What this study suggests is that, at least in the short term, children will be less kind and more cruel to peers as a result of watching licensed mayhem.

Blunting of sensitivity to violence. Rabinovitch, McLean, Markham, and Talbott (1972) conducted a laboratory experiment that addressed the question: Can TV violence blunt children's sensitivity? Sixth grade children saw either a violent program (an episode of *Peter Gunn*) or a nonviolent one (an episode from *Green Acres*). Then each child was tested using a stereoscopic projector which simultaneously presented different images to each eye for such a brief exposure that only one is seen. The two images were very simi-

Table 4.3. Description of Pairs of Slides Used in Free Response Measure of Violence Perception.

Number	Violent slide	Nonviolent slide
1	One man hits the other over the head with a gun.	One man helps the other pound a pole in the ground with a gun butt.
2	One man shoots the other with a rifle.	Both men walk. One carries a rifle.
3	One man pushes the other off a bridge.	Both men walk on the bridge.
4	One man kicks the other off a merry-go-round.	Both men ride on a merry-go-round.
5	One man hits the other over the head with a book.	One man shows the other something in a book.
6	One man, tied up, tries to hit the other man.	One man holds a rope. The other looks at the rope.
7	One man hits the other over the head with a car jack.	One man helps the other take a car jack out of the car trunk.
8	One man hits the other over the head with a rock.	Both men help to lift a rock.
9	One man holds the other and takes money at gunpoint.	One man gives the other man money from his wallet.

Source: Rabinovitch, McLean, Jr., Markham, and Talbott (1972).

lar, but one was violent and one nonviolent (see Table 4.3). For example, one slide showed a man hitting another over the head with a gun; the corresponding nonviolent slide showed a man helping another pound a pole into the ground with a gun butt. Another pair contrasted hitting someone with a book and showing the book to him (see Fig. 4.5). After each slide pair was presented, the child wrote down a description of what he or she had seen. Those who had seen the episode from *Peter Gunn* were less likely to report violence, suggesting that they had become at least temporarily less sensitive to it.

Aggressive and prosocial play among preschoolers. Stein and Friedrich (1972) compared the effect of "prosocial" or socially desirable programs, aggressive programs, and neutral films on preschool viewers' behavior. This was the first study to examine the potential positive effects of television on children's naturally occurring social behavior. (Many studies followed it, as will be seen in Chapter 8.)

Stein and Friedrich studied 97 preschool children, ranging in age from three years ten months to five years six months. They were enrolled in a special summer nursery school program established for the study. The range of

Fig. 4.5. Sample slide pair from Rabinovitch's study of the perception of violence.
Source: Courtesy of Martin Rabinovitch.

social class background was relatively wide, since special efforts were made to recruit children from poorer homes. The children were divided into four classes of about 25 children each and met for two and one-half hours in either the morning or afternoon three times a week.

The experiment took nine weeks to complete: 3 weeks of baseline observation, four weeks of controlled television viewing (the period of experimental manipulation), and two weeks of postviewing observation. During the period of television viewing, children were randomly assigned to one of three groups according to type of programs seen: aggressive, neutral, and prosocial. Aggressive programs consisted of six *Batman* and six *Superman* cartoons, each containing several episodes of verbal and physical aggression. Prosocial programs were 12 episodes of *Mister Rogers' Neighborhood* which emphasized cooperation, sharing, delay of gratification, persistence at tasks, control of aggression, and similar prosocial themes. Neutral programs were children's films of diverse content, emphasizing neither aggression nor prosocial behavior. Almost no aggression occurred in these films, but some prosocial behavior was present. Each program lasted between 20 and 30 minutes; children in all groups saw one program a day, three days a week.

The most important measure was observations of the children either during free-play or in the classroom. Each child's behavior was observed and recorded for three, 5-minute periods each day. Behaviors were scored in five general categories: aggression, prosocial interpersonal behavior, persistence, self-control, and regression. Each category was further divided into more specific behaviors; for example, self-control included rule obedience and delay of gratification, regression included crying or pouting and withdrawal. Observers were "blind" to experimental conditions; that is, they did not know to which treatment the child they were observing had been exposed. Before analyzing their data, Stein and Friedrich further categorized their subjects by dividing them at the median (mid-point) on the basis of their scores on three variables: IQ, socioeconomic status, and initial (pre-experimental) level of aggressive behavior. (Subjects in experimental conditions were about equal in amount of aggression displayed during the pre-experimental period.)

The results of this study showed that children who viewed aggressive programming were more likely to be aggressive in interpersonal situations than those who viewed neutral or prosocial television. However, the effect had a clear limitation: it held only for those children who were in the upper half of the sample (above the median) in initial level of aggression.

Socioeconomic status and IQ, previously assessed by the investigators, influenced which prosocial lessons were learned. Self-control was influenced in the predicted ways: children in the prosocial condition increased while those in the aggressive condition decreased. On the prosocial interpersonal measure, only the children in low socioeconomic classes responded as might be expected by increasing in prosocial behavior.

Children's responses to commercials

Concerns about commercialism on children's television came in with the first broadcasts, but it remained for an ambitious young faculty member at the Harvard Graduate School of Business Administration, Scott Ward, to pioneer the study of children's responses to commercials for the Surgeon General's Report. Until Ward's work, surprisingly little was known about the effects of commercials. Research conducted by the networks and advertisers is unavailable to the public.

Ward and his associates addressed all of the following questions: How much attention do children pay to commercials? How well do they understand them? How much credence do they put in the message? Centrally important, do the commercials lead children (who themselves have little money) to pressure their parents to buy advertised products?

Children's attention to commercials. In one study by Ward, Levinson, and Wackman (1972), mothers served as observers, recording whether their children attended to the commercials (had their eyes consistently on the screen), liked the commercials, and other information about the commercial itself. Each mother observed her child's behavior during a minimum of six but no more than ten one-hour periods spread over ten days.

The most frequently watched commercials occurred during children's programs and movies, although there were age differences reflecting changing tastes in programming. The types of commercials naturally varied with the type of program, so that younger children were more likely to see commercials for food, gum, toys, and games, while older viewers were more likely to be exposed to commercials for personal products. For all children the commercials at the beginning of the program held attention best, although children paid less attention to all commercials than to the program itself.

Other results, some of which are shown in Table 4.4, indicate that attention often falls off when the commercial comes on. Among the older children who were engrossed in the program that preceded the commercial, barely more than half (57%) continued to devote their full attention to television when the commercial appeared.

Children's understanding of commercials. Looking back at the Surgeon General's Report, it is remarkable how little attention was given to children's comprehension of what they saw on television. Leifer and Roberts gave children's understanding of motives and consequences some atten-

Table 4.4. Children's attention to commercials.

		Saturday morning (6 A.M.–1 P.M.)		Weekday evening (6 P.M.–1 A.M.)	
		Age		Age	
		5–8	9–12	5–8	9–12
Attention	Full	50%	33%	46%	45%
during	Partial	15	20	21	24
commercial	Up, in room	3	13	11	4
	Talks	18	16	16	18
	Up, leaves	9	9	2	3
	Not in room	6	9	4	6
		100%	100%	100%	100%

Attention stimulation by commercials: behavior during commercials among children paying full prior attention to programming, by age group.

		Age group		
		5–7	8–10	11–12
Subsequent	Full attention	78%*	70%	57%
attention to	All other (partial			
commercial	attention, talking,			
	up in room, leaves			
	room)	22	30	43
		100%	100%	100%

*Should be read: Of all observations of 5–7-year-old children paying full prior attention to programming, 78% of the subsequent observations indicated that these children continued to pay full attention to commercials.

Source: Adapted from Ward, Levinson, and Wackman (1972).

tion in their project, but their only consistent finding, that older children understand better, could not be immediately linked to the issue of TV violence and aggression.

At the time Ward and his associates could not have predicted the future political significance of their work, but their studies showing that young children do *not* understand the basic nature and "selling intent" underlying commercials formed the cornerstone of one of the biggest confrontations between the FTC and private business in U.S. history. The gist of Ward's results is captured in the following characterizations of how children of different ages perceive the intent of commercials:

Kindergarten: confused (some thought "information," others "didn't know"), semirecognition that ads were intended to sell.

Example: (Q: What are commercials for?) "If you want something, so you'll know about it. So people know how to buy things. So if somebody washes their clothes, they'll know what to use. They can watch what to use and buy it."

Second grade: clear recognition that advertisements were intended to sell; semi-recognition of advertisers' motives.
Example: (Q: What are ads for?) "To make you buy (product)." (Q: Why do they want you to buy it?) "So they can get more money and support the factories they have."

Fourth and Sixth Grades: clear recognition of purpose of commercials, motives of advertisers, and emerging understanding of the techniques advertisers use in constructing commercials.
Example: Fourth Grade: "They put the free things inside so you'll buy it (cereal box)." (Q: referring to discussion of the staging, "tricks" etc., advertisers use: Why do they do that?) "Because they want you to buy it." Sixth Grade: "To advertise the product, to make people buy it, to benefit them because then they get more money" [Blatt, Spencer, Ward, 1972, p. 457].

In a more extensive investigation by Ward, Reale, and Levinson (1972), a larger sample of children responded to similar questions. As can be seen in Table 4.5, clear age differences again emerged in children's understanding of the purpose of commercials. Most of the youngest children's responses were in the lowest category of understanding, e.g., "commercials are to help and entertain you." In contrast, by age 11 to 12 most children understand the nature of the adman's mission, e.g., "commercials are to make people buy things." A similar age trend was found for the perceived credibility of

Table 4.5. Children's Understanding of the Purpose of Commercials, by Age Group.

	Degree of Understanding.		
	Low (Confused, unaware of selling motive; may say "commercials are for entertainment.")	Medium (Recognition of selling motive, some awareness of profit-seeking; "commercials are to make you buy things.")	High (Clear recognition of selling and profit-seeking motives; "commercials get people to buy and they pay for the show.)
Age			
5–7	55%	35%	10%
8–10	38%	50%	12%
11–12	15%	60%	25%

Source: Ward, Reale, and Levinson (1972).

commercials (see Fig. 4.6). Note the striking and growing cynicism which appears even before adolescence. Why do children lose faith in commercials? Ward and his associates report:

> When asked why commercials tell the truth or do not tell the truth, 24 of the 33 older children (ages 9–12) said they feel that the commercials are untrue because the motives of the commercials are suspect—e.g., "they just want to make money" [p. 485].

Effects of commercials on purchasing. The ultimate test of commercials, of course, is in the arena of purchasing. Ward and Wackman (1972) questioned mothers about the frequency of their children's attempts to influence purchases. The highest frequency of requests was for games and toys by the youngest children. Food products, especially those relevant to children such as breakfast cereal, snack foods, candy, and soft drinks were requested very frequently by children in every age group; otherwise, younger children were generally more likely to try to influence parental purchases than older ones. But even though they tried harder, they were less successful than their more persuasive seniors: mothers reported yielding more often to the requests of older than of younger children.

In sum, by age eleven children have become cynical about the purpose and credibility of commercials, feeling that they are being lied to in an attempt to get them to buy products which are not as desirable as the adman's

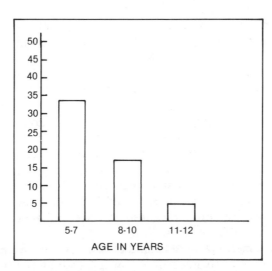

Fig. 4.6. Percentage of children who believe that commercials always tell the truth, as a function of age.

Source: Based on data presented in Ward, Reale, and Levinson, 1972.

copy would have it. It is not surprising, then, that children do not pay full attention to the ads, and that as they grow older they try less often to influence parental purchases.

CREATING THE REPORT

It is desirable at this point to describe the to-be-published report from the vantage point of the committee in mid-1971. In addition to some ancillary documents (such as an annotated bibliography of studies done prior to the report), all of the technical papers submitted to the Committee would be published in the five technical volumes we mentioned before. Much more important than these complex and weighty reports (which ran to more than 2,000 pages when printed) was the official report of the Committee to the Surgeon General. The Committee had to read, study, and discuss all the technical reports, consider their implications, and offer interpretations and conclusions in a report of their own. What conclusions were reached in this official report and exactly how they were worded would doubtless be extremely important in how the press and public interpreted the overall inquiry.

A general understanding prevailed among the principal investigators, staff, and the committee that no statements about the science *or* politics of their work would be made to the press or public until the technical reports had been completed, read, discussed by the Committee, and the official statement had been completed.

A very important issue was at stake until the last minute: whether or not the Committee (composed as it was of industry people and the independent academics with varying views on the issues among them) would agree on a single report. The alternative, a commonplace result of blue-ribbon government inquiries, was to produce several conflicting reports. In such circumstances the industry people would likely collaborate on one report and the independents on one or two others. The press and administration critics would have a field day, and the whole thing would be dismissed cynically as a predictable failure. Eli Rubinstein, as the government's representative, was adamant in his pursuit of a single report, and applying a hand both skilled and subtle, he and his staff managed to hammer out a document everyone would sign on December 31, 1971, the deadline that Rubinstein had insisted from the outset was absolute. (Federal funds ran out, technically at least, at midnight on the 31st.)

All committee meetings were behind closed doors at this point. The private goings on were surely not dull. According to John P. Murray, research coordinator for the project and one of the few non-committee members who was present during the deliberations (Paisley, 1972):

There was a big move by Government officials to get a consensus report. There was a lot of anger, the meetings were extremely tense with the warring factions sitting at either end of the table, glaring at each other, particularly toward the end [p. 28].

The result was undoubtedly a compromise, with the "network five" scoring its share in the battle. According to *Newsweek* (1972):

At one point during the committee meetings . . . former CBS consultant Wiebe raised his eyes from a particularly damning piece of evidence and grumbled: "This looks like it was written by someone who hates television." But the most ardent defender of the industry was CBS research director Joseph Klapper, who lobbied for the inclusion, among other things, of a plethora of "howevers" in the final report [p. 55].

The committee did sign a unanimous report just before the deadline and, of course, it took time to print, bind, and duplicate the document. During this waiting time, committee members were concerned that each hard-bargained subtlety they had won actually appeared in the published wording. Everyone was sensitive to the possibility of intrigue.

Television and growing up: *The impact of televised violence* was the title the committee gave its official report. Though manageable compared to the thousands of pages of technical reports, this 169-page work did not make for light reading either. So an 11-page summary of the report was published, both separately and as the first chapter of *Television and growing up*: *The impact of televised violence*.

Except for the committee members and staff, this brief but all-important 11-page statement by the committee was not seen by the researchers until a summary of the summary was published by Jack Gould in the *New York Times* on January 11, 1972, under the headline: TV VIOLENCE HELD UNHARMFUL TO YOUTH.

Chapter 5
Aftermath of the Report: TV Violence

OVERVIEW

Sufficient controversy surrounded publication of the Surgeon General's Report to warrant follow-up hearings, which were held in March 1972. The hearings led to a "new consensus" among social scientists and government officials that TV violence had been shown to be one of several significant contributors to aggressive and antisocial attitudes and behavior, and that a time for action had come. In the mid-1970's, significant efforts were aimed at monitoring and curbing the amount of violence on TV. A major commitment was made to obtain periodic measures of TV violence and Gerbner's Violence Index became the tool for accomplishing that. In terms of public reactions, both the AMA and the PTA came out strongly for a reduction in TV violence. Others, however, felt that the issue of TV violence was being pursued at the expense of more pressing issues (e.g., unemployment, inadequate educational opportunities). Meanwhile, research into the effects of TV and film violence continued. Although in a few of the studies discussed TV violence did not appear to influence subsequent behavior, the overwhelming majority of new studies suggested that the viewing of violent entertainment did produce noticeable increases in aggression in many youngsters. Evidence also continued to mount that exposure to TV violence "cultivates" attitudes regarding viewers' perceptions of and reactions to real life situations.

Our conclusion is that TV and other media violence can arouse children and youth, instigate copying of aggressive and antisocial acts, and shape the values of the young regarding a variety of undesirable and antisocial behaviors. However, viewing TV violence always works in conjunction with other factors. TV violence has a large effect on a small percentage of youngsters and a small but significant effect on a large percentage of youngsters; the reactions of individual youngsters are almost never predictable in advance.

In three major court cases the possible effects of TV violence have been pitted against broadcasters' First Amendment rights. In each case, First Amendment considerations prevailed.

The first public disclosure of the conclusions recorded in the Surgeon General's Report was written by a newspaper reporter, Jack Gould of the *New York Times*. Gould had somehow managed to get his hands on a copy of the 11-page summary of the Surgeon General's Report, and on January 11, 1972, published a front page story in the *Times* under the headline, "TV

VIOLENCE HELD UNHARMFUL TO YOUTH." The first paragraph of
the article stated:

> The office of the United States Surgeon General has found that violence in tele-
> vision programming does not have an adverse effect on the majority of the na-
> tion's youth but may influence small groups of youngsters predisposed by many
> factors to aggressive behavior.

Speaking more clearly and explicitly than social scientists ever do, Gould
claimed that only children already inclined toward aggression would be affected by TV violence and that their number was small. These claims were,
of course, arguable. In fact, Gould's article produced an enormous furor
and accusations that the Surgeon General's Report had been an industry
"whitewash." As a result, more public attention was focused on TV violence
in the spring of 1972 than ever before.

It is appropriate to step back for a moment to examine the problems reporter Gould faced. First, he was reading a summary of a summary, inasmuch as he had seen a summary of the Surgeon General's Report which itself was largely an effort to integrate and interpret a set of technical reports.

One thing the technical reports to the committee made clear was that TV
violence did not have a uniform effect on all children. In many ways this is
unsurprising, because very few factors do have uniform effects. Thus, the
technical project reports revealed differences in aggressive attitudes and behavior on the basis of gender, age, social and economic background; moreover, many of these factors influenced the degree to which TV violence had
an effect in experimental studies. In the official committee report, factors
associated with increased aggression were lumped together as "predisposi-
tions," and thus it could be said that TV violence had its greatest impact on
those who were "predisposed" to respond to violent content in the medium.
"Predisposition" turns out to be quite a subtle word, and one way to read
the committee's report was that TV violence was entirely harmless except
for possible effects on rare and troubled children. Presumably this is the
way Jack Gould interpreted the 11-page summary.

The Gould story greatly upset a number of the social scientists who had
authored the technical reports, and many contacted one another and local
newspapers in order to rectify what seemed like a gross misrepresentation of
their efforts. Articles on the subject of TV violence and children appeared
in most of the nation's major newspapers and news magazines. Conclusions
varied widely. Norman Mark (1972), writing in the *Chicago Daily News*,
announced:

> Dynamite is hidden in the Surgeon General's Report on children and television
> violence, for the report reveals that most children are definitely and adversely
> affected by television mayhem.

Many of the researchers associated with the project felt that their work had been represented inaccurately, and at the least minimized what seemed a clear relationship between viewing of TV violence and youngsters' aggressive behavior. Monroe Lefkowitz, Principal Research Scientist at the New York State Department of Mental Hygiene wrote in a letter to Senator Pastore:

> The Surgeon General's Scientific Advisory Committee on Television and Social Behavior in my opinion ignores, dilutes, and distorts the research findings in their report, "Television and Growing Up: the Impact of Televised Violence." As a contributor of one of the technical reports whose study dealt with television violence and aggressive behavior . . . I feel that the Committee's conclusions about the causal nature of television violence in producing aggressive behavior are hedged by erroneous statements, are overqualified, and are potentially damaging to children and society.

Lefkowitz' response is strong, but by no means unique. Matilda Paisley, in a report of Stanford University's Institute for Communication Research entitled "Social policy research and the realities of the system: Violence done to TV research," indicated that fully half of the researchers who replied to her questionnaire stated that the results of their own research had *not* been adequately reported by the committee (Paisley, 1972). Some typical replies, with letters substituted for respondents' names, appear below:

> Respondent B commented that, "In fact, they went too deep on some of our extraneous findings, in order to obscure the main conclusion." Respondents G, L, and P spoke of "strange emphases," "misleading focus," and "selective emphases," respectively. Respondents E and F spoke of errors in reporting their research. Respondent T stated that "the conclusions are diluted and overqualified" (Appendix III, p. 4).

One item on the Paisley questionnaire read: Whatever the findings of your own research suggest, which of the following relationships of violence viewing to aggressiveness do you feel now is the most plausible?*

    (a) viewing television violence increases aggressiveness;
    (b) viewing television violence decreases aggressiveness;
    (c) viewing television violence has no effect on aggressiveness;
    (d) the relationship between violence viewing and aggressiveness depends on a third variable or set of variables;
    (e) other, please specify

---

*Almost half of the investigators were involved in projects that did not bear directly on this question.

None of the 20 investigators who responded to this question selected answer (b) or selected (c). Clearly, then, these researchers felt that there was a relationship between TV violence and aggressiveness, and that the catharsis hypothesis was untenable. Seventy percent of the respondents simply selected response (a) — viewing television violence increases aggressiveness. All of the remainder qualified their replies with some version of alternatives (d) or (e).

Two passages from the committee's official report will exemplify the cautious flavor of its tone and give the reader a sense of why it stimulated such controversy.

In sum. The experimental studies bearing on the effects of aggressive television entertainment content on children support certain conclusions. First, violence depicted on television can immediately or shortly thereafter induce mimicking or copying by children. Second, under certain circumstances television violence can instigate an increase in aggressive acts. The accumulated evidence, however, does not warrant the conclusion that television violence has a uniformly adverse effect nor the conclusion that it has an adverse effect on the majority of children. It cannot even be said that the majority of the children in the various studies we have reviewed showed an increase in aggressive behavior in response to the violent fare to which they were exposed. The evidence does indicate that televised violence may lead to increased aggressive behavior in certain subgroups of children, who might constitute a small portion or a substantial proportion of the total population of young television viewers. We cannot estimate the size of the fraction, however, since the available evidence does not come from cross-section samples of the entire American population of children [p. 7].

Thus, the two sets of findings [correlational and experimental studies] converge in three respects: A preliminary and tentative indication of a causal relationship between viewing violence on television and aggressive behaviors; an indication that any such causal relation operates only on some children (who are predisposed to be aggressive); and an indication that it operates only in some environmental contexts. Such tentative and limited conclusions are not very satisfying. They represent substantially more knowledge than we had two years ago, but they leave many questions unanswered [p. 11].

THE PASTORE HEARINGS

In March 1972 shortly after the publication of the technical reports, Senator Pastore held further hearings to clarify the situation (U.S. Senate, 1972). When questioned by Senator Pastore and members of his subcommittee, Ithiel de Sola Pool, a member of the Surgeon General's Advisory Committee, commented:

Twelve scientists of widely different views unanimously agreed that scientific evidence indicated that the viewing of television violence by young people causes them to behave more aggressively [p. 47].

Alberta Siegel, another committee member, stated:

Commercial television makes its own contribution to the set of factors that underlie aggressiveness in our society. It does so in entertainment through ceaseless repetition of the message that conflict may be resolved by aggression, that violence is a way of solving problems [p. 63].

Pool and Siegel were among the academic members of the committee; they had pressed for a "strong" report on the basis of the data all along. But even Ira Cisin, Thomas Coffin, and the other "network" committee members agreed that the situation was sufficiently serious to warrant some action.

The networks' chief executives also testified. Julian Goodman, President of NBC, stated:

We agree with you that the time for action has come. And, of course, we are willing to cooperate in any way together with the rest of the industry [p. 182].

Elton H. Rule of the American Broadcasting Company promised:

Now that we are reasonably certain that televised violence can increase aggressive tendencies in some children, we will have to manage our program planning accordingly [p. 217].

Surgeon General Jesse Steinfeld made the unequivocal statement that:

Certainly my interpretation is that there is a causative relationship between televised violence and subsequent antisocial behavior, and that the evidence is strong enough that it requires some action on the part of responsible authorities, the TV industry, the Government, the citizens [p. 28].

Although few social scientists would put the seal "Absolutely Proven" on this or any other body of research, the weight of the evidence and the outcry of the news media did become sufficient to produce a belated recognition of the implications of the research.* Testimony and documentation at the Hearings of the Subcommittee on Communications, U.S. Senate, were overwhelming. Senator Pastore now had his answer. It is captured entirely

---

*Cater and Strickland (1975) have noted that it was not until after the report that social scientists and government officials reached a "new consensus" on what the data meant.

in the following interchange, late in the 1972 hearings, between Pastore and Dr. Eli Rubinstein. (Recall that Rubinstein was Vice-Chairman of the Surgeon General's Committee and monitored the research and refereed the Committee in Dr. Steinfeld's absence.)

> Senator Pastore. And you are convinced, like the Surgeon General, that we have enough data now [about the effects of television on children] to take action?
> Dr. Rubinstein. I am, sir.
> Senator Pastore. Without a re-review. It will only substantiate the facts we already know. Irrespective of how one or another individual feels, the fact still remains that you are convinced, as the Surgeon General is convinced, that there is a causal relationship between violence on television and social behavior on the part of children?
> Dr. Rubinstein. I am, sir.
> Senator Pastore. I think we ought to take it from there [p. 152].

EMERGING REACTIONS TO THE SURGEON GENERAL'S REPORT

The wake of the Surgeon General's Report ran wide and deep. We have already seen that there was a great deal of controversy over the report itself, especially regarding the validity of the committee's interpretations of the technical data. This led to additional hearings and then to a number of significant government and industry responses. What the Surgeon General's Report did stimulate was public interest. At the same time, social scientists were actively encouraged to explore the issue of television's effects on children in depth and from many vantage points, with financial support readily available from government agencies and private foundations. The ten-year period from 1970 to 1979 was the golden age of television for social science, if not for the medium itself. We shall discuss the results of many of these efforts in the remainder of the book. All of the major developments reflected their origins in the Surgeon General's Report.

For now, though, we will restrict ourselves mainly to the TV violence issue. The scientific evidence focused attention on the issue and helped to convince the public and Congress that TV violence should be reduced. As we will see in this chapter, the pressures generated by these groups actually resulted in industry action. Anticipating external controls, the broadcasting industry adopted self-regulatory measures in response to clear pressures from Congress, the public, and advertisers.

The report also stimulated research and funding in the area. In 1975, the Ford Foundation, National Science Foundation, and Markle Foundation sponsored a major conference in Reston, Virginia, to establish research priorities and increase funding on television and human behavior. In 1976, the National Science Foundation announced its support of a $1.5 million grant program entitled "Policy Related Research on the Social Effects of Broadcast Television." Also in 1976, the American Broadcasting Company provided modest funding for university research on television effects.

The sheer quantity of research on television and social behavior demonstrates the incredible growth of interest in the area. As Murray (1980) points out, a 1972 bibliography (Atkin, Murray, & Nayman, 1971) contained 285 core citations, and his own in 1980 contained 2,886 citations, 60% of which had been published over the preceding five years.

AFFIRMATIVE ACTION

Affirmative action was a banner phrase in the earlier part of the 1970s, and its spirit is reflected in much of the aftermath of the TV violence issue. In 1973, Jessie Steinfeld, recently retired from his official capacity as Surgeon General, wrote an article for *Readers Digest* entitled "TV Violence *Is* Harmful," in which he declared: "It is time to be blunt. We can no longer tolerate the high level of violence that saturates children's television" (p. 37).

The violence index

In Senator Pastore's March 1972 hearings, in which it might be said that the new consensus emerged, one specific idea was heavily promoted by foundation officials, government officers, and social scientists: a regular violence index.

Lloyd Morrisett, President of the Markle Foundation, which had a long interest in children and television, said at the hearings:

> We are impressed by the need for techniques to monitor on a continuing basis the amount and quality of violence on television as a means of informing the public and allowing a more complete understanding of the problem. In suggesting an attack on this problem we fully understand the complexity of the issue. It will be difficult to design sound measures of violence on television and the first ones will undoubtedly be imperfect and need to be improved over time. Despite this and other problems we believe the issue is important enough to warrant immediate action [cited by Cater and Strickland, 1975, p. 93].

Such a violence index was established, and not surprisingly the investigator to take on the task was George Gerbner. Every year since 1967 George Gerbner and his colleagues have continued to monitor the amount of violence on prime-time and weekend daytime (children's) shows. Using the same procedures over time (described in Chapter 4), this work represents the longest running record of TV violence portrayals. Table 5.1 presents an

Table 5.1. Percent of Programs Containing Violence and Number of Violent Acts per Hour (1967-1979).

Year	Percent of Programs Containing Violence			Number of Violent Acts per Program		
	All Programs	Prime Time	Weekend Daytime	All Programs	Prime Time	Weekend Daytime
1967	81.3	75.0	93.8	4.98	5.11	4.72
1968	81.6	75.4	93.3	4.53	3.89	5.73
1969	83.5	70.3	98.3	5.21	3.63	6.98
1970	77.5	62.3	96.0	4.49	3.31	5.92
1971	80.6	75.8	87.8	4.69	3.85	5.95
1972	79.0	71.7	90.0	5.39	4.90	6.13
1973	72.7	59.7	94.9	5.29	4.47	6.68
1974	83.3	77.6	92.1	5.44	5.66	5.11
1975*	78.1	66.7	94.9	5.38	5.51	5.18
1975	78.4	69.7	91.1	5.64	5.47	5.89
1976*	76.5	67.7	89.4	4.86	5.22	4.34
1976	89.1	80.3	100.0	6.18	5.61	6.90
1977**	76.9	66.2	90.6	5.20	5.46	4.87
1978	84.7	74.6	97.9	5.79	4.52	7.46
1979	80.9	70.3	91.9	4.98	5.37	4.58
Total	80.3	70.8	93.6	5.21	4.81	5.77

*Spring sample; all others are fall sample.
**Does not include second week of prime-time programming used in sampling experiment.
Total N = 1603 Programs (935 Prime-Time, 668 Weekend Daytime).
Source: Adapted from Signorielli, Gross, & Morgan (1982).

overview of Gerbner's findings from 1967–1979, including both percent of programs containing violence and number of violent acts per program for prime-time and weekend daytime programs. Over the twelve-year period, there has been a remarkable consistency in levels of violence by Gerbner's measure. The percent of programs containing violence only fluctuated from 72.7% (1973) to 89.1% (1976), and the range for the number of violent acts per program was 4.49 (1970) to 6.18 (1976). The consistencies are particularly striking in light of the number of Congressional hearings and network promises for reductions in TV violence since 1968.

Also consistent over the years has been the social groups that tend to be the victims of violence. The groups that are most likely to be the victim rather than the perpetrator of violence include women (of all ages, but especially young adult and elderly women), young boys, nonwhites, foreigners, and members of the extreme upper and lower classes.

Critics have found Gerbner's work vulnerable on several counts. Most important, perhaps, is that his violence scoring system includes humorous acts and accidents. As a result, Gerbner's analyses are often at odds with those of other studies using the more conventional definition of "acts intended to harm or threaten people or property." For example, a contrast between Gerbner's classification and one done by the *Christian Science Monitor* revealed that Gerbner classified light-hearted but innocent sit-coms such as *Flying Nun* and *That Girl* as violent shows, whereas the *Monitor* study more realistically characterized them as nonviolent (Coffin & Tuchman, 1973).

The Reston Conference

As we mentioned earlier in this chapter, in 1975 three foundations (Ford Foundation, National Science Foundation, and Markle Foundation) held a conference on television and human behavior. The conference had two objectives: (1) to organize a broad range of people (including representatives of academia, private and public foundations, media advocacy groups, the broadcasting industries, advertising, and government regulatory agencies) to develop a set of guidelines for future TV research, and (2) to frame the guidelines to maximize the utility of social science research for television policymakers within the government and the broadcasting and advertising industries. Relatively little consensus on specific issues was reached at the conference, but it became plain that all the researchers were quite interested in the role of television in the socialization of young persons. There also seemed to be some agreement that a causal link between TV violence and aggressive behavior had already been established, and that little more could be learned given the ethical and practical limitations of research. Thus, many researchers were inclined to try to harness TV's potential for various goals of society, an effort which we shall discuss in detail in the last chapter of this book.

The new activists

The new consensus also spurred a new set of activists, with a variety of ambitions for television. Many of these efforts, as we will see in Chapter 8, were designed to harness television's potential, but a few were trying to see TV violence curbed by more direct means. Most prominent in this regard are the efforts of the American Medical Association and the National PTA.

The AMA. In December 1975, the publication of an article by a Seattle physician in the *Journal of the American Medical Association* marked the beginning of a national movement by the AMA to curb TV violence. Dr. Michael Rothenberg, a pediatrician, had given a few lectures on the effects of TV violence on children. He then used the materials he collected for his talks to write a review article for the prestigious medical journal. The article was accepted immediately and made the lead article, cover picture and all. His conclusions, printed in bold type on the first page of the article stated:

> One hundred forty-six articles in behavioral science journals, representing 50 studies involving 10,000 children and adolescents from every conceivable background, all showed that violence viewing produces increased aggressive behavior in the young and that immediate remedial action in terms of television programming is warranted. . . .

> The time is long past due for a major, organized cry of protest from the medical profession in relation to what, in political terms, I consider a national scandal [p. 1043].

Rothenberg's concerns and suggestions that remedial action be taken were soon after echoed by another pediatrician, Dr. Anne Somers, in the April 1976 edition of the *New England Journal of Medicine*. After documenting the dramatic rise in violent crimes by youthful offenders and reviewing the research evidence linking TV violence to aggressive behavior in children, Somers spelled out the role that she felt the American Medical Association should take to reduce TV violence:

> The essential first step is general professional acceptance of the role of television violence as a risk factor threatening the health and welfare of American children and youth and official organizational commitment to remedial action. Recent publication of Dr. Rothenberg's brilliant "call to arms" on this subject was an important beginning.

> Next, it is essential that the American Medical Association and other organizational spokesmen for the profession make their views known to the industry—both to the networks and local stations, to the FCC, and to federal and state legislators, especially the two responsible committees of Congress. The approach should be twofold: a reduction of violence in general entertaining programming and support for the concept of the Family Viewing Hour.* The primary argument for the latter is not that it will save children from exposure to violence; it will not. But its very existence commits the industry to values other than commercialism and may force them, and the rest of us, to come up with some positive guidelines for realizing television's enormous positive cultural and educational potential [p. 816].

---

*The Family Viewing Hour was a National Association of Broadcasters guideline set forth in 1975 which stated that the 8–9 P.M. broadcast period should be free from themes that would be objectionable for child viewers (i.e., sex and violence). The interesting story behind this guideline will be discussed later in this chapter.

Aside from organizational action, Somers urged individual practitioners dealing with children and adolescents to make available to parents the guides to children's television published by media/child advocacy groups such as Action for Children's Television.

Perhaps the most emotional statement voiced by the medical profession against TV violence came from another physician, Dr. F.J. Ingelfinger (1976), who published an editorial called, "Violence on TV: An Unchecked Environmental Hazard" in the *New England Journal of Medicine*. Only his exact words can capture the sentiment expressed:

Diseases caused by the environment — for some reason called environmental rather than envirogenic — are prime public concerns. Hardly a day passes without some pesticide, industrial agent, drug or apparatus being indicted as responsible for some human disorder. These indictments, however, are not without their dilemmas, for the suspect agent is often beneficial as well as purportedly harmful. Without pesticides, nutritional crops are at risk, without drugs, illness may go unchecked and without nuclear power plants, the economy may falter. Thus, society is forced to arrive at difficult risk/benefit decisions. Ironically enough, however, while chlordane is banned and aspirin impugned, an environmental hazard of far greater magnitude and with no redeeming benefits whatsoever (except for fattening a few pocketbooks) goes unchallenged. The hazard is the exaltation of violence on television, its victims are all our children, and the disease is a distortion of values, attitudes and morality. . . .

If the medical profession is truly interested in curtailing the environmental hazard of excessive TV violence, it must make sure that the voices of protest multiply geometrically, from one to two to four, and so on, so that eventually the swell of the chorus can no longer be ignored. But noise, even loud noise, will probably not suffice. "An organized cry of protest" requires by definition organization, which in turn requires leadership and money. Doctors and their families must act as advocates and enlist not only other doctors but patients as well. Letters, as Anne Sommers suggests, must bombard our representatives in Congress. . . .

The AMA, if it is really ready to fight this environmental disease, should appoint a panel that will identify the programs most notorious for their routine and persistent portrayal of violence. Once these programs have been so identified, let the list be posted in doctors' offices. The application of the boycott is then straightforward: those who believe that violence on TV must be contained will simply pledge themselves not to purchase products promoted in association with the offending programs. Our dogs, after all, can survive even if they have to do without any canine gourmet dish that happens to underwrite a weekly gangland-police shoot-out, and our kitchens will function without electronic devices promoted between gory executions and garrottings.

Or shall we medicos and our spouses and friends sit back, as we have been doing, and fold our hands over contented bellies, while the after-dinner entertainment of our children shows that nothing can be accomplished in this world without brass knucks, kicks in the groin, switch blades or Saturday Night Specials [p. 837–838].

These articles were effective in summoning support. During 1976 and 1977, the AMA took several actions as a stand against TV violence. In 1976, the House of Delegates of the AMA resolved that it would:

1. Declare its recognition of the fact that TV violence is a risk factor threatening the health and welfare of young Americans, indeed our future society.
2. Commit itself to remedial action in concert with industry, government and other interested parties.
3. Encourage all physicians, their families and their patients to actively oppose TV programs containing violence, as well as products and/or services sponsoring such programs [American Medical Association Policy, 1976].

The report of a content analysis by the National Citizens Committee for Broadcasting released in July of 1976 helped to pinpoint the sponsors of TV violence on whom the AMA would focus. The public interest organization, headed by a former FCC commissioner Nicholas Johnson, monitored TV entertainment for six weeks and identified the companies that advertised on the most violent programs. They found the following companies to be most often associated with violent programs: Tegrin, Burger King, Clorox, Colgate-Palmolive, and Gillette (Brown, 1976).

In February 1977 Dr. Richard E. Palmer, President of the AMA, declared TV violence a "mental health problem and an environmental issue" and asked ten major companies to examine advertising policies that support TV programs high in violence (*Newsday*, 1977). Further AMA action took the form of national workshops to inform physicians about TV violence effects, research to monitor the amount of TV violence, and encouragement to the National PTA to organize its own campaign.

The PTA. The cornerstone of the National PTA's efforts to deal effectively with TV violence was a survey in which 3,000 parents of school age children were asked to rate prime-time programs for six weeks, between October 22–December 2, 1977. The final report (National PTA, 1978) identified the top twenty quality programs, the ten worst quality programs, and the ten most violent programs. Examples of "excellent" programs (defined as "positive contribution to the quality of life in America, lack of offensive content, and high program quality") are: *Little House on the Prairie, Eight is Enough, Waltons, Donnie and Marie*, and *World of Disney*; "poorest" programs included *Maude, Kojak, Three's Company*, and *Welcome Back Kotter*; the most violent series included *Kojak, Charlie's Angels, Police Woman, Six Million Dollar Man*, and *Starsky and Hutch*.

In the context of these events, a study by the leading advertising firm,

J. Walter Thompson, provided economic reasons for reducing TV violence. Ten percent of the adult sample surveyed considered not buying a product because it was advertised in violent programming, and 8% said they actually had refrained from purchasing a product for that reason. The President of the agency, Don Johnston, presented these results at a meeting of the American Advertising Federation. He stated, "We are counseling our clients to evaluate the potential negatives of placing commercials in programming perceived as violent. Our motivation is primarily social, but there are certain business considerations that confirm our recommendations" (Dougherty, 1976). He warned that public aversion to violent programs was growing and might result in protest letters and product boycotts.

The Heller manual

The industry undertakes relatively few affirmative action steps on its own and for the most part responds only when pressed. A noteworthy exception is a manual written by Dr. Melvin S. Heller, at the behest of ABC, to assist ABC Broadcast Standards personnel in their jobs. Heller wrote a 99-page manual based on his seven years of experience consulting with the Code Authority of the NAB and then with ABC's Broadcast Standards Department and on his own research on children and television for ABC. In Heller's words, "What was needed was a way to begin applying the findings of our own research, as well as that reported by others, to the practical tasks of broadcast standards editors" (Heller, 1978, p. 2). The manual emphasizes the portrayal of violence on television but also contains sections on sexual, stereotypic, and prosocial content, as well as a special section on the child audience. While the manual exudes with psychodynamic theories and rationales (e.g., Oedipal stage, unconscious mechanisms) no longer highly regarded by many psychologists and psychiatrists, the effort as a whole is commendable and offers some excellent suggestions to editors on how to make decisions about controversial content. For example, Heller suggests these questions when evaluating content that presents mischievous or dangerous behavior:

a) Does the portrayal of the act, or a modification of it, carry with it the possibility of similar imitations of mischief, potentially dangerous or reprehensible behavior?
b) Would juveniles and other vulnerable viewers tend to think that such portrayals might be fun, or result in kicks or quick publicity?
c) If the portrayed behavior might appeal to a small group of predisposed youngsters or childish adult viewers, are the downside risks, dangers, and potential untoward consequences clearly and sufficiently elaborated in the storyline?

d) Is the result of an easily replicated deed, such as pushing someone off a crowded subway platform in the path of an oncoming train, presented as a spectacular, formidible and shocking act which might tempt a predisposed individual to imitate it? In other words, is the effort so small and the result so awesome and grotesque as to promise cheap, instant publicity or notoriety, no matter how reprehensible the act might be?

e) If the act as portrayed caused no actual harm, was this due to a lucky escape, and could a possible modification or miscalculation in imitating it be fraught with danger and risk?

f) Finally, would you knowingly allow your children to attempt this stunt, risking their own or someone else's welfare?

An unsatisfactory answer to any of the above questions readily labels it as an unacceptable or borderline portrayal. The risk quite likely outweighs any possible gain in its showing, even in an unusual dramatic vehicle of artistic merit. If high action requires high risk, the risk must be portrayed as absolutely essential to survival, and must be carefully scrutinized as to its potential for capricious imitation by impressionable viewers [p.65–66].

While the manual does not take into account all of the existing research on television's effects, it does encourage a much more sensitive evaluation process for the broadcast standards personnel than that based on the general NAB guidelines.

Kaplan and Singer's critique

As might be expected, not everyone greeted this new activism with enthusiasm. Writing in a 1976 issue of the *Journal of Social Issues*, Robert Kaplan and Robert Singer offered a scalding critique of those who had become preoccupied with TV violence to the exclusion of other, more pressing and important matters. They wrote:

It is fascinating that so many hours of research and so many funding dollars have been directed at the possible effects of TV violence on aggressive behavior when it seems most likely that television is not a major cause of human aggression, an activity which considerably antedates audio-visual media. It is unlikely that war, murder, suicide, the battered child syndrome, other violent crimes, and man's inhumanity to man stem to any marked degree from television viewing. Many social scientists may have become victims of the "bearer of bad news" syndrome. Like the Persian emperor beheading messengers who brought bad news, we berate television, which, it is true, shows us ad nauseam and out of all proportion the aggression which man commits against man.

Instead of castigating the networks it might be more useful to ask why the public is so fascinated by programs portraying violence. We would like to suggest investigations into the connection between violence and unemployment, racial prejudice, poor housing and lack of medical care, the prevalence of guns and the ease of obtaining alcohol, the high mobility of the population, the prevalence of broken families, the role of age, the still partly subservient role of women, the lack of public school courses in child-rearing, and a possibly declining faith in the just nature of our political and judicial system [pp. 63–64].

FURTHER ANALYSIS AND RESEARCH

Network sponsored research on TV violence

Despite the apparent unresponsiveness of the networks to the criticisms and warnings voiced at the numerous Congressional hearings since the early 1960s, the networks did undertake research of their own to evaluate the claim that TV violence resulted in aggressive behavior by its viewers. While several of the studies were initiated in the late 1960s, none of them were completed until after the Surgeon General's Report had appeared. Therefore, we have waited until this point in our discussion to describe them.

In 1969, CBS sponsored two major studies. The first, by Milgram and Shotland, was published in 1973. The second, by Belson, was published in 1978.

The Milgram and Shotland studies. Milgram and Shotland (1973) conducted a series of studies addressing the question: To what extent would viewers imitate an antisocial act seen on television in real life? The major portion of the $500,000 study focused on the antisocial act of stealing from a charity donation box. This was a unique experiment in that CBS actually produced the experimental programs. Three versions of a *Medical Center* episode were produced which modeled such stealing in varying ways. The overall plot revolved around Tom, an orderly who worked at the hospital and faced extreme economic and emotional pressures. His hardship occurred at the time when the hospital was running a charity drive. One version showed Tom stealing money from several hospital charity boxes and subsequently going to jail for it; in a second version, he stole the money and got away with it; in the third version he was shown being tempted to steal the money but then donating a coin. In the fourth condition a neutral episode was shown.

In three experiments varying in the specific versions shown, audiences viewed a *Medical Center* episode in a theater. In each experiment, several hundred participants ranging in age from high school seniors to a heterogeneous sample of adults, were offered a free radio which was to be picked up a week later at another location. The situation was designed to be a frustrating one. When participants arrived at the location where they were to get their radios, they found only an empty office and a sign indicating that there were no more radios. The office also contained a charity box containing coins, a $10 bill, and several $1 bills, one of which was protruding from the box. Concealed cameras recorded the subject's behavior. Hence, a situation was created which paralleled key elements of the TV program—there was a frustrating situation and the temptation to take money from a charity box.

Milgram and Shotland found that overall there were trivial amounts of money taken and what little stealing occurred did not vary significantly with the episode version shown. An example of the amounts of money taken is that in one experiment 5.2% of the subjects stole all the money, 3.5% stole the protruding dollar, and 6.9% tried to break into the box but failed. Further, they tested for immediate effects in a fourth experiment which involved viewing versions of the episode in the office containing the charity box. Again, no version effects were found. A fifth experiment used a home viewing situation and the same assessment situation of being offered a gift and finding an empty room with a charity box. Again, no significant differences between episode versions were found. The authors conclude,

> First, the evidence . . . generated must be taken seriously, and serve as a constraint on discussion of television's effects. For the results of the present experiment are not that we obtained no findings, but rather that we obtained no differences in those exposed to our different stimulus programs. . . . [I]f television is on trial, the judgment of this investigation must be the Scottish verdict: Not proven.

In a critique of the Milgram and Shotland study, Comstock (1974) cogently points out its many flaws. First, the question addressed by the research reflects a narrow perspective:

> It would seem to represent a rather singular thrust—the test of the hypothesis that any specific antisocial act shown on television will have fairly immediate and quite widespread imitation. Now that's a scary proposition, but if true we'd long be well aware of it with every evening's dramatizations predicting the next few days' newspaper headlines [p. 136].

Second, the sample was biased in that only 5 to 7% of those recruited actually showed up for the study. One wonders how representative the participants were. Third, the fact that several studies showed no results implies a corroboration of findings which is misleading since essentially the same design (with all its flaws) was used throughout. Perhaps the most basic potential problem was the use of a medical charity which, given societal values, might have been too strict a test; in other words, the pressure not to steal might have been too great, thus producing a relatively insensitive measure of willingness to steal. Then, too, it should be remembered that the subjects were all adults or older adolescents, rather than children.

The Belson study. Belson (1978) collected information about television viewing, aggressive behavior, and other personal characteristics of more than 1,500 male adolescents in London. After equating for a variety of variables related to aggressive behavior, the extent of aggressive behavior of the heavy and light TV viewers was compared. Belson concluded that the evidence "is very strongly supportive of the hypothesis that high exposure to television violence increases the degree to which boys engage in serious violence" (p. 15). (The antisocial behaviors included deeds which were serious enough to be labeled juvenile delinquency such as inflicting bodily harm to others and damage to property.)

While the Belson study was impressively large scale and sophisticated statistically, it was not a true experiment. CBS chose to view the findings as inconclusive, and the study did not receive much publicity. (Just as a note of interest, this study took eight years to complete and cost CBS $300,000.)

The Heller and Polsky study. In 1970, ABC commissioned a series of studies on TV violence effects by two consultants, a psychiatrist, Marvin Heller (who later wrote the *Broadcast Standards Editing* manual for ABC described earlier) and a lawyer, Samuel Polsky. The Heller and Polsky study (1975) was never available for sale at book stores or through any distribution outlet. Rather, ABC had copies of the Heller and Polsky report printed for private distribution. It was, however, widely cited by people in the industry as showing that TV violence was not a matter to be concerned about any longer. One of us (RML) was sent a review copy of the report by a major journal and asked to review it. The result was an essay published in 1977 critically reviewing the report (Liebert, Cohen, Joyce, Murrel, Nisonoff, & Sonnenschein, 1977). The following excerpts from the essay "Predisposition Revisited" provide the essence of the Heller and Polsky study and its limitations as my students and I saw it:

> The central thesis of this [report] is that televised examples of aggression, violence, and mayhem can only have an effect on those who are already "predisposed" in some way to be influenced by them. A violent disposition, as Heller and Polsky portray it, arises from one's basic personality structure and early childhood experiences. It follows from this position that television viewing in later childhood and adolescence could not possibly "cause" or "instigate" aggressive or antisocial behavior, though the demonstrations and examples which television provides may be copied by criminal types and may lead to increases in rough "horseplay," hostile verbalizations, and other not very serious effects among a wide range of vulnerable youngsters. . . .

[The purpose of Project II, a continuation of Project I] was to "evaluate the effects of cartoon-portrayed violence in comparison with human-acted or non-cartoon programs". . . . When the institutionalized children in this study showed significantly greater aggression after seeing cartoons than after seeing the non-cartoon material (on the much praised Feshbach Behavior Rating Scale the authors had selected), Heller and Polsky dismiss the finding as not surprising because the non-cartoon material was so bland. They go on to conclude that "even though increases in a variety of aggressive behaviors and attitudes were indeed noted following exposure to cartoons, these increases were still a relatively unimpressive percentage of the potential number of incidents" (p. 77). Both here and in subsequent projects, Heller and Polsky find significant changes or differences in overt aggression on measures they themselves have devised or chosen, and then dismiss the differences as "mild" or "unimpressive."

Projects III and IV both report interview data and related information obtained from youthful violent offenders. What is most impressive about Project III, a small study of 35 offenders which the authors consider a pilot for Project IV, is that more than a third of these boys "indicated they had been consciously aware of acting out the techniques of a crime which they had previously seen 'demonstrated' on television!" [p. 94, exclamation in original]. In their conclusions regarding this project, however, Heller and Polsky are inclined to minimize the importance of television violence for these boys because none of the youngsters attributed his own criminal propensities to television. The pattern is continued in Project IV, a study of 100 youthful violent offenders, 98 of whom were black. (One of the interesting artifacts emerging from this overwhelming racial bias in the sample is that the young men in this group said they were 12 times more likely to imitate Flip Wilson than Humphrey Bogart.) Roughly paralleling the findings of Project III, 22 of these offenders reported actually trying criminal techniques they had seen on television, and 19 of them said their television-inspired crimes were carried out successfully and without detection. Another 22 men reported contemplating crimes they had seen on television and more than half of the total sample (52 percent) felt that television had changed their thoughts or beliefs. Despite these findings, Heller and Polsky conclude Project IV by saying that the data do not warrant ascribing any "causative role" to television viewing.

The Milavsky, Kessler, Stipp, and Rubens study (1982). In 1970, NBC supported a three-year longitudinal study of the relationship between TV violence viewing and aggressive behavior in children and teenagers. The project was headed by J. Ronald Milavsky, a Ph.D. sociologist who is the Vice President for News and Social Research at NBC. The results will be published in a forthcoming book. The study was conducted in two cities, Minneapolis, Minnesota and Fort Worth, Texas. Over the course of three years (1970–1973), the researchers collected measures of both aggressive behavior (using peer nomination and self-report methods) and exposure to

TV and televised violence in particular (using a self-report method) up to six times from 2,400 elementary school children (7–12 years old) and 800 teenage boys (12–16 years old). As had been found in many prior studies, the relationship between viewing TV violence and aggressive behavior measured at the same point in time was significant ($r = +.11$ for elementary school age boys, $+.23$ for elementary school age girls, and $+.13$ for teenage boys). However, the authors then made a variety of statistical adjustments they felt were needed, after which the results were no longer statistically significant.

Independent experimental studies paralleling the report

Apart from industry-sponsored studies, independent experimental studies of TV violence continued to be published through the 1970s, dealing with the instigation of physical aggression, criminal behavior, and the cultivation of attitudes that might directly or indirectly foster socially disapproved behavior. Around the time of the Surgeon General's Report, two experiments which had been proceeding independently of the government investigation or industry support were published. Like the studies appearing in the Surgeon General's Report, these investigations represented a clear advance over earlier work in that they aimed to investigate the effects of TV violence on naturally occurring behavior and in natural viewing situations.

Steuer, Applefield, and Smith (1971) investigated the effects of aggressive and neutral television programs on the aggressive behavior of ten preschoolers in their school environment. These boys and girls comprised a racially and socioeconomically mixed group and knew each other before the study began. First, they were matched into pairs on the basis of the amount of time they spent watching television at home. Next, to establish the degree to which aggressive behavior occurred among these youngsters before any modification of their television diets, each was carefully observed in play with other children for ten sessions, and the frequency of aggressive responses recorded. (This part of the study is referred to as the *baseline* observation phase.)

Steuer and her associates used a demanding measure of physical interpersonal aggression, including: (a) hitting or pushing another child, (b) kicking another child, (c) assaultive contact with another child which included squeezing, choking, or holding down, and (d) throwing an object at another child from a distance of at least one foot. The baseline established a high degree of consistency within each pair prior to the modification of the television diet.

Next, Steuer and her colleagues investigated the effects of television. On 11 different days, one child in each pair observed a single aggressive program taken directly from violent Saturday morning program offerings, while the other member of the pair observed a nonaggressive television program. Subsequent observations of the children at play provided continuous measures of interpersonal physical aggressive behavior by each child. Changes from the original measures, if any, would have to be caused by TV effects.

By the end of the 11 sessions, the two groups had departed significantly from one another in terms of the frequency of interpersonal aggression. In fact, for every pair, the child who observed aggressive television programming had become more aggressive than his mate who watched neutral fare.

While this study has been criticized on the basis of the small number of children involved, it is important to emphasize that the size of the sample is taken into account in the statistical tests. A stronger effect is necessary to produce significant results with such few cases; therefore, the aggression effect found is convincing evidence of the impact of TV violence.

As you will recall from Chapter 3, the Feshbach and Singer (1971) field study found that adolescent boys who were shown aggressive programs became less aggressive than those shown neutral fare. However, we indicated that the study was plagued by differences in the boys' interest in the programs comprising the two TV diets (the aggressive programs were liked more), and the fact that the boys in the neutral condition convinced the investigators to allow them to watch the popular and aggressive program *Batman*. Wells (1972) replicated the study eliminating these problems. He found that boys who watched only television fare from which all "action and adventure had been expunged" were somewhat more aggressive *verbally* than those who watched a heavy diet of aggression. But from various other lines of evidence, he reports "that the greater verbal aggression [from this group] may have come from complaints about the 'lousy' shows they were required to watch." His other results and an interpretation of them were presented this way by the Surgeon General's Advisory Committee on Television and Social Behavior (Cisin et al., 1972):

> In a direct reversal of Feshbach and Singer—Wells found significantly greater physical aggressiveness among boys who viewed the more violent television programs . . . the differences . . . were limited to boys who were above average in aggression before the study began. . . . [Wells] interprets the greater physical aggression elicited by the more violent program diet as a tendency for the action-adventure content to stimulate aggressive behavior. He found no evidence [in this replication of Feshbach and Singer] that would support a catharsis interpretation, unless the differences in regard to verbal aggressiveness were so interpreted [p. 66].

Later field experiments

The Surgeon General's Report and the reactions to it prompted independent investigators to look for more convincing evidence that TV violence influenced "hard" measures of aggression. During the 1970s several large-scale field experiments were conducted to probe the question further.

The Parke-Berkowitz studies. A series of three field experiments conducted in the United States and Belgium studied the effect of full-length violent films on the aggressive behaviors of male adolescent juvenile delinquents residing in minimum security institutions (Parke, Berkowitz, Leyens, West, & Sebastian, 1977). In all three studies, the youngsters were observed in naturalistic (i.e., not contrived) situations before and after the film exposure. Film effects on aggressive behavior were apparent in all three studies.

In the first study, which was conducted in the United States, 30 boys in each of two living unit cottages participated, one group forming the aggressive film and the other the neutral film condition. In setting up the units originally, boys were randomly assigned to the cottages. For three weeks before and after a one-week film treatment period, the boys' social and non-interpersonal aggressive behaviors were observed for three consecutive nights each week. During the treatment week, the boys saw a different movie every weekday evening. Those in the aggressive film group watched *The Chase, Death Rides a Horse, The Champion, Corruption,* and *Ride Beyond Vengeance.* The neutral films were: *Buena Serra Mrs. Campbell, Ride the Wild Surf, Countdown, Beach Blanket Bingo,* and *A Countess from Hong Kong.* Behavioral observations were taken before, during, and after the movie viewing each evening. The investigators found that the boys who saw the aggressive films behaved more aggressively than those who viewed the neutral films on measures of general aggression (defined as the sum of physical threat, physical attack, verbal aggression, noninterpersonal physical and verbal aggression, and physical and verbal self-aggression) and physical aggression (defined as the sum of physical attack, noninterpersonal physical aggression, and physical self-aggression). There was no evidence of the prior aggression levels having an impact on magnitude of effect or of a cumulative effect of viewing (i.e., aggression remained stable and did not increase over the viewing period).

The second American study was conducted in the same institution with 120 boys who did not participate previously. Aside from a few changes, the study was a replication of the first. The modifications included increasing the number of observations, changing a few neutral films to equate more for interest level between the two film groups, and adding two conditions. To determine the effect of repeated exposures, an aggressive and a neutral film group were added in which only one film (either aggressive or neutral) was viewed. For the single exposure conditions, boys initially high in aggression became more physically aggressive after exposure to the aggressive film than to the neutral film. A similar pattern was found for the repeated exposure groups. Contrary to expectation, the aggression effects were not greater for multiple than for single exposures to film aggression; in fact, the reverse was true for general and physical aggression measures.

The third study which was conducted in Belgium followed essentially the same multiple exposure procedure, except the observation period before and after the film week was condensed from three weeks to one, and the films used were changed to be more appropriate for Belgian audiences. (The aggressive movies were *Iwo-Jima, Bonnie and Clyde, The Dirty Dozen, Zorro,* and *The Left-Handed Gun.* The neutral movies were *Lily, Alexandre le Bienheureux, Daddy's Fiancee, Sebastien Parni Les Hommes,* and *La Belle Americaine.*) The results, similar to the first two studies, indicated that the boys exposed to the aggressive films became more physically aggressive relative to those who viewed the neutral films. (See Figure 5.1.) Initial aggressiveness influenced the results for the other aggression measures; the boys initially high in aggression showed a greater increase in general and verbal aggression after exposure to the aggressive film than to the neutral film. An additional feature of the Belgian study was that it included an assessment of group membership characteristics—the boys provided rankings of each other based on dominance and popularity. Interestingly, it was

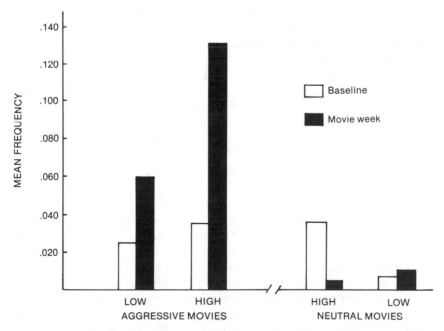

Fig. 5.1. Physical aggression index (immediate effects) for initially high- and low-aggressive boys in Parke, Berkowitz, Leyens, West, & Sebastian (1977) study.

found that the most dominant, popular, and aggressive boys showed the strongest aggression effects. Also affected to a large degree were the least popular youths.

The South Africa study. In all the studies we have discussed so far subjects had considerable experience with television before their participation. (Recall from Chapter 1 how much television most children watch and how young they start.) This prior experience might mute or amplify the effects of TV violence. What would happen if youngsters who had never seen television before saw violent or nonviolent programs on a regular basis?

Although the opportunity to do such a study appeared long gone by the time of the Surgeon General's Report, in fact one industrialized nation of the world had fought successfully to isolate itself from television in tacit acknowledgment of the potential power of the medium. The nation was arch-conservative South Africa.

The opportunity to do an experimental field test with a group of children who had not yet been exposed to TV seemed a last-chance opportunity to University of California research psychologist, Paul Ekman. For several years Ekman actively devoted himself to encouraging and assisting three South African social scientists to do such a study before it was too late. (When the first man landed on the moon in 1969, the historically momentous event could be seen almost everywhere in the world via satellite, but not in South Africa where television had been barred. The government finally decided to let TV in, and was persuaded by Ekman and the prospective South African researchers to permit the study to go ahead before the medium was introduced into the country.) The large-scale field study was conducted in 1975 and reported in 1980 (de Konig, Conradie, & Nell, 1980). The study was conducted in two provinces in South Africa, which up to the time of the study did not have television transmission. This feature gave the research the unique advantage of assessing television's influence on TV-naive youngsters rather than on the TV-saturated youths tested in the American and European studies. Three TV diets were constructed, each composed of 18 American TV programs. One diet contained aggressive programs, one "prosocial" programs, and the other neutral programs. Content analyses conducted by American researchers ensured that the aggressive diet presented high levels of aggressive behavior, the prosocial diet presented high levels of prosocial behavior (such as cooperation, helping and sharing) and little or no aggression, and the neutral diet contained low levels of aggressive and prosocial behaviors. About 700 children ranging in age from five to thirteen years viewed programs from one of the three diets for one hour daily, four days a week in their school. The youngsters' behavior (both aggressive and prosocial) was rated before and after the viewing periods. Few significant differences between viewing groups were found. It appeared that the neutral diet decreased aggression against peers, and the prosocial diet increased aggression toward authority figures; the latter finding was explained as resulting from the fact that the youngsters did not like the prosocial programs and reacted negatively to them. The diets did not produce differences in prosocial behavior.

Why did deKonig, Conradie and Nell fail to observe any significant effects in contrast to the great majority of studies of roughly similar design? It is difficult to be sure. It is possible, of course, that TV does not have a differential content effect in some cultures, or that the subjects were temporarily overwhelmed by the sheer novelty of television. Also, the imbalanced popularity of the two diets may have tempered or masked other effects. Further, the behavioral ratings may have been insensitive. The children's teachers, who provided some of the ratings, indicated how often (never, seldom, or often) each student engaged in each listed behavior for the week before and the week after the TV treatment. Such ratings may have been too global and vulnerable to preconceptions about the behavior of individual students to detect behavioral differences. (Other studies, it will be recalled, employed more fine-grained and detailed measures of participants' actual behavior.)

Later field correlational studies

Two major field correlational studies of TV violence viewing and aggressive behavior were performed after the Surgeon General's Report. There was an interest in studying children younger than those focused on in the 1972 report as is evident in the two studies reported here.

Eron and Huesmann (1980). As a follow-up to the ten-year longitudinal study done for the Surgeon General's Report, Eron and Huesmann (1980) conducted a three-year longitudinal study on a new and younger sample of children. The researchers collected TV viewing information and aggressive behavior measures (based on peer ratings) from 700 first and third graders once each year for three years. Their findings regarding the relationship between TV violence viewing and aggressive behavior largely corroborated the earlier ten-year study. However, while the earlier study reported that the relationship held only for boys, the more recent study showed significant relationships between viewing TV violence and aggressive behavior for girls as well.

Singer and Singer (1980). Dorothy and Jerome Singer (1980) of Yale University did a one-year longitudinal study of the relationship between television viewing and aggressive behavior in three- and four-year old preschool children. They determined the children's TV viewing habits from viewing diaries that were completed by the parents of the participating children for three, two-week periods over a year. The youngsters' aggressive behavior during free play periods in school was observed and recorded three times throughout the one-year period. Then the relationship between TV viewing and aggressive behavior was determined. Because the study was not an experiment and causal statements would be limited by third variable and directionality problems, the Singers used the statistical techniques used for the Surgeon General's Report: partialling and cross-lagged correlations. (Both of these techniques were discussed in Chapter 4.) Partialling out the influence of background factors (socioeconomic status, ethnicity, IQ, and sex) diminished only slightly the significant association between the action-adventure television viewing and aggressive behavior. As in the Lefkowitz et al. (1972) study for the Surgeon General's Report, the cross-lagged correlations indicated that it was more likely that violence viewing led to aggressive behavior than that aggressive children prefer violent programs. The correlation between watching action-adventure television programs at Time 1 (October) and aggression at Time 3 (April) was significant (+ .18) and higher than the correlation between aggression at time 1 and action-adventure viewing at Time 3 (+ .05). It should be noted, though, that from a practical standpoint these relationships are quite small.

Studies of TV's antisocial cultivation effects

Gerbner's studies. In the decade since the publication of the Surgeon General's Report, Gerbner has gone a long way in developing and advancing his cultivation theory about television's influence on viewers' conceptions of social realities. The theory predicts that the more a person is exposed to television, the more likely the person's perceptions of social realities will match those represented on TV ["the more time one spends 'living' in the world of television, the more likely one is to report perceptions of social reality which can be traced to (or are congruent with) television's most persistent representations of life and society" (Gerbner, Gross, Morgan, & Signorielli, 1980, p. 14)]. The procedure used to test the theory involves comparing frequent TV users ("heavy viewers") and infrequent users ("light viewers") on their perceptions of various social events. The social events used reflect those areas that content analyses have shown television to represent in a distorted way. The expectation is that heavy viewers would give more "television answers" (reflecting the TV world) to social reality questions than would light viewers.

Gerbner has conducted this type of analysis on many different samples of people differing in age, income, education, and race, and has found support for his theory. Heavy viewers are more likely than light viewers to have outlooks and perceptions congruent with television portrayals—even after eliminating the influence of variables such as income and educational levels.

A recent study on adolescents serves to illustrate the method used (Gerbner, Gross, Signorielli, Morgan, Jackson-Beeck, 1979). A total of 587 adolescents (average age between 13 and 14 years) from New York City and New Jersey filled out questionnaires which offered two answers to each question; one based on actual facts and one based on the television portrayal ("television answer"). Table 5.2 presents the questions and the percent of heavy and light viewers selecting the "television answer." While the differences are not dramatic, for every question, a greater percent of heavy viewers than light viewers responded with the television answer, whether the

Table 5.2. Percent of Heavy and Light Viewers Giving "Television Answer" to Violence Questions.

		Heavy	Light
1.	"Think about the number of people who are involved in some kind of violence each year. Do you think that 3 percent of all people are involved in some kind of violence in any given year, or is it closer to 10 percent*?"[a]	83%	62%
2.	"Think about the number of people who are involved in violence each week. Do you think one person out of every 100 is involved in some kind of violence in any given week, or is it closer to 10 people* out of every 100?[b]	73%	62%
3.	"About what percent of all people commit serious crimes—is it closer to 3 percent or 12 percent*?[b]	88%	77%
4.	"Would you be afraid to walk alone in a city at night?"[a] (*Yes)	52%	46%
5.	"Are you afraid to walk alone in your own neighborhood at night?"[a] (*Yes)	32%	13%
6.	"Is it dangerous to walk alone in a city at night?"[b] (*Yes)	86%	79%
7.	"On an average day, how many times does a policeman usually pull out his gun—less than once a day or more than five times a day*?)[a]	18%	6%
8.	When police arrive at a scene of violence, how much of the time do they have to use force and violence—most of the time* or some of the time?[b]	56%	45%
9.	"Can most people be trusted, or do you think that you can't be too careful* in dealing with people?"[b]	62%	52%
10.	"Would you say that most of the time people try to be helpful, or that they are mostly just looking out for themselves*?"[b]	64%	56%

*"Television" answer.
[a]Based on New York City sample (N = 140).
[b]Based on New Jersey sample (N = 447).
Source: Adapted from Gerbner, Gross, Signorielli, Morgan, & Jackson-Beeck, 1979.

question was about the number of criminals, the fear of walking alone at night in a city or one's own neighborhood, the frequency of police violence, or general trust in people. Questions about the personal characteristics of the adolescents were also asked, including sex, socioeconomic status, achievement, experience as a victim of violence, and frequency of newspaper reading. Some of these variables influenced the differential responding of heavy and light viewers, and in some cases made the discrepancy much greater than the overall percents reflect in Table 5.2. For example, for the question about the percent of people who are involved in violence in any given year, of the males, 87% of heavy viewers overestimated the violence, while only 58% of the light viewers did so. Of the adolescents who were never victimized by violence, 75% of the heavy viewers gave the TV answer compared to only 29% of the light viewers. Gerbner would say that adolescent males who have not experienced personal violence and don't watch much TV diverge from the "mainstream" cultivated by television; otherwise similar males who watch TV frequently share a relatively homogeneous conception of a violent, mean world. In Gerbner's own words, "The most significant and recurring conclusion of our long-range study is that one correlate of television viewing is a heightened and unequal sense of danger and risk in a mean and selfish world" (Gerbner et al., 1979, p. 196).

Additional evidence supporting Gerbner's cultivation theory is provided in a recent study which used Gerbner's procedures on youngsters in Australia. Pingree and Hawkins (1981) obtained responses to social reality questions (parallel to those used by Gerbner) and television viewing diaries from 1,085 second, fifth, eighth, and eleventh graders residing in Perth, the largest city in Western Australia. As with U.S. samples, heavy viewing was associated with more TV answers. The youngsters in the sample watched TV between two and four hours daily, and during evening prime time 50–70% of the available commercial programming were U.S. reruns. It is interesting that the frequency with which the children viewed U.S. programs related more to the perception of Australia rather than the U.S. as a "mean world."

The evidence does not firmly prove that TV cultivates attitudes, however. Like all correlational studies, those reported by Gerbner and his associates are subject to the directionality and third variable problems (see Chapter 4). For example, it is possible that people who are apprehensive about going out, stay home and watch television rather than hazarding the dangers of the streets; in this case, the attitude would have produced the heavy TV viewing rather than the other way around. Or it could be that TV is more enjoyable or more stimulating for apprehensive people, since it provides safe, vicarious experience. In this case a third variable, the personality trait *apprehensiveness*, would be the cause of exaggerated ideas about dangers in society and would also be the basis for obtaining social gratification vicariously, which is the opportunity TV provides.

Drabman and Thomas' experiments. An ingenious line of experimental research suggesting a cultivation-like effect has been pursued by Drabman and Thomas who have addressed the question: Does TV violence make children more tolerant of real-life aggression?

After exposing children to an aggressive TV program, Drabman and Thomas (1974) tested the children's reponse to a situation in which two younger children behaved aggressively toward one another. Twenty-two male and 22 female third and fourth graders viewed either an aggressive cowboy film or no film. Then the youngsters were left in charge to watch over two younger children whom they could see via a TV monitor. What the subject saw was actually a prepared videotape of two children playing quietly at first and then becoming progressively aggressive toward one another and destructive to property. In fact, the fighting became so vigorous that the camera appeared to be knocked over. The researchers measured how long it took the subject to seek adult help after the aggressive behavior began, and whether the subject intervened before the youngsters abused each other physically. Drabman and Thomas found that relative to the no-film control group, the boys and girls who saw the aggressive cowboy film took longer to seek adult help and were much more likely to tolerate all but the violent physical aggression and destruction before seeking help. Whereas 58% of the no-film children who went for help did so after the children started arguing and destroying each other's property but before the extreme forms of aggression appeared, only 17% of the children in the film group responded to these lower levels of aggression. These results were replicated in a second study by Drabman and Thomas (1976) in which an exciting control excerpt from a baseball game was used instead of a no-film condition. These findings obtained with a more appropriate control group lend further support to the claim that TV violence makes young viewers more apathetic to real-life violence.

Thomas and Drabman (1977) asked in a later study: would TV violence affect children's expectations of other children's aggression? This question resembles that asked by Gerbner and his colleagues in their "mean world" studies; however, Thomas and Drabman addressed this issue using an experimental rather than a correlational strategy. They showed 88 third and fifth grade children either a 15-minute aggressive excerpt from a TV detective series or a nonviolent one from a nature series. Then the children were given the Response Hierachy measure of Leifer and Roberts (1972) in which the child is presented with a series of conflict situations and paired choices of how to handle them including physical aggression, verbal aggression, leaving the field, or positive coping. In the Thomas and Drabman study, the youngsters were asked (1) how they thought other children their age *would* act in the situation, and (2) how they thought other children their age *should* act. They found that relative to the control group, the children who saw the aggressive excerpt were more likely to predict that other children would react aggressively to conflict, but the TV condition did not influence the children's responses about what others should do.

CURRENT STATUS OF THE TV VIOLENCE ISSUE: AN APPRAISAL

After all these years and dozens of major studies, what can be concluded about TV violence and children? Andison (1977) pooled the findings of all 67 studies conducted between 1956 and 1976 on the relationship between TV violence viewing and aggressive behavior. The final tally was 77% of the studies revealed an association, 20% no results, and about 3% an inverse association (i.e., TV violence decreases aggression). Andison found a relationship between the scientific method used and the type of effects reported. Only 13% of the experiments reported no differences or inverse associations, whereas about 30% of the surveys and field experiments yielded such outcomes. However, a relationship between TV violence viewing and aggressive behavior was found consistently across methods, age of subjects, measures of aggression, and time period and country of investigation.

Predispositions to react to TV violence

The idea that certain factors "predispose" a child to react to TV violence was first raised in the Surgeon General's Report and has remained alive to the present. In a recent book on television, *Children and the Faces of Television* (1980), a whole chapter was devoted to reviewing the TV violence literature for predispositional influences. The chapter by Aimée Dorr and Peter Kovaric (1980) entitled "Some of the People Some of the Time—But Which People? Televised Violence and Its Effects," concluded:

> First, we conclude that television violence seems to be capable of affecting viewers of both sexes and varying ages, social classes, ethnicities, personality characteristics, and levels of usual aggressiveness. Second, we conclude that males and females are equally likely to be influenced by exposure but that within each sex those who are more aggressive are more likely to be influenced. We will also advance the tentative conclusion that "middle-aged" children, those between the ages of about 8 and 12, are somewhat more likely to be affected than are either younger or older youth. Third, we conclude that in actual behavior boys are more likely to be aggressive than are girls, and, by definition, delinquents and others who are measured as more aggressive in their daily behavior are more aggressive than are their obvious comparison groups. Fourth, we conclude that in terms of actual viewing of and preference for televised violence, boys are likely to exceed girls and members of the working class are likely to exceed those of the middle class [pp. 193–194].

What are the specific effects of TV violence?

Arousal. First, it seems likely that high action content is arousing to viewers. Arousal dissipates quickly, but for a period of time between a few minutes and a few days after exposure a child may act more aggressively, more vigorously, or more impulsively because he or she has been aroused by TV violence. In rare instances, such arousal may collide with circumstances to produce a tragic result. Presumably this is the price we pay for being aroused, which seems to be a major element in successful entertainment (Tannenbaum, 1980).

Copying. Second, TV violence may be imitated, either impulsively or when environmental circumstances invite or condone acts that have been modeled in TV shows. Many children and adolescents thus gain the *potential* for acting in more aggressive and antisocial ways as a result of exposure to TV violence. Whether these examples will be acted out typically depends on other factors.

Value-shaping. Third, TV violence conveys attitudes and values about violence, aggression, and antisocial behavior. It must be remembered that although older children and adolescents discount particular content as being "just a story," they describe the roles, role relationships, and interactions of characters as highly realistic. Admired characters are presumed to behave in appropriate or desirable ways, and their approval of aggression or antisocial behavior elevates it in the eyes of young viewers.

To be sure, there are many unanswered questions. The precise mechanisms through which TV violence arouses or teaches are still being studied. But it is unlikely that we will learn much more about the social effects of TV violence in the foreseeable future than we know now. TV violence has a large effect on a small percentage of youngsters and a small effect on a large percentage of youngsters. Its influence always works in conjunction with other factors. The reactions of any individual child are almost never predictable in advance. It is against this backdrop of facts that the TV violence issue collided legally with the U.S. First Amendment on three separate occasions.

LEGAL BATTLES OVER TV VIOLENCE: THE FIRST AMENDMENT THRICE PREVAILS

On three separate occasions in the 1970s various efforts to curb TV violence by one means or another collided legally with the protections guaranteed by the First Amendment to the Constitution of the United States.

Family viewing time

The early evening (7 to 9 P.M.) has long been considered the time when the family is most likely to be watching television as a unit. It is the early segment of prime time. As we noted in Chapter 1, it is truly prime time for children, accounting for far more of their television viewing than does watching actual children's shows. An effort to establish a family viewing time, spearheaded by the FCC in response to a variety of pressures, was the first collision between the First Amendment and the TV violence issue.

It all began in 1970 with the Prime Time Access Rule, which stated that stations could only show three hours of network fare per night (8 to 11 P.M.), which meant in practice that the period between 7:30 and 8:00 P.M. was left free for local station use.* As we mentioned in Chapter 2, the intent of this ruling was to encourage the station to serve local community and family needs in this half-hour with public service programming, to break the network monopoly in prime time, to provide independent producers with a new market outside of the three networks, and to encourage the production and airing of new program formats (Brown, 1977). All of this might have decreased violence on television and improved its overall quality. However, inasmuch as the rule itself did not dictate what content could be aired, local stations responded to the ruling as an opportunity to air game shows or syndicated films which are inexpensive and thus highly profitable.

A more daring step was then taken. In 1974, Congress asked that the FCC report on the "specific positive actions taken or planned by the Commission to protect children from excessive programming of violence and obscenity" (Broadcasting, 1974). This message had clear implications for future fiscal appropriations to the FCC. The FCC chairman at the time, Richard E. Wiley, called several meetings with the three network presidents. Arthur E. Taylor, then president of CBS Television, proposed a plan in which the networks would keep the evening hours from 7:00 to 9:00 free from themes that would be objectionable for child viewers (i.e., sex and violence). Actually, this amounted to only one hour; the first half-hour is programmed with news, and the 7:30 to 8:00 slot had already been taken from the networks with the Prime Time Access Rule.

This period was called the "family viewing" time, and by 1975 the National Association of Broadcasters included it in its code. This was the closest that the FCC ever came to try to control TV content directly. It used the National Association of Broadcasters as an intermediary mechanism, but the pressure the FCC exerted was undeniable. A poll conducted by the Opinion Research Corporation for *TV Guide* in October 1975 showed that

---

*The period between 7:00–7:30 P.M. had been the long-time domain of the news.

the public supported the family hour guidelines; 82% of adult Americans were in favor of them (Hickey, 1975).

But the family viewing hour was seen as a threat to First Amendment rights, and it was challenged in court by Hollywood's TV writers and producers. On November 4, 1976, Judge Warren G. Ferguson ruled against the FCC, the NAB and the three networks' efforts to uphold the family viewing time because (1) the government pressure violated the First Amendment, (2) the FCC proceeded in an unofficial manner, and (3) the networks were a party to restricting individual broadcasters in their First Amendment rights. The only way that the family code could be adopted was by individual broadcasters voluntarily abiding by it.

The Zamora trial

During a two-week period in October 1977, TV violence was a codefendant in a murder trial. On June 4, 1977, Ronald Zamora, 15, killed his next door neighbor Elinor Haggart, 82, a Miami Beach widow, in the process of burglarizing her home with a friend. Finding the boys in the midst of their burglary, she warned them that she was going to call the police, whereupon Zamora shot her to death. Four days later, Zamora confessed to the murder and four months later went to trial for charges of first-degree murder, burglary, robbery, and possession of a firearm while committing a felony.

Zamora's Defense Attorney, Ellis Rubin, pleaded that his client was temporarily insane at the time of the murder because he was "suffering from and acted under the influence of prolonged, intense, involuntary, subliminal television intoxication." Zamora's parents described their son as a "TV addict" who watched six hours daily and favored cops-and-robbers programs such as *Kojak*, *Baretta*, and *Starsky and Hutch*. Kojak was his idol, and Zamora's parents testified that the boy went as far as to ask his father to shave his head so he would look more like his hero. A psychiatrist, Dr. Michael Gilbert, examined the boy and testified that Zamora had compared the situation to an episode of Kojak: "He recalled some program where women who had been shot got up and walked away, and he said he felt that might happen" (Buchanan, 1977a). Dr. Gilbert further asserted that Zamora's shooting Mrs. Haggart when she threatened to call the police was a "conditional response" similar to that of a dog who automatically responds to a bell to get his meals. In Gilbert's words, "The woman's statement 'I'm going to call the police' was a symbol of everything Zamora had seen on television, and he reacted to rub out the squealer" (Buchanan, 1977a). This was claimed to be the result of Zamora's "addiction" to television and his long years of watching crime shows and horror movies.

Rubin labeled television an "accessory to the crime" throughout the trial and stated: "It is inevitable that TV will be a defendant. I intend to put television on trial" (*Time*, 1977b, p. 87). In his closing remarks, Rubin said: "If you and I can be influenced by short commercials to buy products, certainly an hour 'commercial' on murder could influence this boy when he's seen them over and over" (Buchanan, 1977b). The title of a *Time* (1977b) article on the trial reflects the nature of the trial: "Did TV make Him Do It? A Young Killer — and Television — Go on Trial for Murder."

Testimony by other psychiatrists and psychologists challenged Gilbert's testimony and Rubin's defense claims. Several mental health professionals rejected Gilbert's "conditioned response" theory and the temporary insanity plea. Further, the conditioned response theory was brought into question by the testimony of a psychiatrist, Dr. Albert Jaslow, who said that Zamora's own report of the incident indicated that one and one-half hours elapsed between Mrs. Haggart's threat to call the police and the murder; such a delay is not feasible if his shooting were a conditioned or automatic response. Dr. Jaslow also reported that he asked Zamora, "Did television teach you to kill anybody?" and that the boy answered "No." Further, Jaslow said Zamora told him that the one thing he had learned on television was, "The bad guys didn't get away with it" (Buchanan, 1977b). Another psychiatrist, Dr. Charles Mutter also testified that Zamora did not blame television for his actions but provided evidence that Zamora imitated TV characters. Zamora was reported by Mutter to have said, "Sometimes I'd be a cop and sometimes a bad guy" and that he "wished the shooting had been like a TV show where the dead get up when the show is over" (Buchanan, 1977b).

In terms of knowing right from wrong and the nature and consequences of his act (the criteria for sanity in Florida law), the weight of the mental health professionals' testimony sided with Zamora being sane. However, this is not to say that the consensus was that Zamora was a typical 15-year-old boy. Dr. Helen Ackerman, a psychologist who examined Zamora on three occasions, testified that the defendant was "emotionally disturbed, erratic and unpredictable," referring to alleged suicide attempts including "riding his bicycle into heavy traffic and standing under knives he had thrown into the air" (Buchanan, 1977a).

After nearly two weeks of testimony, the jury deliberated for slightly less than two hours and found Ronald Zamora guilty of murder, burglary, armed robbery, and possession of a firearm. The verdict resulted in Zamora facing an automatic life sentence with chance for parole after 25 years. Apparently the state had not sought the death penalty because of Zamora's age.

A bit of irony is that the nine-day trial of Zamora (and television) was broadcast on a public television station. Given television's role in the case, Judge Paul Baker banned all TV viewing by the jury members on the first day of the trial. As one would expect, the jurors complained, and the judge compromised by allowing them to watch anything but news shows and taped excerpts of the trial. The jurors then requested being allowed to watch tapes of the trial without the sound so they could see what they looked like on TV. Their request was denied (*Sarasota Journal*, 1977).

Niemi vs. NBC

In 1974 a nine-year-old girl, Olivia Niemi, was attacked by three older girls and a boy on a beach in San Francisco in the process of which she was artificially raped with a bottle. Four days before the incident a movie, *Born Innocent*, portraying a girl being similarly raped with a plumber's helper, was aired by an NBC San Francisco TV station, KRON-TV. Olivia's mother and her lawyer, Marvin Lewis, claimed that Olivia's assault was provoked by the movie and demanded $11 million in damages from NBC and the affiliate station due to the broadcasters' alleged negligence in showing the movie, especially during prime time when children and adolescents comprise a fair share of the audience. The following description of the movie scene in question comes from the judge of the California appeals court that considered the lawsuit: An adolescent girl, played by Linda Blair (then 15 years old), is seen taking a shower in the shower area of a girls' reform school (Daltry, 1978):

> Suddenly the water stops and a look of fear comes across her face. Four adolescent girls are standing across from her. One of the girls is carrying a plumber's helper, waving it suggestively at her side. The four girls attack and wrestle her to the floor. She is shown naked from the waist up, struggling as they force her legs apart. Then the television film shows the girl with the plumber's helper making intense thrusting motions with the handle of the plunger until one of the four says, "That's enough." The young girl is left sobbing and naked on the floor [p. 69].

The legal term for the alleged negligence is "vicarious liability"; it is based on the presumed incitement of a criminal act if it is vividly depicted in a book, TV show, or other medium, the source of that depiction being responsible for damages to the victim. The alleged involvement of the TV broadcast in this violent act was immediately dramatized by the press with headlines such as: "Television on Trial: The Tube Made Me Do It" (Daltry, 1978, p. 69), "TV on Trial" (Levering, 1978, p. 5), and "Was TV Born Guilty?" (Mandel, 1978, p. 35). It is important to realize that unlike the Zamora case, TV in general was not on trial; rather, the broadcasters of a specific program were charged with negligence for presenting an explicit depiction of a violent/sexual act.

The First Amendment was the major argument of the defense lawyers of NBC. They argued that a ruling in favor of Niemi would stifle journalists, broadcasters, and publishers. The only legal basis for holding someone responsible for what he/she wrote (or showed on TV) is if the content is obscene or libelous, neither of which pertains to the case. There are other exceptions to protection by the First Amendment as we pointed out in Chapter 2. For example, speech that is "directed to inciting or producing imminent lawless action and is likely to incite or produce such action" is not protected. Intent to incite is a critical component of this First Amendment exception. The head NBC defense attorney, Floyd Abrams, argued that NBC did not advocate or intend to incite rape with its broadcast. Siding with the NBC defense, several organizations filed friend-of-the-court briefs against the suit arguing about the dangers of infringing on First Amendment rights. NBC's allies included the other two networks, the Writers Guild of America, the Directors Guild of America, the National Association of Radio and FM Stations, the Motion Picture Association of America, the National Association of Broadcasters, and the American Library Association. CBS argued that if Niemi won, "journalists and creative artists would be forced to avoid factual reporting on, or fictional portrayal of, violent acts for fear of incurring enormous liability if some jury could be convinced that some anti-social act somewhere was 'inspired' by the drama or the report in question" (cited in Levering, 1978, p. 5).

Concerning the First Amendment issue, Marvin Lewis argued, "Our forefathers would roll over in their graves if they saw the use that the First Amendment is being put to. They did not design the First Amendment to allow the graphic portrayal of the gang rape of a child before a nationwide children's audience" (Daltry, 1978, p. 69). Lewis also argued that NBC's promotion of the movie showed that they were trying to attract a young audience. They scheduled the movie immediately after *The Wonderful World of Walt Disney*, and they ran an ad in *TV Guide* promoting *Born Innocent* on the same page as *Born Free*, an innocuous wildlife movie to be aired the night before. Lewis contended that the similarity of names may have led people to believe that *Born Innocent* was a sequel to *Born Free*. Further, before its broadcast there were clear signs that the movie (or at least the rape scene) was objectionable. Lewis had evidence that after pre-screening the movie, fifteen national advertisers refused to sponsor the movie, and NBC's broadcast standards department had misgivings about it. The California Medical Association was the only group to file a friend-of-the-court brief on Niemi's behalf which argued that "the First Amendment cannot be a shield from civic responsibility for forseeable consequences of harmful acts" (cited in Levering, 1978, p. 6).

On another level, the defense also claimed that the assailants denied ever watching *Born Innocent*. Marvin Lewis contested that with the statement of a National Park Service Officer who said that the attackers told him they had seen the movie and specifically referred to the rape scene. The defense also claimed that the girl who led the attack was an emotionally disturbed youngster with a history of sexually deviant activities. Marvin Lewis argued that broadcasters should not air explicit, violent, or sexual scenes such as that in *Born Innocent* precisely because there are many disturbed people in the audience who might be inspired to imitate what they viewed.

NBC offered to settle out of court shortly after the suit was filed. When Olivia's mother refused, NBC retaliated by charging the mother with being an "unfit guardian" for subjecting her daughter to the trauma of such a legal proceeding. The judge found their charges to be unacceptable. What followed was a series of actions in which the case was thrown out of court (on First Amendment grounds), then appealed and put back in court, and then challenged to be thrown out of court, all of which lasted about three years and involved two rulings by California's highest court and one by the United States Supereme Court.

During the summer of 1978 the case went to court in San Francisco, and on August 8, before witnesses were even heard, the negligence suit was thrown out of court because Judge Robert Dossee ruled that the plaintiff had to prove that the network intended its viewers to imitate the violent sexual attack depicted. With the case being treated by the judge as a strict First Amendment case, Marvin Lewis could not win; it was not feasible to prove that NBC intended its viewers to copy the rape scene.

Notes of interest: One week after, the U.S. Supreme Court ruled that Niemi was entitled to a court hearing; Ronald Zamora, who was serving his life sentence, filed a $25 million lawsuit against all three commercial networks claiming they were responsible for his murdering his neighbor in 1975. One of Olivia's attackers was sent to a federal reformatory for three years, and the other three were put on juvenile probation. NBC aired *Born Innocent* a second time, but at 11:30 P.M. and with most of the offensive rape scene edited out.

Chapter 6
Television Advertising and Children

OVERVIEW

Action for Children's Television (ACT) has been the major force in tempering advertising directed at young children in the United States. In addition to scoring a number of direct victories (such as reducing the amount of time devoted to advertising on Saturday morning), ACT was instrumental in prodding the National Science Foundation to fund and then review research on the effects of TV advertising on children.

The research, reviewed in this chapter, shows that young children are unable to understand the "selling intent" of TV commercials, and that misleading impressions are often created by these commercials despite the disclaimers (e.g., a quick announcement stating "Partial assembly required"). It is equally clear that commercials "work" for the advertiser (studies show that children ask their parents to buy many advertised products), and that occasional conflict between parents and children can be linked to the demand for something advertised on TV.

Until recently the FTC was empowered to prohibit commercials that were "unfair, misleading or deceptive." Arguing on the grounds that TV advertising is demonstrably unfair to children who are too immature to understand what the advertisers are up to, the FTC proceeded in 1978 to hold hearings on children's TV advertising with an eye toward possible rule making. The industry *counterattacked* successfully, for the most part through direct pressure on members of Congress. Congress, which approves the FTC's budget annually, forced the Commission to abdicate its previous authority to prohibit "unfair" advertising and thus effectively quashed the FTC hearings. Though capitulation to industry pressure weighed heavily in the decision to let advertisers have free reign, First Amendment considerations were also cited frequently.

Some researchers have begun to develop curricula for teaching children about the TV business, partly as an effort to balance the advantages that advertisers seem to enjoy in their communications to children.

There is no doubt that the TV habits of children make the medium an attractive place to advertise. Graphics, camera work, and old-fashioned cleverness make TV commercials a potent way of advertising to the credulous young child. In fact, a children's TV commercial is carefully written, designed, and usually musically scored with the help of private research agencies so as to maximize its impact on the young viewer.

The economic outcomes of TV advertising are truly impressive. Effective use of commercials has rapidly transformed some companies into major concerns. For example, in 1955 Mattel launched a TV-based advertising program that propelled it from a $500,000 company to a truly big business of $12 million almost over night (Jennings, 1970). Advertising and broadcast industry spokesmen typically argue that the economic advantages of using TV advertising get passed onto the consumer in the form of lower prices for advertised products (see Table 6.1).

Everyone agrees some restrictions are necessary. Certain abuses tarnish the image and diminish the effectiveness of all advertising. Either government-imposed or self-imposed regulations and restrictions on advertising for children are necessary for any competitive free enterprise system to function effectively.

This chapter is devoted to the topic of TV advertising and children in all its aspects, including the prevailing guidelines for industry self-regulation, a review of the research evidence pertinent to these guidelines, and a discussion of a major effort by the FTC to increase its control over children's TV advertising, which was ultimately set aside, partly on First Amendment grounds.

BACKGROUND

As we pointed out in the first two chapters, the earliest complaints about TV ads came from ACT in the late 1960s. By the early 1970s, ACT brought the issue of the problems of advertising to children to the attention of both the FCC and FTC.

Another pressure group looking to reform children's advertising has been the Council on Children, Media, and Merchandising (CCMM), headed by Robert Choate, former White House staff member of the Conference on Food, Nutrition, and Health. Choate's concerns focused primarily on the poor eating habits encouraged by children's ads, and his efforts included petitioning the FCC and FTC and providing testimony at congressional hearings.

Supported by the less visible activities of people like Choate, ACT's efforts resulted in a number of highly significant victories:

1. Voluntary withdrawal of commercials for children's vitamins.
2. The NAB prohibition of host selling on children's programs.
3. A reduction in the maximum advertising time on weekend children's programming.

An even more important contribution of groups such as ACT and CCMM was to increase the salience of the issues involved in advertising to children. Up through the 1960s, research interest in children's TV advertising had

Table 6.1. Advertisers' Arguments Supporting TV Advertising

There has been little or no attention paid by critics to the benefits that proceed from our industry's advertising and merchandising system, and to the increased costs to the consumer that would inevitably occur, we feel, if toy advertising were limited or unduly restrained or proscribed.

Toys are advertised on television to the consumer — to the child and his parents. This creates awareness on the part of child and parent and provides them with choices.

The mass merchants — chain, discount, variety, and department stores — who sell the overwhelming bulk of the toys in this country take advantage of the advertising-created awareness by featuring the TV toys in their newspaper price ads. The more attractive his price, the more likely the merchant is to draw the toy-shopping parent into his store.

The outcome of this system, it has been our experience, is a narrow spread between the manufacturer's price to the store and the ultimate cost of the toy to the consumer. The Marketing Sciences Institute of Harvard University has quantified these relationships in studies of marketing productivity. The evidence is powerful. Before television advertising of toys, in the mid-1950's, the distribution markup was 100 percent; that is, the price paid by the consumer was about double the price paid by the retailer to the manufacturer. Today, that 100-percent markup has shrunk to about 36 percent. To put it another way, the toy that a manufacturer sold to the trade 20 years ago for $3 cost the consumer $5.98. Today, it costs him only $4 or so because of this unique TV/mass merchandising/price-feature system. . . .

---

been almost nil. Aside from advertising agencies' in-house research, the research that Ward and his colleagues conducted for the Surgeon General's Report (described in Chapter 4) was the only systematic examination of children's reactions to TV advertising. In a review of research on children and televised advertising, Sheikh, Prasad and Rao (1974) concluded that the lack of interest in the area was due to the belief by academics that the area was not "respectable" enough, and that research would not be used effectively by policymakers.

Respectability came to the area when the National Science Foundation commissioned a distinguished panel to review the research on the effects of television advertising on children and to recommend areas for future research. The panel members included:

- *Richard P. Adler*, Graduate School of Education,
     Harvard University
- *Bernard Z. Friedlander*, Department of Psychology,
     University of Hartford

(**Table 6.1** Continued)

Is television advertising harmful to children? According to expert scientific opinion, toy commercials have few effects, if any, either helpful or harmful, on the mental health or emotional development of the viewing child. Further, the right kind of advertising can add some positive values to viewing. Children, like adults, enjoy good TV commercials. To be sure, there are commercials they dislike, and others they hate, but many they find interesting, and highly engaging. They develop favorites, and consider many of them delightful, irrespective of whether or not they wish to buy the product featured. Also, they often learn from them, which is why *Sesame Street* borrows so heavily from commercial TV in devising its learning messages, which attempt to teach children the alphabet, or to count. . . .

What would happen to children's television programs if commercial sponsorship were to cease or decline? Programs of particular interest to children on commercial television would be dramatically reduced, if not eliminated.

The reason for this is that television—like radio, magazines, newspapers, and other communications media—depends on advertising revenue to finance program development, production, facilities and talent. Certainly reduction or elimination of commercial sponsorship would seriously curtail the opportunities for better programming on children's television in the future. [Quote from the testimony of Aaron Locker, representing the Toy Manufacturers of America at hearings before the House of Representatives Subcommittee on Communications of the Committee on Interstate and Foreign Commerce; Locker, 1975, pp. 349–352.]

- *Gerald S. Lesser*, Graduate School of Education,
     Harvard University
- *Laurene Meringoff*, Graduate School of Education,
     Harvard University
- *Thomas S. Robertson*, The Wharton School,
     University of Pennsylvania
- *John R. Rossiter*, The Wharton School,
     University of Pennsylvania
- *Scott Ward*, Graduate School of Business,
     Harvard University

The review was organized around ten policy issues, which maximized its usefulness to policymakers (National Science Foundation, 1977):

1. Children's ability to distinguish television commercials from program material.
2. The influence of format and audio-visual techniques on children's perceptions of commercial messages.
3. Source effects and self-concept appeals in children's advertising.

4. The effects of advertising containing premium offers.
5. The effects of violence or unsafe acts in television commercials.
6. The impact on children of proprietary medicine advertising.
7. The effects on children of television food advertising.
8. The effects of volume and repetition of television commercials.
9. The impact of television advertising on consumer socialization.
10. Television advertising and parent-child relations [p. ii].

Twenty-one relevant studies were reviewed (the majority of which were conducted after 1974), and the general conclusions of the scientific panel were:

It is clear from the available evidence that television advertising *does* influence children. Research has demonstrated that children attend to and learn from commercials, and that advertising is at least moderately successful in creating positive attitudes toward and the desire for products advertised. The variable that emerges most clearly across numerous studies as a strong determinant of children's perception of television advertising is the child's age. Existing research clearly establishes that children become more skilled in evaluating television advertising as they grow older, and that to treat all children from 2 to 12 as a homogeneous group masks important, perhaps crucial differences. These findings suggest that both researchers and policymakers give greater attention to the problems of younger viewers, since they appear to be the most vulnerable. . . . Research can guide policy by providing concrete information on the actual impact of television advertising on children. In the long run, such research can provide essential factual guideposts for directing policy toward adequate safeguards against economic exploitation of these young viewers [p. i–ii].

Undoubtedly the most significant event in the history of children's advertising occurred quite recently. In 1978 the FTC published a Staff Report (Federal Trade Commission, 1978) that recommended the banning of all commercials directed to children too young to understand their selling intent. Empirical research played an extremely important role in this drama. We will unravel the interesting story of the events leading up to the FTC actions, the hearings, and the outcome later in this chapter. First, though, it is important to consider the existing industry guidelines, the policy issues identified by the 1977 NSF report, and the relevant research evidence in the light of existing guidelines.

Industry guidelines

The first industry action with regard to children's TV advertising was in 1961 when the NAB adopted its Toy Advertising Guidelines and subsequently added guidelines to cover the advertising of all products intended for children. The advertising guidelines are presented following the program standards in the NAB Television Code. The advertising section, which is periodically revised, contains guidelines concerning the frequency and spacing of commercials, restricted product categories (e.g., hard liquor, gambling aids), unacceptable advertising techniques, presentation of product claims and premium offers, and special considerations for children-oriented commercials. The NAB Code Authority reviews all nationally advertised children's toy advertisements and the premium segments of nontoy ads to help assure compliance with Code standards. These commercials are reviewed in preliminary stages before the final product is produced and in its final state. However, one recalls from Chapter 2 that adherence to the NAB Code is purely voluntary.

Another self-regulatory mechanism has emerged from the advertising sector. In 1974, a Children's Advertising Review Unit was established within the Council of Better Business Bureaus' National Advertising Division (NAD). With input from an advisory committee composed of several academic consultants (including Eli Rubinstein, Jerome Singer, and Scott Ward mentioned earlier in this book), the Children's Advertising Review Unit issued a set of Children's Advertising Guidelines (National Advertising Division, 1975) which are similar but not identical to the NAB guidelines. Like the NAB standards, those of the NAD rest on voluntary compliance.

What is a commercial?

A commercial is intended and specifically designed to produce an effect. They are intended to sell particular products or services; their effectiveness is ultimately measured in sales. Adults are presumed to recognize commercials and to grasp the selling intent. We discount part of what is said when we know someone is just making a pitch or trying to sell us something. If children do not understand that commercials differ from entertainment programming in this way, then any TV advertising directed at them may be unfair. With this argument in mind, researchers have sought to establish (1) whether children perceive *any* difference between entertainment programming and commercials, and (2) whether children perceive and understand the selling intent of commercials.

What restrictions should be placed on children's TV commercials?

In addition to research that attempts to determine whether children understand commercials, investigators have sought to interlock their studies with the efforts of the industry to provide appropriate guidelines to advertisers. Thus in the late 1970s there emerged a body of research relating to a variety of specific propositions about what constituted appropriate television advertising to children.

RESEARCH EVIDENCE

Are commercials seen as different from regular programming?

Ward and his colleagues reasoned that if the attention of children didn't change when TV content shifted from programs to commercials, that would be evidence that children couldn't discriminate between the two. Their early studies (Ward, Levinson, & Wackman, 1972; Ward & Wackman, 1973) showed just that: the attention of children under seven years of age did not change when commercials came on the screen, although the attention of older children did. In fact, partly due to these findings, the FCC in 1974 required that all licensees "insure that a 'clear separation' be maintained between program content and commercial messages" (Federal Communications Commission, 1974, p. 215). In response to the FCC 1974 ruling, the three commercial networks inserted program/commercial separators into children's weekend programming. The networks varied in their separating technique: ABC and CBS used audio and video presentations while NBC used video only; ABC and NBC inserted them before the commercial while CBS inserted them before and after the commercial.

To test the effectiveness of these separators, Palmer and McDowell (1979) did an experiment in which sixty kindergarten and first graders were shown two program segments (one animated and one live format) containing commercials and using a separator from one of the three networks or no special separator. At various predetermined points during the viewing, the video-cassette was stopped and the children were asked whether the part they just saw was "part of the show" or a "commercial." Correct identification of the commercials averaged only 53% of the time they were shown. The children who were not exposed to a separator were no worse and at times were better at identifying commercials than were those shown a network separator. Clearly the network separators were not effective in aiding discrimination. The cue that helped children most to discriminate commercials from programs was the length—i.e., commercials are "short." Further, when questioned about what the commercial was telling them to do, only half of the youngsters who recognized the commercials showed any awareness of their selling intent. Therefore, children recognized a commercial *and* realized its purpose only about a quarter of the time. The researchers concluded, "our research indicates that the beginning of the commercial itself seems to provide more contrast than the separators; children have a greater likelihood of recognizing a commercial if it is *not* 'introduced'" (p. 200).

More recent studies bring into question children's apparent lack of discriminating ability. Children under eight or nine years old have been found to shift attention away from the TV at the onset of a commercial (Winick & Winick, 1979), while children as young as three or four have been found to increase their attention at this point (Zuckerman, Ziegler, & Stevenson, 1978).

However, if children know and recognize some distinctions between commercials and programs, they may still not understand the selling intent.

Selling intent

Research clearly supports the claim that young children do not comprehend the selling intent of commercials. Why this issue is considered important is best explained in the 1974 FCC report on Children's Television (Federal Communications Commission, 1974). In justifying the Federal Communications Act requirement that all TV and radio advertisements clearly indicate that they are paid for and by whom, the Commission observes:

> The rationale behind this provision is, in part, that an advertiser would have an unfair advantage over listeners if they could not differentiate between the program and the commercial message and were, therefore, unable to take its paid status into consideration in assessing the message [p. 215].

In several interview studies (Bever, Smith, Bengen, & Johnson, 1975; Robertson & Rossiter, 1974; Sheikh, Prasad, & Rao, 1974; Ward, Wackman, & Wartella, 1977) children were asked why commercials are shown on TV or what commercials try to do. All found that youngsters under eight years of age cannot explain the selling intent of commercials. Children between six to nine years of age seem to understand more than four to five year olds, but there are variations between studies in exactly how much they understand.

One criticism of these studies is that young children have difficulty explaining anything, and that the results could be due to the youngsters' general lack of verbal ability. Dorr (1978) tested this possibility by using a multiple choice test rather than the open-ended questioning used previously. She still found that the majority of eight to nine year olds did not understand the selling intent of commercials.

As one might expect from the increasing comprehension of selling intent with age, children's trust in commercials declines with age. Blatt, Spencer, and Ward's (1972) findings have been corroborated in other studies (Robertson & Rossiter, 1974; Ward et al., 1977). When asked whether commercials tell the truth, most five to seven year olds reply that they do, while only a minority of youngsters over eight years old give this response.

The influence of format and audio-visual techniques on children's perceptions of commercial messages

Both the NAB and NAD have recognized and acknowledged the danger of children being deceived by audio-visual techniques that exaggerate product characteristics or fail to communicate important product information contained in disclaimers (e.g., "batteries not included," "accessories not included," "assembly required").

For example, the NAB code states (National Association of Broadcasters, 1976):

> Advertising shall present the toy on its actual merit as a play thing. It shall neither exaggerate nor distort play value.

> Audio and visual production techniques shall not misrepresent the appearance and performance of toys. Any view of a toy or any demonstration of its performance shall be limited to that which a child is reasonably capable of reproducing. . . . There shall not be any implication that optional extras, additional units or items that are not available with the toy, accompany the toy's original purchase [pp. 194–195].

The Children's Review Unit of the National Advertising Division of the Council of Better Business Bureaus established similar guidelines (National Advertising Division, 1975):

> Copy, sound and visual presentations—as well as the advertisement in its totality—do not mislead on performance characteristics such as speed, method of operation, size, color, durability, nutrition, noise, etc.; on perceived benefits such as the acquisition of strength, popularity, growth, proficiency, intelligence, and the like; or on the expectation of price range or cost of the product.

> The advertisement clearly establishes what is included in the original purchase of the advertised product, employing where necessary positive disclosure on what items are to be purchased separately in a way that will be understood by the child audience to which the advertisement is primarily addressed. All advertising for products sold unassembled should indicate that assembly is required. If any other product is essential in order to use the advertised product—such as batteries—this should be disclosed [p. 203].

In a review of content studies of children's advertising, Barcus (1980) found that "hard" product information (price, materials used or construction, performance qualities, intended age level) was rarely provided. What was emphasized were themes of "appearance," "action," and the "fun" nature of the product. He also found that qualifiers about batteries, accessories, and assembly appeared in about two-thirds of all toy commercials, and they were usually presented just auditorily. Atkin and Heald (1977) performed a similar analysis of child-oriented commercials, summarized in Table 6.2.

Table 6.2. Percentage of Children's Toy Commercials Containing Information Needed to Evaluate the Toy.

	Toy ads (N = 270) %
Mention of price	0
Mention of "hard" qualities*	11
Mention of appropriate age	1
Mention of skill needed	32
Suggestion of difficulty to duplicate toy demonstration	27

*Information about materials or durability.
Source: Adapted from Atkin & Heald, 1977.

Prior to the NAB and NAD 1975–1976 guidelines, disclaimers were often presented only visually. A study by Atkin (1975a) showed that audio-visual disclaimers were far more effective. He showed a Mattel "Vertibird" commercial to 500 preschool and grade school children. For half the children, the video disclaimer "batteries not included" was presented only visually (in a superimposed video display), and the rest were exposed to an audio-visual presentation. The children in the audio-visual group were more than twice as likely to report that batteries weren't included than the video-only group. After vigorous complaints by consumer advocacy groups that young children cannot read the disclaimers, the codes required that both audio and visual messages be presented. Apparently there is not complete compliance with the guidelines because many advertisers use only audio messages.

Another issue concerning disclaimers is the specific language used — whether it is understandable to young viewers. Liebert, Sprafkin, Liebert, and Rubinstein (1977) did a study in which 240 six and eight year olds saw two toy commercials containing either no disclaimer, a standard audio disclaimer ("some assembly required"), or a modified audio disclaimer ("you have to put it together"). In terms of understanding the disclaimer message, children in the standard disclaimer group were no better off than those in the no disclaimer group, while the modified disclaimer resulted in significantly better comprehension for both age groups. These findings emphasize the importance of using language appropriate to the age of the intended audience.

Extravagant performance demonstrations are clearly discouraged by both the NAB and NAD guidelines. A study by Atkin (1975a) demonstrates that even from the manufacturer/advertiser's side, such practices are undesirable. Atkin showed a large sample of preschool and grade school children a

commercial for a block game in which two children were shown constructing either (1) a tall elaborate structure, with the voice-over encouraging
players to build "a sky-high tower so you can be the champion," or (2) a
modest structure, with the voice-over emphasizing "it's fun . . . anyone can
play." Then the viewers were observed playing with blocks. The children in
the extravagant presentation group were more likely than those in the modest presentation group to display hostile behavior (verbal and physical aggression). Further, the extravagant version produced only half the level of
brand name recall as the modest version, and the youngsters were slightly
less likely to state that the blocks would be fun to play with. So the extravagant claims resulted in worse recall, less desire to play with the toy, and
more aggression.

Source effects and self-concept appeals

The National Science Foundation report identified four issues related to the
kinds of characters that can be used in children's commercials: (1) host selling; that is, the use of program personalities in commercials (2) the use of
celebrities or authority figures to endorse a product or just to be associated
with the product, (3) the presentation of social stereotypes, and (4) the use
of appeals to enhance personal characteristics or social status.

These practices are addressed in the industry's self-regulatory codes:

1. Both the NAB and NAD codes prohibit program personalities to de-
liver commercial messages within the star's program or in commercials ad-
jacent to that program.

2. The NAD code prohibits commercials to "falsely imply that purchase
and use of a product or service will confer upon the user the prestige, skills,
or other special qualities of characters appearing in the commercial or ad"
(National Advertising Division, 1975, p. 203). The NAB code does not prohibit the effect per se but sets limitations on the type of endorser and endorsement.

3. While the NAB code does not mention social stereotyping, the NAD
code states, "Social stereotyping which is demeaning or derogatory to any
group should be avoided" (National Advertising Division, 1975, p. 203).

4. Both the NAB and NAD codes allow the use of claims that the product
enhances personal attributes as long as they are accurate and not misleading. However, both codes prohibit the use of claims that a product enhances
social status or its lack reduces social status.

To what degree are these guidelines followed? While host selling was a
popular advertising technique up to the early 1970s, their prohibition in the
NAB and NAD codes resulted in a substantial decrease in their use. Examining Saturday morning network advertisements, Atkin and Heald (1977)
found that only 3% of toy ads and 8% of food ads contained testimonials

or celebrity endorsements. With regard to the prohibition of social status claims, 8% of the toy ads and 4% of the food ads implied that the product increased social status.

Social stereotyping in commercials occurs in the form of underrepresentation of females and minority characters. Between 60% and 70% of all characters on child-oriented commercials are male, and 75% to 95% are white (Atkin & Heald, 1977; Barcus, 1975a, b; 1978a; Schuetz & Sprafkin, 1978). In terms of race portrayal, Schuetz and Sprafkin (1978) found that while blacks occupied 40% of all human parts in commercials for records, they constituted less than 6% of all human roles in commercials for box and board games.

The NAB and NAD prohibitions of host selling, direct endorsements by authority figures or celebrities, and claims of social status enhancement were not instituted on the basis of research findings indicating the harm or deceptiveness of such practices. The NSF review presented studies with mixed results or serious limitations for all of these areas.

Some support for an indirect endorsement effect came from a study by Iskoe (1976) who found that first, third, and fifth grade children's product preferences were significantly affected by the mere juxtaposition of a product with an "endorser." Some endorsers were more effective than others; for example, Mohammad Ali had a greater effect on product preference than Lucille Ball. Recall that while direct endorsements are prohibited, the NAB code allows celebrities or authority figures to appear in children's commercials and thus to be associated with advertised products.

Research on the adverse effects of social stereotyping has concentrated on programs rather than commercials. The next chapter is devoted entirely to the complex issue of race and sex stereotypes on television.

Effects of advertising containing premium offers

Critics of premium offers (which have been used mostly in cereal commercials) argue that they distract children from considering relevant product attributes. The FTC questioned the use of premiums in a proposed trade regulation in 1974, stating that such offers most likely increase the chance of confusion and poor purchase decisions by children. The use of premium offers declined after 1975. Among cereal ads, 47% contained premium offers in 1975, but this figure had dropped to 25% by 1977 (Barcus, 1980).

Both the NAB and NAD guidelines allow premiums to be offered, but provide some restrictions on their presentation. For example, the NAD guidelines state (National Advertising Division, 1975):

Care should be taken that the child's attention is focused primarily on the product rather than the premium. Therefore, major emphasis should be given to the

product and its benefits. Emphasis on the premiums should be clearly secondary
[p. 205].

That premium offers influence children's product requests was shown in
an interview study by Atkin (1975e) in which 70% of the mothers of three to
eleven year olds reported that their children "sometimes" requested specific
cereals seen advertised on TV, and 47% of these said that the premium was
the reason for the request. The premium was mentioned more often than
any other reason.

Atkin (1975d) also did mother-child observations in the cereal aisle at the
supermarket. It was found that 9% of all cereal requests explicitly mentioned the premium. Further, mothers were more likely to yield to cereal requests that were not based on expressed desire for the premium; however,
denied requests based on desire for the premium most frequently resulted in
open conflict between parent and child in the supermarket.

Effects of violence or unsafe acts in television commercials

Both the NAB and NAD codes prohibit the portrayal of violent, antisocial,
or unsafe acts in commercials. For example, the NAB code states (National
Association of Broadcasters, 1976):

> Material shall not be used which can reasonably be expected to frighten children
> or provoke anxiety, nor shall material be used which contains a portrayal of or
> appeal to violent, dangerous, or otherwise antisocial behavior.

> Advertisements and products advertised shall be consistent with generally recog-
> nized standards of safety. Advertisements shall not include demonstrations of
> any product in a manner that encourages harmful use or dramatizations of ac-
> tions inconsistent with generally recognized standards of safety [p. 194].

Despite these guidelines, Schuetz and Sprafkin (1979) found 113 aggressive acts in a single Saturday morning sample of 414 commercials. The
amount of aggression in the commercials was about three times that found
in the programs surrounding them. Further, there was the greatest concentration of aggressive acts in cereal commercials. Presumably these elements
were included to capture the attention of the young viewer.

Due to problems with definition, it is more difficult to determine the inci-
dence of unsafe acts in commercials. Certainly the FTC has received complaints about various ads, but the decision about safety remains subjective.
In at least one case, however, the FTC requested that research be conducted
to determine the risk. Poulos (1975) examined a series of cereal commercials
that showed an adult picking wild berries or a part of a pine tree, noting that

the vegetation was good to eat and in some cases adding some to this cereal bowl. The FTC had received several complaints from parents who were concerned about the demonstration of eating wild vegetation. Children between five to eleven years old were asked to judge whether each of a series of familiar and unfamiliar plants was good or bad to eat. They then saw the commercials and were tested again. While the commercials did not change the youngsters' judgments about familiar plants (e.g., carrots, blackberries), they did produce a more accepting attitude toward the unfamiliar (and nonedible) plants, especially those most similar in appearance to those shown in the commercials. The results therefore suggested that after viewing these commercials, children would be more inclined to eat potentially harmful wild vegetation. The cereal company withdrew this series of commercials.

Impact on children of proprietary medicine advertising

Both the NAB and NAD codes prohibit ads for medicines and vitamin supplements on programs designed primarily for children under 12 years old. The problem is that children watch programs not intended for them and are therefore exposed to commercials for medicinal products.

Atkin (1975c) looked at the relationship between fifth, sixth, and seventh grade children's exposure to medicine advertising and their beliefs about medicine. High exposure to medicine commercials was very slightly associated (correlations under $+.15$) with the perception that people are often sick and take medicine, the belief that medicine gives quick relief, and concerns about getting sick. However, exposure was not related to medicine usage. Atkin did find a moderately strong relationship between viewing commercials for deodorants, mouthwash, and acne cream, and the frequency of using these products.

In a three-year study of the effect of TV drug advertising on teenage boys, Milavsky, Pekowsky, and Stipp (1975–76) found a weak but significant relationship between exposure to drug commercials and use of proprietary drugs; the relationship was stronger for boys whose homes had many such drugs available. Further, they found a weak inverse relationship between exposure to drug commercials and the use of illicit drugs; in other words, boys who saw many drug advertisements tended to be infrequent illicit drug users.

Effects on children of television food advertising

Commercials for food products comprise a large portion of children's TV advertising. Barcus (1978b) analyzed 33 hours of children's weekend morning programming and found that on the network affiliated stations, 34% of the commercials were for cereals, 29% for candies and sweets, 3% for snack foods, 1% for other foods, and 15% for eating places, primarily fast food chains. Nonfood product commercials were for toys (12%) and other products (6%). Eighty-two percent of the commercials on network affiliated stations were for manufactured food products, the majority of which were highly sugared. Natural foods such as dairy products, fruits, vegetables, or meats were rarely advertised. Aside from the emphasis on highly sugared manufactured foods, the presentation techniques used in the food ads also give reason for concern. Food ads focused on taste, especially sweetness and texture (e.g., chewy) and provided little, if any, information about nutritional content or attributes, except perhaps "fortified with essential vitamins" or "part of a balanced breakfast."

It is not surprising that children rarely mention nutritional reasons as the basis for a particular cereal request or that they have nutritional misconceptions. As mentioned earlier, Atkin (1975e) found that mothers reported the premium as the most frequent reason given by their child. Also, Atkin and Gibson (1978) found that in a study of four- to seven-year-old children, less than half realized that presweetened cereals produced more cavities than nonsweetened cereal. They also found that the disclosure "part of a balanced breakfast" was ineffective. Two-thirds of the four- to seven-year-old sample could not recall any of the foods shown with the cereal and showed no understanding of the term "balanced breakfast."

Correlational studies in which amount of exposure to television advertising is related to various behaviors and attitudes has shown that frequent viewers more than infrequent viewers reported liking frequently advertised foods (Atkin, Reeves, & Gibson, 1979), requesting advertised cereals and other advertised foods (Atkin, 1975e,c; Atkin et al., 1979; Clancy-Hepburn, Hickey, & Nevill, 1974) asking to go to frequently advertised fast food restaurants (Atkin, 1975c), and consuming advertised cereals, candies, and snacks (Atkin, 1975c; Atkin et al., 1979; Dussere, 1976). Furthermore, heavy viewers are less knowledgeable than light viewers about nutritional aspects of food (Atkin et al., 1979; Sharaga, 1974) and attribute more credibility to animated characters selling the products (Atkin & Gibson, 1978). For example, Atkin et al. (1979) found that youngsters who are heavily exposed to food ads were twice as likely as those less frequently exposed to believe that sugared cereals and candy are highly nutritious.

In a supermarket observation study, Galst and White (1976) showed three to eleven year olds commercials in a laboratory and then observed them in a supermarket setting. The children's level of attention to the laboratory-shown commercials was positively related to the number of purchase requests made. Number of purchase requests was also moderately related to the amount of home viewing of commercial programming.

Effects of television advertising on consumer socialization

The issue here is what role television commercials play in the process by which children learn skills, knowledge, and attitudes relevant to their behavior as consumers, both present and future. Existing research we have already reviewed suggests that commercials impact upon children's attitudes and consumer-related behaviors. The NSF report summarizes research in this area as follows:

> If consumer socialization is defined in terms of development of skills, attitudes, and knowledge relevant to consumer behavior, then it is probably safe to conclude that television advertising is one of many influences on the process. What is not clear from existing research is whether television advertising contributes to "effective" or "good" consumer behavior patterns; whether advertising merely provides consumer-related stimuli which provides a catalyst in the process; or whether television advertising's influences contribute to any long-range socialization effects [p. 131].

Television advertising and parent-child relations

Both the NAB and NAD codes state explicitly that commercials should not direct the child to ask the parent to buy the product. Accordingly, recent content analyses seldom find such techniques used in children's commercials (Atkin & Heald, 1977).

Despite the absence of direct appeals to ask parents for products, both children (Atkin, 1975c,e) and parents (Atkin, 1975e; Ward & Wackman, 1972) have reported that product purchase requests are very often based on exposure to TV commercials. Predictably, the products requested are primarily toys and cereal. As reported in the food advertising section, heavy commercial viewers more than light viewers tend to make requests for advertised foods and restaurants (Atkin, 1975c,e; Atkin et al., 1979; Clancy-Hepburn, Hickey, & Nevill, 1974). Direct observations in the supermarket (Atkin, 1975d; Galst & White, 1976) corroborate that children request products they saw advertised on television.

That conflicts ensue when parents refuse their child's product requests has also been reported (Atkin, 1975c,e) and observed (Atkin, 1978). Atkin (1978) found that 65% of all parent denials resulted in observable parent-child conflict in the form of arguments.

A study by Goldberg and Gorn (1977) suggests that negativistic attitudes toward parents are inspired by commercials. Four- and five-year old children saw a program with no commercials, two commercials for a toy, or the programs and two commercials on two successive days. Children were later shown photographs of a father and son and told that the child requested the advertised toy, but the father refused to buy it. Less than 40% of the commercial viewers felt the boy would still want to play with his father, while over 60% of the no-commercial group thought so. Further, the study assessed the possible materialistic effects of commercials on children's peer relations. The children were asked whether they would rather play with friends in the sandbox or with the advertised toy. Preference for the interaction with friends was shown by about twice as many children who were not exposed to the commercials. Further, they were asked if they would rather play with a "nice boy" without the toy or with a "not so nice boy" with the toy. Seventy percent of the no-commercial group selected the nice boy without the toy while only 35% of the commercial viewers selected him.

FTC HEARINGS

The FTC began an investigation of children's television advertising in response to petitions filed in 1977 by two nonprofit organizations: ACT and Center for Science in the Public Interest. (CSPI is a District of Columbia corporation devoted to improving domestic food policies.) Both the ACT and CSPI petitions were directed at broadcasts in which children comprise at least half the audience. ACT's petition sought a ban on televised candy commercials during these periods. CSPI's petition sought the following changes: (1) a ban on TV ads for between-meal snacks for which more than 10% of the calories are derived from added sugar, and (2) mandatory disclosures of the added sugar content of foods and the dental health risks posed by eating sugared products. In July 1977, representatives of several organizations met with then FTC Chairman Michael Pertschuk to endorse the petitions. These endorsers included the American Academy of Pediatrics, the American Parents Committee, and the Dental Health Section of the American Public Health Association.

In response to these petitions, the FTC Advisory Staff in 1978 proposed that the commission should proceed to rulemaking to determine whether it should (FTC, 1978):

> (a) Ban all televised advertising for any product which is directed to, or seen by, audiences composed of a significant proportion of children who are too young to understand the selling purpose of, or otherwise comprehend or evaluate, the advertising.

> (b) Ban televised advertising direct to, or seen by, audiences composed of a significant proportion of older children for sugared products, the consumption of which poses the most serious dental health risks;

(c) Require that televised advertising directed to, or seen by, audiences composed of a significant proportion of older children for sugared food products not included in paragraph (b) be balanced by nutritional and/or health disclosures funded by advertisers [pp. 10–11].

The FTC solicited public comment on the above proposals through the fall of 1978, and during the winter of 1979 six weeks of hearings on children's television advertising were held in San Francisco and Washington D.C. About 200 witnesses representing the broadcasting, food and toy industries, health and education professionals, consumer groups, and parents testified.

Following the hearings, the FTC Presiding Officer, Judge Morton Needelman, reviewed the evidence submitted and issued a statement clarifying the disputed and nondisputed issues. Needelman indicated that the issues that should be pursued are (FTC, 1979):

1. To what extent can children between the ages of 2 and 11 distinguish between children's commercials and children's programs to the point that they comprehend the selling purpose of television advertising aimed at children?
2. To what extent can children between the ages of 2 and 11 defend against persuasive techniques used in these commercials, such as fantasy or cartoon presenters, premiums, limited information, and various associative appeals?
3. What health effects, actual or potential, attach to any proven lack of understanding or inability to defend against persuasive techniques [pp. 6–7]?

The issues that Needelman considered unworthy of further FTC attention included: TV advertising not specifically directed at children, TV advertising's effectiveness in getting children to ask for advertised products (proven), parent-child conflict resulting from such requests (proven to be present but not severe), and the adverse effects of overconsumption of sugar on obesity and the formation of dental caries (proven) (FTC, 1979).

Throughout these events, the broadcasters, advertisers, and targeted manufacturers launched a counterattack. In 1978 they reportedly raised a $30 million "war chest" to fight the FTC (ACT, 1980). Industry groups lobbying in Washington tried to prevent the hearings from ever taking place. They almost convinced the House and Senate appropriations committee members to forbid the FTC from using any funds on the children's advertising rulemaking; they sought to undermine the participation of groups such as ACT by attempting to cut their public participation funds; and they challenged Michael Pertschuk's role, accusing him of being biased.

In December 1979, the Court of Appeals ruled that while Pertschuk's participation was lawful and appropriate, he had to withdraw from further participation in the proceedings. The industry lobbyists continued their opposition during and after the hearings. By May 1980, their pressures in

Washington culminated in Congress passing a bill that eliminated the power of the FTC to rule on "unfair" advertising practices, thus confining its powers to "deceptive" practices. Further, the proceeding was suspended until the FTC developed specific rules concerning deception.

In June 1980, the FTC Commissioners instructed the staff to present recommendations for the future conduct of the proceeding. On March 31, 1981 the FTC staff released its report and recommendation. The recommendation that appears on the cover page of the report succinctly states: "Recommendation: That the Commission Terminate Proceedings for the Promulgation of a Trade Regulation Rule on Children's Advertising" (Federal Trade Commission, 1981a). In its report, the staff acknowledged that there were many problems with children's advertising, but that they were not in a position to do anything about it at the time. The following is a summary statement of the bases for this rather defeatist recommendation (FTC, 1981b):

Staff recommends that the Commission terminate the children's advertising rulemaking proceeding. While the rulemaking record establishes that child-oriented television advertising is a legitimate cause for public concern, there do not appear to be, at the present time, workable solutions which the Commission can implement through rulemaking in response to the problems articulated during the course of the proceeding. . . .

The record developed during the rulemaking proceeding adequately supports the following conclusions regarding child-oriented television advertising and young children six years and under: (1) they place indiscriminate trust in televised advertising messages; (2) they do not understand the persuasive bias in television advertising; and (3) the techniques, focus and themes used in child-oriented television advertising enhance the appeal of the advertising message and the advertised product. Consequently, young children do not possess the cognitive ability to evaluate adequately child-oriented television advertising. Despite the fact that these conclusions can be drawn from the evidence, the record establishes that the only effective remedy would be a ban on all advertisements oriented toward young children, and such a ban, as a practical matter, cannot be implemented. Because of this remedial impediment, there is no need to determine whether or not advertising oriented toward young children is deceptive. Staff's recommendation for this portion of the case is that the proceeding be terminated.

Other major concerns expressed in the proceeding were that advertisements for sugared products directed to children under twelve may have adverse effects on their nutritional attitudes, and may undermine children's health because such advertisements do not warn children of the possible effects of the over-consumption of sugar on their nutritional and dental well-being. The rulemaking record established that advertising for sugared products is concentrated during children's television programming and that this advertising persuades children to ask for the advertised products. However, the evidence on the record is inconclusive as to whether this advertising adversely affects children's attitudes about nutrition. Therefore, staff recommends that rulemaking be terminated on this issue.

With regard to dental health, the rulemaking record establishes that dental caries is a major childhood disease, and that the consumption of sugar contributes to the formation of dental caries. Evidence on the record also establishes that there are a number of factors other than the sugar content of a food which are important contributors to the formation of dental caries. However, it became apparent during the course of the proceeding that there is no scientific methodology for determining the cariogenicity of individual food products which is sufficiently scientifically accepted to justify formulation of a government-mandated rule. Since such identification would be a threshold step in the implementation of any proposed rule, the lack of a methodology precludes regulation through rule-making of child-oriented advertising for food products on the ground that such products contribute to dental caries. Thus, staff recommends that the rulemaking be terminated on this issue [pp. 2–4].

On September 30, 1981 the FTC announced that "It is not in the public interest to continue this proceeding. . . . We seriously doubt . . . whether a total ban should ever be imposed on children's advertising at the end of rulemaking proceedings. . . . We cannot justify sacrificing other important enforcement priorities to its continuation" (*Daily News*, 1981, p. 40).

It is interesting that even before the FTC staff report was released, Robert Choate,* the avid child advocate and founder of the Center for Children, Media, and Merchandising, sensed that regulatory action was unlikely and that parents would have to assume the responsibility to protect their children against the abuses of commercials. Choate (1980) wrote:

the handwriting on the wall is clear: Parents must help their children to comprehend the totality of the message in the more than 20,000 commercials per year they view [p. 336].

Work in this direction has begun. An active interest has emerged in developing "critical viewing skills" in children to make them less vulnerable to the persuasive techniques used in television advertising and to potential adverse effects of programming.

---

*It might be of interest that Robert Choate has redirected his efforts in a totally different area. He has established a nonprofit institute under the Academy for Educational Development called Institute for Gender Equity which deals with men's attitudes toward the changes occurring in women's lives.

DEVELOPING CRITICAL VIEWING SKILLS

With the clear indication that government will not control program or commercial content, there has been an increasing interest in developing children's "critical viewing" skills to enable them to protect themselves from adverse TV influences. The assumption of this approach is that if children can be taught to be critical evaluators of television, they will be less vulnerable. Many funding agencies have supported this notion. In 1978, the Idaho Department of Education funded an ESEA Title IV-C Innovative Education project to promote the viewership skills of the youngsters in the third through sixth grades. Similar funding was made available by the National PTA, the National Education Association, the Office of Education, and even ABC.

Classroom curricula

Dorr, Graves, and Phelps (1980) were pioneers in developing a critical viewing curriculum. Based on extensive interviewing of children, these researchers identified four critical evaluation skills which would be the objectives of the curricula: (1) decrease children's belief that TV programs are real, (2) increase children's tendencies to compare what they see on TV with other information sources, (3) decrease television's credibility by teaching children about economic and production aspects of television, and (4) teach children to evaluate television content by making use of the outlined skills.

Two different curricula were developed. The "industry curriculum" was designed to teach children about television's economic structure and production techniques, and how to use this knowledge to evaluate programming as real or fantasy. The training revolved around eight facts:

1. Plots are made up.
2. Characters are actors.
3. Incidents are fabricated.
4. Settings are often constructed.
5. Programs are broadcast to make money.
6. Money for programs comes from advertisers purchasing air time.
7. Ads are to sell products to the viewer.
8. Audience size determines broadcaster income [p. 73].

The "process curriculum" was designed to teach children processes and sources for evaluating TV content. The facts around which this curriculum was developed are:

1. Entertainment programs are made up.
2. Entertainment programs vary in how realistic they are.

3. Viewers can decide how realistic they find entertainment programs.
4. Television content may be evaluated by comparing it to one's own experience, asking other people, and consulting other media sources [p. 73].

The effectiveness of these curricula was compared with a control curriculum on "social reasoning" which developed children's role-taking skills by teaching them how to take other people's feelings and perspectives into account.

All three curricula were taught during the school day in six one-hour sessions to small groups of between four to seven children in kindergarten and second/third grades. The curricula, taught by research personnel with previous teaching experience, used similar methods of instruction: audio-visual materials, role playing, discussion, games, and drawing. In subsequent paper and pencil tests and interviews, the researchers demonstrated that the six-hour curricula successfully taught children much about television and alternative information sources and how to use that knowledge in reasoning about the reality of television content. The researchers concluded that each of the critical viewing curricula contributed unique skills and should be combined into one program.

In a study funded by the American Broadcasting Company, Singer, Zuckerman, and Singer (1980) developed an eight-lesson critical viewing curriculum for third through fifth graders. The lessons were entitled: Introduction to Television, Reality and Fantasy on Television, Camera Effects and Special Effects, Commercials and the Television Business, Identification with Television Characters, Stereotypes on Television, Violence and Aggression, and How Viewers Can Influence Television. The lessons, taught by the regular classroom teachers after rather brief training, lasted about forty minutes each and involved presentation of audio-visual materials (e.g., clips from TV programs), discussions, teaching of lesson-related vocabulary, and engaging in guided activities (e.g., practicing special effects on video equipment in the classroom). Testing of information learned (with a pretest-posttest method) revealed that the program was effective in conveying new information, especially about special effects, commercials, and advertising and in enhancing facility with TV-related vocabulary. What has yet to be determined is the extent to which such critical viewing programs decrease the negative influences or enhance the positive effects of television.

A film: "The Six Billion $$$ Sell"

The effectiveness of showing children critical viewing films was demonstrated in a series of studies by Donald Roberts and his colleagues (Roberts, Christenson, Gibson, Mooser, & Goldberg, 1980). These studies focused on two films, *The Six Billion $$$ Sell* (by Consumer's Union) and *Seeing*

Through Commercials (by Vision Films), both designed to teach children about the selling intent of commercials and the persuasive techniques used in them. (See Table 6.3 for a summary of the content of the two films.) Both before and after viewing one of these films or a control film, children's skepticism toward commercials was measured with items such as "When someone famous tries to get you to buy something in a TV commercial, you can be pretty sure it is as good as he says it is" (agree-disagree), and "Most

Table 6.3. Summary of the Basic Contents of Two Instructional Films.

The Six Billion $$$ Sell	Seeing Through Commercials
Announcer comments on various "tricks" used in commercials and says we will look at some.	A scene shows the making of a commercial in which the actor cannot stand the product and steps out of character to explain that commercials are "pretend."
"Selling the Star" — use of celebrity testimonials.	
"Now You See It, Now You Don't" — exaggerations, irrelevant claims, tricks of camera and lighting.	Shows how addition of song, happy children, play, etc., can make any product look like fun.
"New! New! New!" — use of the word "new" to imply superiority.	Examination of how camera can be used to make product look larger than it really is.
"Word Games" — use of scientific-sounding words to imply superiority.	Discussion of special effects used to make a product look exciting — sound effects, excited spectators, rapidly sequenced visuals shot from many perspectives.
"The Giveaway" — promoting premium offers rather than the product itself.	
"Promises, Promises" — association of product with glamour, success, fun, and the good life.	Discussion of special effects to make a product seem beautiful — set, dramatic lighting, filters on cameras, music and sound.
"Brand Loyalty" — promoting a brand rather than the product itself.	
Children conduct a group discussion about commercials in general and come to the conclusion that people should make their own product choices and should be very careful about the claims made in commercials.	Discussion of implied messages — disclaimers, premium offers, etc. A closing "commercial" full of the "tricks" discussed above — included for discussion by viewers at the end of the film.

Source: Roberts, Christenson, Gibson, Mooser, & Goldberg, 1980.
© 1980 by The Annenberg School of Communications. Reprinted by permission.

of the things they say on TV commercials are true" (agree-disagree). The researchers found that *The Six Billion $$$ Sell* viewers became more skeptical about commercials than the other two groups. In addition to the general questions about commercials, the youngsters were shown actual commercials containing the specific techniques described in the film and were questioned about them. Their responses provided further evidence of the film's effectiveness in increasing viewer skepticism regarding commercials. The film was particularly successful with the youngest children (second graders in one study and fourth graders in another study) and with those who watched the most television.

Chapter 7
Race and Sex on TV

OVERVIEW

The cultivation of children's attitudes through the stories they are exposed to originated with the earliest fairy tale. Today concern focuses on race and sex stereotyping and on the portrayal of sexuality on television.

Clark (1972) observed that there are two ways in which the presentation of women and minorities can be biased: lack of recognition and lack of respect. Recognition refers to the frequency with which a group receives TV roles at all. (One German university professor, who had seen a good deal of U.S. television in the 1960s but had never been to the United States, expressed amazement that more than 10% of the U.S. population was black. Based on the frequency with which blacks appeared on TV, he thought there were very few blacks in this country.) Respect refers to how characters behave and are treated once they have roles.

Although blacks were once almost ignored on TV, this situation has changed markedly as a result of the pressures of black and broader-based civil rights groups. Women and other minorities have not fared so well in terms of recognition. No other group on television is accorded respect even approaching that given to the white male. Moreover, both correlational and experimental studies show that how groups are portrayed on TV can exert a clear influence on the attitudes of the young viewer.

Television has only recently been accused of being "pornographic," and no doubt this is because sexuality was considered taboo by producers and the networks until the mid-1970s. Content analyses show that there has been an increasing emphasis on sexual themes over the past decade (causing critics to hiss that the networks responded to the Surgeon General's Report by trading violence for sex), but most of this sex is merely talk and innuendo. Except for aggressive acts, physical contact on television is usually quite proper or conservatively affectionate.

There is almost no research on the effects of sexual material on children, probably because even soliciting for child participants in such studies would be a violation of deeply held values.

We have already mentioned on several occasions Gerbner's theory that TV content "cultivates" various ideas and attitudes about the world and the people in it. Representation of racial groups, gender roles, and sexual relationships on television potentially cultivate underlying attitudes of children (and perhaps adults) who watch. Thus race and sex portrayals on TV and in other media continue to be researched and discussed even though other issues seem to reach partial resolution.

In this chapter we consider race and sex stereotypes on television, both in terms of their prevalence and their effects, and then consider the highly controversial issue of sex and sexuality on television.

STEREOTYPING

Early television was highly biased in its portrayals of blacks and other minorities. These groups were underrepresented or presented in a very unflattering light. In Smythe's (1954) early study, 80% of all characters were found to be white Americans, and only 2% were black Americans; of the 18% remaining, Europeans (especially English and Italians) appeared most frequently. India and Africa, with more than one-third of the world population, were almost entirely unrepresented, and China provided a mere 0.2% of the television population, even though it represented 22% of the world's population. In terms of stereotyped roles, the analysis also revealed that minorities were more likely than Anglo-American whites to be law breakers. Italians were law breakers over half the time they were presented.

In the 1950s, blacks were rarely presented at all, and when they were, it was either as minor characters or as lovable but stereotyped buffoons (*Amos and Andy*). By the 1960s, partly influenced by the civil rights movement, some of the most blatant forms of discrimination in both portrayals and employment practices had been abated. Recall from Chapter 2 the WLBT-TV case where a station in Jackson, Mississippi lost its license in 1964 on the grounds that it did not serve the city's black community. A few years later, in 1968 the National Advisory Commission on Civil Disorders accused the news media of distorting racial problems and inadequately representing black people's complaints. In entertainment programming during the 1960s, blacks still had minor roles and were rarely portrayed as powerful or prestigious. This situation has changed as we will see shortly.

Similarly, the women's movement is largely responsible for an increasing interest in TV's portrayals of sex roles. In the early 1970s the National Organization for Women launched several campaigns against advertisements portraying women as mindless sex objects. There were also complaints about programs and commercials presenting women in limited roles, primarily housewife and mother. Independent sex role analyses of prime-time television conducted by Women on Words and Images (1975), a feminist organization, and the Women's Division of the United Methodist Church (United Methodist Women's Television Monitoring Project, 1976) revealed an extreme under-representation of females, a biased portrayal of occupational and interpersonal roles, and distorted images of male/female personal characteristics.

With few execptions, research on the portrayals of minorities and women and their influence on the TV viewer did not begin to appear until the early 1970s. The research culminated in a report by the United States Commission on Civil Rights (1977). The Commission was concerned about the violation of civil rights in broadcasting, both the biased portrayal of minorities and women on network television programs and discriminatory employment practice at television stations. The Commission based its report on the 1969–1974 content analyses data of George Gerbner and his colleagues, an analyses of a week of network news, and an examination of broadcasting industry employment statistics. The Commission later issued an update report (1979) which examined the 1975–1977 television seasons and 1977 employment statistics.

Racial and ethnic stereotypes

Content analysis in the early 1970s found that except for blacks, most ethnic minorities were practically ignored on television (Gerbner, 1972; Mendelson & Young, 1972; Ormiston & Williams, 1973). Where nonblack minorities did appear, they were presented in a very unfavorable light. In prime-time programming, non-Americans were more often cast as villains and as the victims of violence (Gerbner, 1972). On children's programming "good" characters almost invariably spoke standard English, whereas more than 50% of the "bad" characters had foreign accents (Mendelson & Young, 1972).

Due to pressure from black groups, the proportion of blacks on television increased to approximate their number in the U.S. population; however, blacks were more likely than whites to be cast in minor roles, and only eight of a sample of 133 evening network programs featured a black character as a regular (Hinton, Seggar, Northcott, & Fontes, 1973). The formal social-occupational status of blacks has also been elevated since the early days of television. While they used to be cast as servants or entertainers, blacks in the late 1960s and early 1970s were presented as "regulators" of society in positions such as teachers or law enforcers (Clark, 1972; Roberts, 1970). However, although these black characters were portrayed as good and likeable, they were neither forceful nor powerful. Donagher, Poulos, Liebert, and Davidson (1975) found that black men were nonaggressive and altruistic, and black women were shown quite often trying to resolve conflict by expressing feelings. Hinton et al. (1973) found that TV blacks were presented as industrious, competent, and law abiding. On children's programs, blacks were found to be "good" people but never in a leadership position in the absence of a white co-leader (Mendelson & Young, 1972). Blacks typically did not speak or hold the product in commercials and rarely appeared without whites (Dominick & Greenberg, 1970).

The 1977 U.S. Commission on Civil Rights report (1977) used Gerbner's Cultural Indicators Project 1969–74 content analysis data on network prime-time dramatic programs (which include situation comedies, dramas, and movies, but exclude variety shows) and children's noncartoon Saturday morning programs. The analysis revealed that 89.1% of the TV characters were white. Nonwhite females were the most under-represented group, comprising only 2.3% of the character sample. More than half of the nonwhite characters were black, while individuals of Hispanic origin were rarely seen. There was a significant increase in the proportion of nonwhite characters between 1969 (6.6%) and 1974 (12.5%). In terms of portrayal, a greater proportion of nonwhites than whites were depicted as heroes, killers, in comic roles, as very poor, as service workers, and associated with illegal activity. An analysis of fifteen 1974–1975 newscasts, 5 from each network, revealed that 94.1% of the news correspondents were white; furthermore, 88.7% of the newsmakers (defined as being identified by the anchorperson or correspondent and appearing in a video display) were white. The update reported in 1979 (U.S. Commission on Civil Rights, 1979) representing the 1975–77 seasons supported the earlier results and failed to find any significant changes in race portrayals. (See Figure 7.1 and Table 7.1.)

Gender stereotypes

Content analyses invariably show that there are far fewer females than males in the world of television; males fill between 66–75% of all television roles (Gerbner, 1972; Head, 1954; Tedesco, 1974; U.S. Commission on Civil Rights, 1977, 1979). These studies have asked, "What does the TV world convey about appropriate roles for males and females? How should they conduct their lives according to the TV world?" In terms of formal occupational roles, TV males are generally employed and enjoy highly prestigious positions such as doctors, lawyers, and law enforcement officials. In contrast, most TV women are assigned marital, romantic, and family roles; only about one-third the TV roles with a definite occupational activity are held by women, and those jobs are rarely prestigious ones (DeFleur, 1964; Gerbner, 1972; Seggar, 1975; Long & Simon, 1974; Tedesco, 1974). On Saturday morning, Busby (1974) found a greater diversity of male jobs — there were 42 different male jobs and only nine different female jobs.

In terms of how they behave, TV males are portrayed as more powerful, dominant, aggressive, stable, persistent, rational, and intelligent than females. Females are portrayed as more attractive, altruistic, sociable, warm, sympathetic, happy, rule abiding, peaceful, and youthful than males (Donagher et al., 1975; Long & Simon, 1974; Tedesco, 1974, Turow, 1974).

Similarly, on exclusively children's programs, females are shown as generally passive, deferential, and very likely punished for displaying high levels of effort, while males are planful, constructive, and generally rewarded for their efforts (Sternglanz & Serbin, 1974). On Saturday morning cartoons, males enjoy wide occupational variety, whereas females are almost always pretty teens or housewives, if adults (Levinson, 1975).

In 1975, the National Advertising Review Board issued a report based on an analysis of portrayals of females in TV commercials. They concluded that women were inaccurately presented as sex objects and rarely as professionals. Several of the airline commercials illustrate their claim. Recall National Airlines "Fly me" campaign and Continental Airlines' "We really move our tail for you." An earlier study sponsored by NOW (Hennessee & Nicholson, 1972) reported similar results and published their findings in a *New York Times* magazine article, "N.O.W. says: TV Commercials Insult Women." A 1974 review of four studies on sex role portrayals on TV commercials (Courtney & Whipple, 1974) reported the consistent finding that "women are not portrayed as autonomous, independent human beings, but

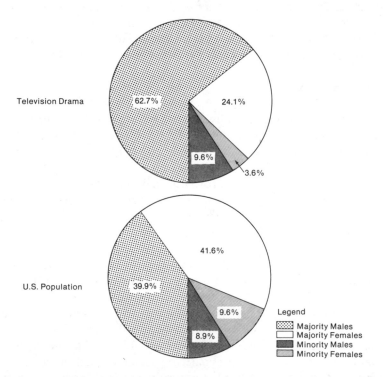

Fig. 7.1. Sex and Race of Major Characters in Television Drama, 1975–77, and of the U.S. Population, 1976.

Source: U.S. Commission on Civil Rights, 1979.

Table 7.1. The 10 Most Frequently Appearing Occupations on Prime-Time Television by Race and Sex (Specific Occupation Title Data)

Majority Male		Majority Female		Minority Male		Minority Female	
Occupation	Percent	Occupation	Percent	Occupation	Percent	Occupation	Percent
1. Police	16.0	1. Unknown*	32.3	1. Unknown*	19.8	1. Unknown*	37.4
2. Unknown*	13.3	2. Secretary	7.3	2. Police	15.1	2. Student	10.4
3. Criminal	8.0	3. Student	6.4	3. Criminal	8.2	3. Homemaker	6.0
4. Self-Employed	4.8	4. Homemaker	5.5	4. Other	7.0	4. Household Worker	6.0
5. Doctor	3.8	5. Nurse	4.8	5. Student	5.8	5. Nurse	4.9
6. Enlisted/Noncom	3.8	6. Criminal	3.4	6. Self-employed	5.6	6. Criminal	3.8
7. Student	3.4	7. Unemployed	2.7	7. Miscellaneous Service Worker	3.7	7. Secretary	3.3
8. Miscellaneous Managers	3.2	8. Hotel/Restaurant Service Worker	2.5	8. Doctor	2.7	8. Self-employed	2.7
9. Journalist	2.5	9. Military Nurse	2.4	9. Hotel/Restaurant Service Worker	2.7	9. Hotel/Restaurant Service Worker	2.7
10. Hotel/Restaurant Service Worker	2.2	10. [Police; Household Worker; Self-employed]	1.7	10. Enlisted/Noncom	1.9	10. Other	2.7
SUBTOTAL	61.0	SUBTOTAL	72.4	SUBTOTAL	72.5	SUBTOTAL	79.9
5 other occupations	39.0	38 other occupations	27.6	36 other occupations	27.5	17 other occupations	20.1
TOTAL	100.0	TOTAL	100.0	TOTAL	100.0	TOTAL	100.0

*The Unknown category includes all those characters for whom no occupational information is available.
Source: U.S. Commission on Civil Rights, 1979.

are primarily sex-typed." While males are presented as worldly, dominant authority figures, females are shown as domesticated and submissive.

Finally, studies show that TV conveys different messages for males and females in terms of the values attached to both youth and marriage. While youth is emphasized for both sexes, the emphasis is considerably greater for females: in an analysis of dramatic programs, 40% of the male characters but only 15% of the females were over 40 (Tedesco, 1974). In terms of the desirability of marriage, television marriages typically reduce a man's power but enhance a woman's power; single men are portrayed as more powerful than married men, but single women are more likely to be the victims of violence than married women (Gerbner, 1972). McNeil (1975) found that TV women more than TV men are concerned with family and marital/romantic problems, have problems solved with the help of others and, if employed, were supervised by others.

So the overall picture of what one should be like is limiting for both females and males. According to TV, a male should strive for power and aspire to highly prestigious occupations; to do so, he can be aggressive and break rules and has to be smart, stable, persistent, and remain unemotional. A female should strive for marriage, and to attract a man she must be warm, sensitive, altruistic, and attractive; further, if she tries to accomplish something, she is likely to fail due to others' discouragement and her own personal limitations.

The U.S. Commission on Civil Rights reports (1977, 1979) based on the period 1969–1977 corroborated the earlier studies. During this period, females occupied only about 27% of the TV roles. (See Figure 7.1 for the 1975–77 period.) Males predominated in the 31–40 year old range while females were heavily concentrated in the 21–30 year old range. Females far more than males tended to be cast in comic roles, as married, and as the victims of violence. While almost 70% of males had identified occupational roles, over half the females had none. (See Table 7.1.) Males far more than females were aggressive, associated with illegal activity, and with law enforcement occupations. The news analysis revealed that only 11.8% of the correspondents and only 13.5% of the newsmakers were female.

Effects of stereotyped portrayals

In the mid-1970s research reports started to appear that examined the impact of television's sex role and race stereotypes on child viewers. What is striking is the meager amount of research evidence in the face of major protests by special interest groups.

The potential influence of television entertainment on racial attitudes was shown most dramatically by Sheryl Graves (1975) who studied how positive and negative portrayals of black characters in cartoons affected white and black children's attitudes toward blacks. She selected eight previously broadcast cartoons which varied in the portrayal of blacks (positive or negative). The positive portrayals showed blacks as competent, trustworthy, and hardworking. The negative portrayals showed them as inept, destructive, lazy, and powerless. Graves found that there was a positive attitude change for the black children who saw either portrayal and for the white children who saw a positive portrayal. However, white children exposed to a negative portrayal changed the most and in a negative direction. Overall, these results suggest that while the mere presence of black TV characters may have a positive impact on black children, the type of characterization of blacks is critical in terms of the potential negative impact on white children. Graves' findings are particularly striking because the attitude changes occurred after only a *single* program exposure.

Children's acceptance of televised stereotypic sex role portrayals was explored by Frueh and McGhee (1975), who reasoned that if children accept TV's sex role messages, frequent TV viewers should have more stereotypic beliefs (such as girls should play with dolls, dishes, and dresses and boys should play with trucks, guns, and tools) than infrequent TV viewers. They found that for both boys and girls in kindergarten, second, fourth, and sixth grades, frequent viewers were far more likely than infrequent viewers to identify with the sex stereotyped roles associated with their own gender. Similarly, Beuf (1974) found that three to six-year-old children who were heavy TV viewers made more sex-typed occupational choices than light viewers.

An experimental study by Tan (1979) found that adolescent girls exposed to a heavy dose of beauty commercials were more likely than a control group of girls not exposed to the commercials to believe that being beautiful is an important characteristic and is necessary to attract men. Twenty-three high school girls (16–18 years of age) viewed 15 commercials which emphasized the desirability of sex appeal, beauty, or youth (e.g., ads for toothpaste or soap), and 33 girls viewed commercials which did not contain beauty messages (e.g., ads for dog food, soy sauce, or diapers). They were then asked to rank order the relative importance of ten attributes (e.g., pretty face, intelligence, sex appeal, hard-working, youthful appearance, competence) in each of four areas (career/job, wife, to be liked by men, and desirable personal attribute). The beauty ad group ranked the importance of the sex-appeal qualities significantly higher than the neutral ad group for the item "to be liked by men"; marginal significance in the same direction was found for the item "personally desirable."

Counter-stereotyped models also seem to have an impact. A study by Atkin (1975b) revealed that children who were shown a commercial featuring a female judge were more likely than a no-exposure control group to rate the profession as an appropriate one for females. Miller and Reeves

(1976) found that grade school children who viewed more non-sex stereo-typed programs were more likely to accept nontraditional sex roles as ap-propriate. Davidson, Yasuno, and Tower (1979) found that five to six-year-old girls who saw a nontraditional cartoon showing females as competent athletes subsequently gave less stereotyped responses on a sex role attitude measure than those who saw a neutral or sex role stereotyped cartoon. Fi-nally, *Freestyle*, a TV series designed to reduce sex role stereotypes in nine to twelve year olds, had positive results which will be discussed in Chapter 8.

Employment of women and minorities in the television industry

Equal employment opportunity for women was a major goal of the feminist movement in the late 1960s, as it was for blacks and other minorities in the civil rights movement. These movements were effective in applying pressure on the television industry, which heretofore had been quite biased in its em-ployment practices. (A characteristic, we should note, which it shared with academia and many other industries.)

Partly as a result of the pressures we have mentioned, the FCC in 1969 adopted a nondiscrimination rule prohibiting discrimination in employment by broadcast licensees on the basis of race, color, religion, or national origin. Partly in response to pressures from the National Organization for Women, in 1971 the FCC included women in its nondiscriminatory ruling, stating "It is fully appropriate, in our judgment, for the attention of broadcasters to be drawn to the task of providing equal employment opportunity for women as well as for Negroes, Orientals, American Indians, and Spanish Surnamed Americans" (FCC, 1971, p. 709). The FCC ruling required broadcast li-censees with five or more full-time employees to furnish equal employment opportunity statistics with their license renewal application.

As part of its 1977 and 1979 reports, the U.S. Commission on Civil Rights conducted a study of the employment status of women and minorities on 40 television stations in major markets throughout the nation, including the 15 network owned and operated stations, 15 network affiliates, and 10 public stations. The Commission on Civil Rights wanted to determine the effec-tiveness of the FCC equal employment opportunity ruling. It found that the minority and female employment at the 40 stations increased between 1971 and 1975, and that the increases occurred in the upper job categories. How-ever, the job categories were designated such that 75% of all employees were in upper level jobs. The most significant finding was that females and minority members were almost absent from the decision-making positions, which were the domain of white males. In the 1979 update (representing 1977 statistics), the Commission did not find significant increases in the proportion of minorities and females employed as managers and officials.

Figure 7.2 shows the employment distribution of officials and managers by race and sex. Furthermore, the Commission on Civil Rights found that many females and minorities were given impressive titles and salaries, but that their position in the organizational structure was relatively low, suggesting that the stations were artificially creating the impression of an equal employment situation.

According to the Commission, the real problem in getting an equal employment program to work is the biased attitude of station managers. The Commission report states (U.S. Commission on Civil Rights, 1977):

> The overriding deterrent to assuring equal employment opportunity for minorities and women in the television industry is not necessarily the failure of the FCC's EEO guidelines to be specific and result-oriented. It is not entirely the failure of the licensees to implement affirmative measures to assure nondiscrimination; nor is it the ineffectiveness of each of the affirmative measures they do undertake. All of these factors detract from realizing equal employment opportunity, but the real deterrent is the lack of a genuine commitment by licensees which was conveyed in their attitudes toward minorities and women.

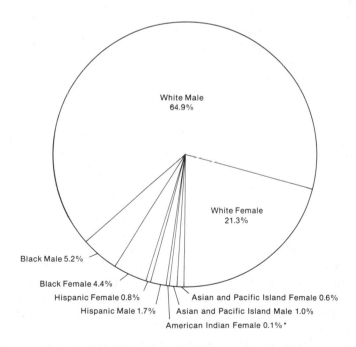

Fig. 7.2. Distribution of Officials and Managers by Race and Sex, 1977 (40-Station Sample).
*American Indian Male: 0.0%.

Source: From U.S. Commission on Civil Rights, 1979, p. 35.

The station managers were convinced that these groups lacked the appropriate qualifications or experience necessary for managerial, professional, or technical positions at their stations. While some conceded that past employment practices in the industry have traditionally limited opportunities for minorities and women, their attitudes as well as the ineffective affirmative measures they have undertaken suggest that they are allowing these practices to continue. Three general managers emphasized that in the "real world" there were very few qualified minorities and women whom they could hire.

Station managers often perceived women as lacking initiative and being incapable of asserting themselves. They attributed the fact that women were often not hired or promoted to their lack of assertiveness rather than to the stations' failure to provide equal employment opportunity [pp. 84–85].

SEX AND SEXUALITY

Human sexuality is a highly charged topic. Obscenity, one type of speech *not* protected by the First Amendment (see Chapter 2), has been taken by the courts to refer to sexual material. (Occasionally, critics of TV violence have labeled such material "obscene," but the courts generally take obscene to imply a sexual component.)

How and to what extent is human sexuality displayed on TV, and what effects do these portrayals have? These are the questions with which we will be concerned in this section.

Emerging interest in TV sex

Only in recent years has the issue of sex on prime-time television warranted much attention in a book about television. Aside from stereotypic sex role portrayals, there wasn't much sexual content on TV. Throughout early TV history, the standards and practices departments in the broadcasting industry perpetuated and maintained a very puritanical TV world in which use of words such as "pregnant" were taboo, and all married couples apparently slept in separate beds. In the late 1960s and early 1970s, when public criticism was firmly centered on the issue of televised violence, network censors and TV producers were already engaged in behind-the-scenes battles over the limits of sexual reference (Cowan, 1978). The resulting gradual and progressive relaxation of strictly-held taboos passed with little reaction from the general public until 1977 when *Soap*, a sex-oriented prime-time situation comedy was aired.

Even before its airing, the promotional releases for *Soap* were sufficient to incite demonstrations, a deluge of complaint letters, and the withdrawal of some advertising support largely due to anti-*Soap* campaigns launched by the National Council of Churches and other religious groups (*Time*, 1977a). Several of ABC's affiliates did not air the premiere episode of *Soap* and many aired it an hour later (presumably to reduce the child audience). Shortly thereafter, TV began to be closely scrutinized for sexual content by religious-based organizations and public interest groups. One of them, the National Federation for Decency (NFD), counted and published the number of sexual references on individual prime-time TV series along with the names and addresses of the "top sponsors of sex on television." The NFD report called for action: "When you purchase products from a company which advertises on programs which exploit sex and make it a commercial product, you help promote such shows. Make your purchases in the marketplace in keeping with your convictions concerning sex on television" (National Federation for Decency, 1977, p. 1). The NFD based its findings on its own monitoring study of 15 weeks of prime-time programming. The report found 2.81 references to sex per hour of prime-time viewing, which ment, "At that rate, over a period of one year viewers would be exposed to 9,230 scenes of suggested sexual intercourse or sexually suggestive comments." It was also pointed out that "89% of all sex shown on prime time television is presented outside marriage." The NFD used its own findings to exert direct pressure on TV's "sex sponsors." In mid-1978, the NFD picketed the Sears Tower in Chicago and Sears-Roebuck stores in 34 cities to protest Sears' sponsorship of *Three's Company* and *Charlie's Angels*, two programs rated as highly sexual by the NFD. Sears then withdrew its sponsorship from these shows. Other "sex sponsors" received similar treatment.

Shortly thereafter the NFD's findings were corroborated by a survey conducted by minister John Hurt who asked his Church of Christ congregation in Joelton, Tennessee to list the five most morally offensive TV programs. The results were: *Soap, Three's Company, Dallas, Saturday Night Live*, and *Charlie's Angels*. Dissatisfied with the responses of the executives at several of the sponsoring companies, Hurt got several thousand Churches of Christ to take part in a boycott of the products of the sponsors of the offensive shows. The church members received wallet-sized lists of the targeted products. Advertisers seemed concerned, but it was unclear whether the boycott affected sales (*Time*, 1980).

By 1981, another group, the Coalition for Better TV, emerged. Backed by the Moral Majority and headed by Rev. Donald Wildmon (the NFD leader), the group met with corporate representatives from the offending companies (according to the monitoring study lists) and threatened a boycott in July 1981. However, it was postponed pending anticipated changes in sponsorship and programming practices regarding sexual content (*Time*, 1981a,b).

Numerous newspaper and magazine articles appeared in the late 1970s concerning TV's apparent obsession with sex, with headlines such as "TV is

Getting Tough on Violence and Loose with Sex" (*New York Times*, September 11, 1977), "TV Tunes in Sex as Crime Fades" (*New York Times*, March 20, 1978), "The Jiggly Effect Takes Off" (*Newsday*, April 23, 1978), and "The Year TV Turned to Sex" (*TV Guide*, May 6, 1978). Perhaps most visible was *Newsweek's* February 20, 1978 feature story, "Sex and TV," which showed scantily clad Suzanne Somers on the cover.

Many of the articles were tinged with criticism about TV's new emphasis on sex. While most network officials denied it, a CBS censor admitted to a *Newsweek* reporter: "With the mix of programming today, sexuality has taken the place of violence" (*Newsweek*, 1978, p. 54).

Criticism came from public officials as well. Margita White, a member of the FCC, wrote a harsh editorial in the *New York Times* (White, 1978):

> The name of the network ratings game for the coming seasons is *sex*. There is every indication that the networks, in shifting from violent themes, will be falling all over each other to see which can expose most often the most of the female anatomy. . . .

> I'm not sure whether I'm more outraged because the medium has missed the message of the antiviolence campaign, or more offended because women are to be battered through a new low in sexploitation. But I do know that the networks will be hearing a new chorus of "I'm mad as hell and I won't take it any more."

What was all the fuss about? Both the sheer amount and the hysterical tone of much of the criticism might cause one to wonder whether TV suddenly had become a pornographic medium. In the mid-1970s, TV researchers embarked on answering the question, "How does television portray sexuality?" Before the answers were available, however, the Family Viewing Time Code, which as you may recall from Chapter 5 prohibited sexual and violent content from 7–9 P.M., went into effect. It is interesting that the ruling emerged in response to public interest group protests and in the absence of objective evidence of (1) the nature or extent of televised sexuality, (2) negative opinions of TV sex by a representative viewer sample, or (3) adverse effects of such content on viewer attitudes or behaviors. At least some evidence in all of these realms was available for TV violence, the content area also affected by the Family Viewing Code.

Content analyses of sex on television

What have TV researchers found out about how sexuality is presented on TV? Considering the problem of defining categories of sexuality that could be *objectively* recorded (i.e., perceptions of sexuality are highly subjective), many consistent findings emerge across different studies (Fernandez-Collado & Greenberg, 1978; Franzblau, Sprafkin, & Rubinstein, 1977;

Gerbner, 1980; Silverman, Sprafkin, & Rubinstein, 1979; Sprafkin & Silverman, 1981). Table 7.2 presents the findings of three analyses covering the period 1975–1978.

First, explicit sexual intercourse has not been shown on network television. References to intercourse occur verbally through descriptions and innuendos or are contextually implied through indirect scenic and behavioral cues that a sexual act has or will take place. While such verbal and contextual references have become commonplace, the overwhelming majority of interpersonal touching on TV is nonsexual in nature. The most frequent type of physical contact is "ritualistic," including such casual acts as handshakes, pats to get someone's attention, and touches to emphasize a point.

Table 7.2. Mean Number of Acts (Per Hour) of Selected Physically Intimate and Sexual Behaviors over Three Prime-Time Seasons.

Behavior	Mode of presentation[a]	1975	1977	1978
Kiss	P	3.32	4.06	7.30
Hug	P	2.65	3.36	4.96
Nonaggressive touching	P	68.07	66.06[b]	62.35[b]
Suggestiveness	P	.79	3.26	2.75
	V	1.27	7.38	10.82
Intercourse	P	0	0	0
	V	.04	.10	.90
	I	0	.24	.43
Aggressive touching	P	5.33	11.06[c]	6.17[c]
	V	.15	.88	.74
Discouraged sexual practices[d]				
Homosexuality		0	.20	.31
Incest			.02	.01
Pederosis			0	.01
Prostitution			.30	1.38
Aggressive sexual contact		.27	.18	.54
Exhibitionism			.02	.09
Fetishism			0	.07
Masturbation			0	.01
Transvestism/transsexualism			.64	.23
Voyeurism			.17	.01
Pornography/striptease				.34

[a]P = physical; V = verbal; I = implied.
[b]Frequency of ritualistic touching plus supportive touching plus affectionate touching.
[c]Frequency of nonsexual aggression plus aggressive child contact.
[d]Most discouraged sexual practice categories were only examined in the two later seasons. The categories are collapsed over physical, verbal, and implied modes of presentation due to small frequencies.
Source: Sprafkin & Silverman (1981).

Also quite common are touches that are supportive or affectionate gestures. Viewers are exposed to a fair number of kisses (about seven per hour in a 1978 sample) and hugs (about five per hour) between adult characters during the prime-time hours (Sprafkin & Silverman, 1981).

These casual contacts aside, the majority of the sexual portrayals on television are verbal presentations in the form of sexual innuendos. The frequency of such allusions has increased steadily over the past few years, with hourly rates of about one per hour in 1975 (Franzblau et al., 1977) to 11 per hour in 1978 (Sprafkin & Silverman, 1981). Throughout the years, the bulk of the innuendos have occurred in a humorous context, appearing almost exclusively in situation comedy and variety shows.

Although the predominance and steady increase of "sex-with-a-titter" characterizes much of prime time, recently there has been a cautious attempt by broadcasters to present sexual references in serious contexts. Unlike the sex typical of comedies, sexual presentations in movies and dramatic series most often take the form of direct verbal references to or contextual implications of intercourse. Both types of portrayals have appeared with much greater frequency in recent years, though remaining hardly comparable to the overall frequency of comical sex. The 1975 study of prime-time television (Franzblau et al., 1977) did not record a single instance of contextually implied intercourse during the week sampled. In the week-long samples of 1977 (Silverman et al., 1979) and 1978 (Sprafkin & Silverman, 1981), a total of 15 and 24 TV scenes respectively contained cues that heterosexual intercourse had just occurred or was about to occur. Even more striking is the increased use of direct verbal references to heterosexual intercourse during prime time. The weekly frequency of such references increased from two in 1975, to six in 1977, to 53 in 1978, most of which appeared in movies and dramas.

Clearly, broadcasters have become bolder in their treatment of sexuality, presenting it more and more frequently in both humorous and serious contexts. Perhaps the most socially significant aspect of such portrayals is the relationship of the individuals involved. One study that examined this aspect (Fernandez-Collado & Greenberg, 1978) found that the number of references to premarital and extramarital sexual encounters far surpassed those to marital sex.

What other traditionally discouraged sexual behaviors are shown or implied on prime-time TV? Based on prime-time analyses conducted on the 1974–79 broadcast seasons, (Franzblau et al., 1977; Silverman et al., 1979; Sprafkin & Silverman, 1981), socially taboo sexual behavior is more often talked about than acted out on TV. Frequencies of such references (either as a direct verbal reference or humorous innuendo) vary, depending on the specific topic. The prime-time viewer is rarely, if ever, exposed to televised allusions to incest, pederosis, exhibitionism, fetishism, masturbation, or voyeurism. However, during a typical evening of prime-time viewing, the viewer could experience at least one reference to homosexuality, prostitution, rape, transvestism, transsexualism, and pornography or striptease. Most of these references are concentrated between 9–11 P.M. The type of program largely determines the kind of sexual reference that appears. There is a tendency for situation comedies to contain the references to homosexuality and transvestism/transsexualism, crime/adventures to deal the most with aggressive sex, and dramas to present the majority of references to prostitution.

Sex on afternoon soap operas has also received attention. Katzman (1972) found that the predominant theme in these daily serials was characters' romantic and marital affairs. Greenberg, Abelman, and Neuendorf (1981) analyzed sexual references directly in a sample of 65 hours of soap operas in 1976, 1979, and 1980. They found afternoon soap operas to contain more sexual references than prime time but less intimate acts; while the afternoon had frequent petting episodes, references to intercourse were more common in the evening programming, along with references to sexual deviance.

Studies of public reactions to TV sex

Several public opinion surveys substantiated that objections to TV sex were widespread and not confined to an outspoken few. As early as 1960, Steiner (1963) found that about half the people he polled thought TV was harmful to children because "they see things that they shouldn't," and two-thirds of those respondents were concerned about immoral behaviors (suggestiveness, vulgarity, and wrong values). Three separate surveys conducted by *TV Guide* in 1975 (Hickey, 1975) 1976 (Ryan, 1976) and 1979 (Callum, 1979), showed that more than half (53–58%) of the respondents felt that there was too much sexually oriented material on television, and yet the majority opposed control mechanisms involving government censorship of such content.

Such reactions most likely reflect the fact that many parents believe that television plays a significant role in the development of their children's attitudes and values toward sexuality. Roberts, Kline, and Gagnon (1978) reported that in a sample of 1,400 parents of three- to eleven-year-old children, television was ranked second only to parents themselves as the primary source for their children's sexual learning. The proportion of parents reporting their child learned the most about sexuality from television was greater than the proportion that reported siblings, peers, older children, books/magazines, movies, other relatives, other adults, a school program, church or physician/doctor.

A study by Sprafkin, Silverman, and Rubinstein (1980) explored further the possibility that the objections to TV sex are rooted in the age of the

potential audience. Several hundred adults in the community watched a
sample of 15 prime-time programs and indicated the degree to which they
thought the sexual content was suitable for an adult, a teen, and a child audience. The respondents also answered a variety of questions concerning
programming policy issues, the degree to which TV sex is a problem, the
perceived impact of TV sex on children, and how suitably they thought TV
had presented 13 specified sexual themes for the three age groups.

Overall, 63% of the respondents thought there was too much sex on TV.
To varying degrees the adults read sexuality into many of the programs they
were shown. For example, the respondents "saw" sexual intercourse when
the scenes contained not intercourse, but affectionate touching, suggestive
behavior, and kissing. Programs containing frequent displays of kissing, affectionate touching, suggestiveness, and references to prostitution or other
"atypical" sexual behaviors were considered unsuitable. As might be expected, the suitability ratings became increasingly conservative as the considered audience went from adult, to teen, to child. In the general evaluations of TV's past presentations of 13 sexual themes, children were
considered to be an inappropriate audience for most of the topics. Many of
the respondents thought programs dealing with rape, prostitution, extramarital sex, striptease, and child molesting were unsuitable for teenagers.
By contrast, the majority of respondents deemed all 13 themes suitable for
an adult audience. (See Table 7.3.)

Despite a general agreement about what topics are suitable for children of
different ages, there was no consensus about what is likely to happen if children are exposed to sexual themes on TV. Forty-eight percent of the re-

**Table 7.3. Percent of Adults Judging TV's Presentations of Various Sexual Topics
to be Unsuitable for Three Audiences.**

Topic	Average Adult	Average Teen	Average Child
Childbirth	6	12	32
Birth Control	6	15	44
Abortion	13	27	58
Necking or Petting	6	20	53
Premarital Sex	16	39	69
Marital Sex	8	21	43
Extramarital Sex	17	41	69
Homosexuality	21	35	61
Prostitution	17	41	72
Striptease	19	46	65
Transsexualism	15	32	57
Rape	22	43	71
Child Molesting	27	40	58

Source: Sprafkin, Silverman, & Rubinstein, 1979.

spondents felt the children would "ask questions about topics they were too young to understand," 41% said they would be "confused or upset," 41% said they would "use language that is unacceptable to the parents," and 35% said they would "tolerate behaviors or lifestyles in others that are unacceptable to the parents." However, 45% said the children would "initiate useful discussions with their parents," and 19% that they would "learn something positive." Consistent with these latter findings, 73% of the respondents indicated that at some time sexual content on TV had prompted a discussion in their household; of these, 51% reported that the ensuing discussion was a positive or useful experience.

Effects of sexual content

Speculations on the effects of TV sex on young viewers abound. However, the crucial issue of how children react to TV sex remains to be systematically studied. To date, there have not been any studies of how children's attitudes or behaviors are affected. Due to moral and ethical issues, it is extremely difficult to do such studies. One study, however, examined adolescents' comprehension of televised sexual innuendos, the most prevalent form of TV sex.

Adolescents' comprehension of TV sex. Supported by the American Broadcasting Company, Silverman and Sprafkin (1980b) asked adolescents between 12 and 16 years old to explain the meaning of 24 sexual innuendos excerpted from prime-time situation comedy programs. (See Table 7.4 for examples of innuendos.) Not surprisingly, it was found that the 12 year olds understood far less than the 14 to 16 year olds; however, even the 12 year olds evidenced a high degree of comprehension, correctly describing at least part of the sexual meaning in each of the presented innuendos. Of the different topics referenced, the adolescents considered innuendos about intercourse as funniest. However, this topic showed the lowest comprehension

Table 7.4. Examples of Televised Sexual Innuendos.

1. An attractive woman asks her boss to change his mind about something. He responds, "Once I make a decision, it takes a lot to get me to change it . . . and you certainly have a lot," as he leers at her ample chest.
2. A marriage counselor asks a couple "How's your love life," to which the husband replies, "I do my duty." The counselor remarks, "You must not think of it as a duty." The wife exclaims, "Don't tell him that. It's the only edge I've got."
3. Two single women caught up in a robbery scene discuss what they will miss out on if they get killed. One remarks, "Once in our lives we should have 'fo-do-de-do-doed' . . . . if we die now we saved it for nothing!"

Source: Courtesy of Silverman & Sprafkin.

scores, most likely due to their embarrassment in talking about it. Best understood and also considered very funny were innuendos about the discouraged sexual topics, primarily homosexuality. In contrast to their discussion of heterosexual intercourse, the adolescents evidenced both clear comprehension and comfort in explaining innuendos that referenced sexual taboos.

National Commission on Obscenity and Pornography Report. An interesting historical contrast for the story of televised sex is the Report of the National Commission on Obscenity and Pornography. Established in 1967 by Congress in response to widespread complaints by people who objected to receiving unsolicited pornography in the mail, the Commission was to analyze (1) pornography control laws, (2) the extent of pornography distribution, and (3) the effects of pornography on the public, particularly on minors and in relationship to crime and other antisocial behavior and to recommend appropriate legislative and/or administrative action.

Based on a review of the relevant research, the Commission stated (Commission on Obscenity and Pornography, 1970):

> The Commission believes that there is no warrant for continued governmental interference with the full freedom of adults to read, obtain or view whatever such material they wish. Extensive empirical investigation, both by the Commission and by others, provides no evidence that exposure to or use of explicit sexual materials play a significant role in the causation of social or individual harms such as crime, delinquency, sexual or nonsexual deviancy or severe emotional disturbances [p. 58].

There were many critics of the Commission's report. Victor Cline (1974a) carefully reviewed the research data upon which the Commission report was based and concluded that the interpretations were biased in the direction of protecting freedom of speech. Cline points out inaccuracies in the Commission's report of the research, unwarranted conclusions, lack of discrimination between poor and good studies, and failure to report findings indicating a significant relationship between exposure to pornography and either sexual deviance or affiliation with criminal groups.

As a matter of interest, the report of the Pornography Commission was rejected by President Nixon and the U.S. Senate. At the root of the rejection was one of the Commission's recommendations that all existing laws restraining access to explicit sex materials by consenting adults be repealed even though the Commission also recommended stronger legal prohibition against distribution of such materials to minors.

Project on Human Sexual Development

While many have opposed the boycotting strategies of the current anti-TV sex and violence groups, the TV sex issue has lacked a spokesperson defending the free speech issue to the extent demonstrated by the mail pornography issue. The one possible exception is Elizabeth Roberts, head of the Project on Human Sexual Development (PHSD). Founded in 1974 by John D. Rockefeller III and Population Education, Inc., PHSD has been devoted to expanding the public's understanding of human sexuality, including gender identity, sex roles, and sexual behavioir. PHSD regards television as one of the important agents of sexual learning and has held workshops and seminars with TV producers, writers, and network executives to heighten awareness of TV's portrayals of sexuality. Roberts advocates a broad definition of sex when considering the TV sex issue (Roberts & Holt, 1977):

> Human sexuality . . . is expressed in a set of human relationships, meanings, and feelings. Therefore, television's focus on the relationships between people may be far more important and have far more potential impact on the sexual socialization of children and adults than the portrayal of any one particular nude scene, rape theme, or sexual act. We all spend far more time in the social relationships that lead to sexual expression than we do in sexual activity itself.

> There is no right way for television to handle a bedroom scene or a young boy's first love affair. A list of dos and don'ts might reassure public interest groups and seem to make life easier for industry executives. However, that kind of specificity would only perpetuate the public's misunderstanding of televised sexuality by suggesting that it can be conveniently compartmentalized, monitored, and regulated. To simplify either the meaning of sexuality in our lives or on television is only to add to the confusion and fall into the trap of equating sexuality with the number of kisses on prime-time or orgasms in the bedroom.

> Responsible television entertainment does and must deal with issues of sexuality. These issues are central to our humanity and the core of human drama. Through discussion and exploration about such issues as intimacy, love, relatedness, vulnerability, and affection, perhaps the public and the TV industry will come to understand the fullness of human sexuality and television's responsibility to present the diversity of this human experience with honesty and accuracy [p. 351].

Chapter 8
Harnessing Television's Potential

OVERVIEW

Interest in harnessing TV's potential to benefit children and society can be traced to the earliest days of the medium. Crude educational television in the 1950s was transformed by the Corporation for Public Broadcasting (CPB) and other sophisticated organizations into a network of public television stations broadcasting "quality" television for a wide audience as well as specialized programs for children. *Sesame Street*, which is exemplary of such programs, has been shown to have some academic and instructional value, but probably has its greatest influence on advantaged children, who are the ones most likely to watch.

Stimulated in part by the goal of harnessing TV's potential more effectively, researchers in the 1970s began to ask about the factors influencing children's attention to, and comprehension of, television programming. The mid-1970s also saw an unprecedented effort to use television as an active force in the socialization of children. Rooted in early laboratory experiments using simulated "TV programs" (which showed that TV models could increase children's generosity and self-control), researchers looked for instances of prosocial behavior in commercial programs and then demonstrated that exposure to shows "naturally rich" in such examples had discernible effects on child audiences. Of greater significance, perhaps, social scientists and producers collaborated in making children's TV programming with the intention of having specific social effects on the attitudes and behavior of the child audience. Moreover, once made, these programs with a social message were tested during production (formative research) and after broadcast (summative research) to assure that the desired effects were occurring while guarding against possible side effects (e.g., inadvertently triggering a child's aggression or creating an inaccurate stereotype). The results must be considered encouraging. While it is doubtful that any one program can have a dramatic or even a lasting effect for many children, it does appear that heavily saturating entertainment television with models who reflect a consistent set of values could greatly influence children. Whether this is progressive education or a chilling new form of brainwashing, and what, if anything, we will do with TV's great potential power over the young have become the great unanswered questions.

The importance of exploring the "prosocial" effects of television was expressed by Surgeon General William Stewart in his testimony before Senator Pastore when the Surgeon General's Report was launched (U.S. Senate Subcommittee, 1969).

> The knowledge that should emerge from this kind of scientific endeavor will be knowledge aimed at understanding. If television can have a negative effect on children, it can also be a positive stimulus. Although television may have power to incite, it also has the power to enlighten and educate. We must learn more about how to promote this latter capability while we learn how to avoid the hazards of the former [p. 339].

Nevertheless, the emphasis of the Surgeon General's Report and the technical reports behind it was on TV violence. Only the Stein and Friedrich (1972) study included an assessment of the effects of socially desirable content, and even this study addressed the effects of aggressive content as well (see Chapter 4). However, shortly after the completion of the Surgeon General's Report there was a reorientation of priorities.

A survey conducted by Comstock and Lindsey (1975) indicated that researchers were shifting their attention from the antisocial to the prosocial effects of television. Believing that existing research on the effect of TV violence was sufficient to warrant programming changes, many social scientists and funding agents reasoned that if prosocial fare could be shown to draw child audiences, there would be less resistance by the broadcasters to present socially valuable programs.

Two different streams can be identified historically in the effort to put television to positive use in children's development. One stream is through public television and the purposeful development of programs carrying planned educational messages; the other is through commercial television. Our aim in this chapter is to provide an overview of all these efforts to harness TV. Our discussion begins with public educational television in the United States and then turns to efforts to teach academically important skills. Thereafter we consider efforts to use television as a tool in transmitting social attitudes and influencing interpersonal reactions, and finally to examine the hard value issues that such possibilities raise.

U.S. PUBLIC/EDUCATIONAL TELEVISION

The educational potential of television was recognized quite early and was initially believed to be a possible panacea for overcrowded schools, poor teacher training, and teacher shortages. In 1958, an American educator wrote, "Education needs television. . . . Television, we hold, while not the *deus ex machina* to solve the crisis, is one indispensable tool that we can and must use to extricate ourselves from the grave trouble we are in, but of which all too few still seem to be aware" (cited in O'Bryan, 1980, p. 6).

In the United States, educational television developed along two types of broadcast systems. One made use of a closed circuit system in which a lesson is broadcast from a central studio to a number of local schools. O'Bryan (1980) describes these broadcasts as featuring "the ubiquitous big talking face" (p. 7), a teacher standing at a blackboard talking. Clearly missing were both the spontaneity of a live audience and the action of commercial broadcasts. So, despite the novelty of the new medium, it is not surprising that research in the early 1960s did not find any teaching advantages of using televised rather than live teachers (Kumata, 1960; Schramm, 1962). Further, perhaps threatened by being replaced by televised education, teachers resisted wide adoption of instructional television in the classroom. The situation has not changed much since the 1950s. A fortune was spent on TV in the schools, but it has not been used very much and the equipment has grown obsolete.

The second broadcast method involved the transmission of a program from an educational television (ETV) station to the general public, just as it is done by commercial stations. Initial attempts to designate channels exclusively for educational programming were bitterly fought by commercial networks who argued that all of television was their domain. But in 1952 the FCC set aside a number of then almost useless UHF channels for educational purposes.*

By 1959 there were 45 educational stations—some community operated, some university owned, and some operated by school systems. On the average, they were on the air five days per week, almost nine hours a day. An analysis of the content of their offerings revealed the following: (1) 40% credit course use, (2) 13% children's (out of school) viewing and (3) 47% adult (noncourse credit) viewing (National Educational Television and Radio Center, 1960).

In 1959, only 8.5 million homes were capable of receiving an educational station; many were not close enough to a transmitter and others could not receive UHF. Still, assuming multiple viewers in each home, educational television then had a *potential* audience of about 25 million. But a survey by the American Research Bureau revealed that only about 2 million people watched at least one program during a typical week. This small group was found to differ from "the average TV viewer" on several dimensions. They tended to be better educated, to come from higher social strata, to spend less total time viewing, and to be more planful and selective in their viewing habits (Schramm, 1960). One likely reason for the limited viewership of educational television was the poor production quality and unappealing programming which was not far removed from the "big talking face" style.

The first decade of educational television saw the entire enterprise on a

---

*At that time very few TV sets had the capability to receive UHF broadcasts.

financial precipice. But in 1962 federal legislation authorized the expenditure of funds for the construction and equipping of stations, and the Carnegie Commission on Educational Television was established in 1965. The Commission looked to expanding and strengthening educational or "public" television as a way to improved content. In 1967, it issued a report calling for the establishment of a system similar to the British one, but which would finance only educational programming (Carnegie Commission, 1967). It also suggested the formation of a trust fund, derived from a tax on the sale of new television receivers (in Britain there is a yearly tax on all television sets), with recommended funding of about 100 million dollars a year.

The Corporation for Public Broadcasting

Instead, the financing for public television has come from annual congressional appropriations to the Corporation for Public Broadcasting (CPB). (See Table 8.1). Formed by a 1967 Act of Congress, CPB is an autonomous board of 15 members appointed by the President. It is a private, non-profit service agency to local stations, supplying money for program development.* In 1970, CPB created the Public Broadcasting Service (PBS) to manage distribution of national program services. PBS is funded by CPB, federal agencies, foundations, private corporations, and dues from member stations.

In addition to congressional appropriations, there are numerous federal agencies that support educational programming. The Office of Education

Table 8.1. Federal Appropriations to the Corporation for
Public Broadcasting 1969-1982 (in $ millions).

Year	Appropriation
1969	5.0
1970	15.0
1972	35.0
1974	47.8
1976	78.5
1978	119.2
1980	152.0
1982	172.0

Note: Certain program or other special project grants from various federal agencies are not included.

Source: Adapted from Rowland (1980).

*The Public Broadcasting Financing Act (1975) and the Public Telecommunications Financing Act (1978) have provided multi-year federal funding to CPB until 1983.

has been a major source of federal funds. A significant portion of its money has been allocated to Children's Television Workshop and to the Emergency School Aid Act (ESAA), both of which will be discussed later in this chapter. ESAA funding has been specifically devoted to multicultural programming. Production groups compete for funds following the release of an ESAA announcement requesting proposals to produce programs or series addressing a specified cultural group/content area. ESAA awards funds for pilot episodes and makes further funding contingent on demonstrating the effectiveness of the program in achieving its stated goals. Other federal agencies have also supported children's programming (e.g., Bureau of the Handicapped, National Institute for Education, National Endowment for the Arts), with the specific programming supported reflecting the priorities of the funding agency.

While the federal government has provided a substantial share of public broadcasting funds, it is not the only source. According to a CPB report (Lee, 1981), public television's income of $507.7 million in 1979 came from the federal government (25.9%), state governments (25.0%), subscribers (12.2%), state colleges (7.6%), business (10.6%), local governments (7.7%), foundations (3.7%), other colleges (.8%), and other sources (3.5%).

While federal and private funding of public television has increased steadily over the years, the total funding for the system is only about 5% of the revenues of the commercial broadcasters. Further, the discrepancy between the number of dollars available for programming by public and commercial television will be even greater as the Reagan administration reduces appropriations to public service and social/cultural agencies.

What kinds of programs appear on public television? Table 8.2 presents the distribution of public television broadcast hours by type of program, producer, and distributor. It is apparent that the largest proportion of programs are produced by public television stations, that the overwhelming majority of programs are distributed by PBS, and that there is an emphasis on cultural and information/skills programming. Thus "educational" television has evolved into public television, with the latter involving social and cultural as well as traditional academic education.

Who watches public television programming? During a one-month period in 1979, 65.9% of all U.S. TV households tuned to at least one public television program, and the average home tuned to public TV a total of nine and one-half hours (Myrick & Keegan, 1981). However, public TV's rating share during prime time is only about 3%, meaning that 3% of all TV sets are tuned to it (LeRoy, 1980). Public television viewing was highest in the northeast region of the country and in homes with children under six years of age, an income of $20,000 or more, and with adults having four or more years of college. Public TV viewing was lowest among homes in the smallest U.S. counties, in the east central region, and in homes with incomes below

Table 8.2. Percentage Distribution of Public Television Broadcast Hours by Type of Program, Producer, and Distribution.

Type of Programs	Percent of all Broadcast Hours
Information/Skills	23.6
Cultural	22.1
Sesame Street/Electric Company	16.1
Instructional Television	14.9
News/Public Affairs	11.0
General Children's	8.7
Other	5.3
PRODUCER	
Public Television Station	52.2
Children's Television Workshop	16.8
Foreign/Co-Production	9.1
Local	5.7
Independent	5.3
Other	8.9
DISTRIBUTOR	
PBS	71.6
Local	7.4
Regional Network	5.4
Other	15.6

Source: Adapted from Lee (1981) for Fiscal Year 1978.

$10,000 per year. Public television usage generally increases as level of education and income rise (Myrick & Keegan, 1981).

In 1968, one year after the CPB was established, the Children's Television Workshop (CTW) was created from the funds of both public and private agencies. (The Carnegie Corporation, Ford Foundation, U.S. Office of Education, U.S. Office of Economic Opportunity, and the National Institute of Child Health and Human Development were all involved). CTW's first program, *Sesame Street*, became the world's most famous and popular children's TV series.*

Sesame Street

Educators have long recognized the importance of preschool experiences for later educational development. But four-fifths of our three- and four-year-olds and one-quarter of our five-year-olds do not attend school. *Sesame*

Sesame Street has been broadcast in English in over 40 countries including Africa, Australia, Canada, the Caribbean, Europe, and the Far East. In another 19 countries, the programs are broadcast in foreign-language adaptations (e.g., French, Spanish, German).

Street was developed to provide preschool experiences at home. CTW's goal was to telecast a daily program that would both entertain and foster intellectual and cultural development (Ball & Bogatz, 1970).

Planning and formative research. Joan Ganz Cooney and Lloyd Morrisett, planners and parents of Children's Television Workshop and *Sesame Street* obtained $8 million in initial funding and two years in lead time. Cooney and Morrisett then brought in Harvard's prominent educational psychologist, Professor Gerald Lesser, to chair a top-notch, hardworking advisory panel. Dr. Edward Palmer was given a fully equipped lab in New York and a free hand to research and criticize production efforts, and regulars such as Jim Henson's muppets, Kermit the Frog, Big Bird, and the infamous Cookie Monster, were accompanied by guests of the stature of James Earl Jones and the popularity of Batman and Robin. At the business and technical level, a prestigious public relations firm was retained, and hard-headed executives were drawn in to criticize, counsel, and sell *Sesame Street* even before the first show was produced. To satisfy the requirements of the Office of Education and various foundations who footed the bill, the Educational Testing Service (ETS) was commissioned to do evaluations of how well the program worked.

A series of planning seminars was held by experts in child development, preschool education, and television production. Out of these meetings came ideas for many of the basic instructional methods and ways of presenting materials. The planning phase went even further. Viewing preferences of youngsters were examined, and the attention-holding power of videotaped materials was assessed by playing them in competition with potential distractors. In 1969, *Sesame Street* was on the air, combining attention-holding tactics (e.g., fast movement, humor, slapstick, and animation) with a carefully planned educational curriculum designed to foster skills such as recognition of the letters of the alphabet, recognition of the numbers 1 through 10, simple counting ability, vocabulary, and the like.

Summative research. The first year's summative research studies were conducted in five widely separated areas of the country. Children were assigned either to a control condition or a viewing condition, involving home or nursery school viewing. In the case of home viewers, parents were told about *Sesame Street*, given publicity material about the program, and visited each week by members of the research team. The control subjects did not receive these treatments. In the school situation the experimental classrooms received two television sets, while control classes did not. According to Ball and Bogatz:

> It was generally understood that the teachers of the viewing classes would use the sets to have their pupils view *Sesame Street* but that the degree to which they

did so, and the way *Sesame Street* was used in the classroom, was their prerogative [p. 19].

In both school and home samples, the experimental treatment lasted about
six months. Altogether, about 950 children participated in all phases of the
study.

Each child was both pretested and posttested. The tests were designed to
measure the specific learning goals; thus, there were subtests on body parts,
letters, numbers, forms, matching, relationships, sorting, and classification. An example is shown in Fig. 8.1.

Here are pictures of shoes. Which picture doesn't belong with the others?
Which is different from the others?

Fig. 8.1. Sample item from the tests given to children to assess the effects of *Sesame
Street*.

Source: Ball & Bogatz (1970), courtesy of Children's Television Workshop.

Parents were also interviewed, both before and after the study, about their attitude toward education, the child's viewing habits, and the "intellectual climate" in the home (e.g., how many books does the family own?).

Ball and Bogatz analyzed their data in several ways. Besides examining a total score and then separate subtest scores, they also looked at the whole sample and then subsets of children.

The original plan to compare viewers to nonviewers turned out to be infeasible because most of the subjects watched at least occasionally. Instead, the sample was divided into quartiles (a quartile contains 25% of the sample) on the basis of amount of viewing. Q_1 rarely watched Sesame Street; Q_2 watched two or three times a week; Q_3 about four or five times a week; and Q_4 more than five times. Because the different quartiles differed in original levels of proficiency on the pretest, the investigators decided to assess change scores, that is, the average differences between pretests and posttests. As Fig. 8.2a. indicates, the more that children watched the program, the more they tended to improve on the total score.

When the total score was broken down, it was clear that the effects of viewing held for all eight major subtests. The gains on some items were quite impressive; alphabet recitation, for example, on which the various groups were about equal at the beginning, had improved dramatically among children who watched Sesame Street regularly. (See Fig. 8.2b.)

Of particular interest in considering the gains in specific subtests were scores on items and skills not directly taught on Sesame Street. For example, Sesame Street apparently had some effect on reading skill and ability to write one's first name, both of which are important for school performance. (See Fig. 8.2c.) For disadvantaged children, the six items in the reading subscale were significantly affected by amount of viewing despite the fact that reading words was not a Sesame Street goal, nor was it directly taught on the show.

A later investigation provided some additional information (Bogatz & Ball, 1972). By this time, Sesame Street itself had changed somewhat; for example, practice in sight-reading a 20-word vocabulary of common words and simple skills in Spanish had been introduced. Evaluation changed to incorporate these expanded goals, but the major focus of the tests was the same. Two other types of measures were also added: questions designed to examine attitudes toward race, school, and other people, and teacher rankings of school readiness at the beginning and end of the school year.

A new sample of children was selected in cities where Sesame Street had not been available the first year. This sample was restricted to urban disadvantaged children. The investigators also followed up 283 of the disadvantaged children studied during the first year. About half of these children had started in nursery school, kindergarten, or first grade.

The results essentially replicated those of the first year study—children

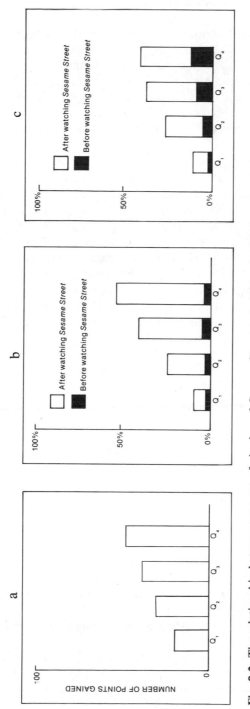

Fig. 8.2. The relationship between amount of viewing of *Sesame Street* and children's abilities.
a. Improvement in total test scores for children grouped into different quartiles according to amount of viewing.
b. Percentage of children who recited the alphabet correctly, grouped according to quartiles of amount of viewing.
c. Percentage of children who wrote their first names correctly, grouped according to quartiles of amount of viewing.
Source: Ball and Bogatz, 1970, courtesy of Children's Television Workshop.

who viewed *Sesame Street* improved more than children who did not. The follow-up study also revealed that heavy viewers were rated by teachers as better prepared for school than low viewers and adapted well to the school situation. The children who viewed frequently continued to outgain low viewers, particularly on the items introduced during the second year of the program. The show influenced other behaviors as well; viewers scored significantly higher on measures of attitudes toward school and toward people of other races.

Sesame Street revisited. Subsequent work casts some doubt as to whether *Sesame Street* was as effective as had been supposed. In the book *Sesame Street Revisited*, Thomas Cook and his associates (1975) claim that in reality rather slight (though statistically significant) increases were actually produced by *Sesame Street*, and note that an equal amount of money spent in other ways might have greater educational impact on children. Even more critical, Cook and his associates suggest the possibility that broadcasting *Sesame Street* may widen rather than narrow the gap between the advantaged and the disadvantaged child. In the research conducted by ETS (described above) participating families were stimulated to watch *Sesame Street* by a variety of incentives provided by the experimenters. In naturally occurring situations with the absence of such incentives, it appears that children in advantaged families will be considerably more likely to watch *Sesame Street* than those in disadvantaged families, and as a result any gap between the groups could be widened. This is both unfortunate and ironic because an apparent goal of *Sesame Street* was to narrow the gap. Joan Cooney had said in her original proposal that the general aim of *Sesame Street* was "to promote the intellectual and cultural growth of preschoolers, particularly disadvantaged preschoolers," and in her conclusion she referred to "the national demand that we give the disadvantaged a fair chance at the beginning."

Electric Company

In 1970, a team from the Children's Television Workshop began planning a program aimed specifically at reading skills. As with *Sesame Street*, *Electric Company* grew out of a series of consultations with experts, this time in the area of reading. Prior to the first appearance of one of the shows, various reading curricula had been evaluated and experimental programs pretested (Fowles, 1971).

In the fall of 1971 the series began with a snappy format. Well-known personalities such as Bill Cosby frequented the show and heavy use was made of animation. The curriculum, directed primarily at second-graders, involved what is termed sound-symbol analysis of the printed word. Children were taught the correspondence between letters (and combinations of letters) and sounds to enable them to decode words. Reading for meaning, using the context of the material, and syntax were also taught. (See Figure 8.3.)

The degree of *Electric Company's* success was evaluated using the same research design and researchers as that for *Sesame Street* (Ball & Bogatz, 1973). On a reading test battery designed specifically for the program by Educational Testing Service, it was found that the first through fourth grade children who viewed *Electric Company* in school attained significantly higher scores than the nonviewers. However, the effect of home viewing seemed to be negligible. No significant effects were found nor did the experimental group, which was encouraged to watch the program, watch significantly more than did the controls. So, it is likely that the effects of the program were enhanced by the teacher and curriculum reinforcement of the TV lessons in the school environment.

Electric Company has earned two Emmys and several other prestigious awards. Within two months of the series premiere, it was used in close to a fourth of the nation's elementary schools, and by the second season in 35% of the elementary schools (Children's Television Workshop, 1976). Furthermore, it is a real "bargain" in terms of its costs: While a typical Saturday morning commercial program costs about $70,000 to produce, an average episode of *Electric Company* only costs about $32,000.

3-2-1 Contact

In 1977, the Children's Television Workshop began to explore the potential of television to motivate children's interest in science and technology. Funded by the National Science Foundation, Department of Education, United Technologies Corporation, Corporation for Public Broadcasting, and CTW, the series of 65 half-hour programs was broadcast   beginning in January 1980. Like *Sesame Street* and *Electric Company, 3-2-1 Contact* was developed out of a collaboration between producers, formative researchers, and content experts. The series was geared toward eight-to twelve-year-olds, and its goals were (1) "to help children experience the joy of scientific exploration," (2) "to help children become familiar with various styles of scientific thinking," and (3) "to help children, with a special appeal to girls and minorities, to recognize science and technology as open to their participation" (Children's Television Workshop, 1980). During its first six weeks of broadcast, the show was seen in more than 15 million homes. Research has yet to determine the degree to which the series achieves its stated goals.

Fig. 8.3. Learning to position adverbs. *The Electric Company* method.
Source: Courtesy of Children's Television Workshop.

HOW CHILDREN LEARN FROM TELEVISION

In the early years of television research, little attention was given to analyzing the process of watching or learning from television. Most investigators relied loosely on social learning theory, which proved sufficient to guide studies of TV violence. (See Chapters 4 and 5.) But after the Surgeon General's Report, it was apparent that much was still unknown about how children learn from television. The demonstrations by CTW of television's positive potential in developing children's academic skills inspired an interest in finding out how to make TV a more effective teacher. Therefore, out of an interest to ultimately enhance the effectiveness of educational and social programming, research emerged on how children attend to and understand television.

Research on children's attention to television

CTW's research during the formative stages of *Sesame Street* was largely devoted to capturing children's attention. Children were shown segments of the program while a series of slides next to the TV monitor were flashed as a distractor. Segments were modified or eliminated based on their power to hold children's attention (Lesser, 1974).

Anderson and his colleagues (Anderson & Levin, 1976; Levin & Anderson, 1976) refined the procedure used for *Sesame Street* and investigated the attention-drawing power of a wide range of program characteristics. Preschool children between one and four years of age watched *Sesame Street* segments, *Misterogers' Neighborhood*, or general audience programs (e.g., *Gilligan's Island*) in a laboratory/den setting with natural distractors (toys, books, etc.). Anderson and Levin surreptitiously monitored the child's pattern of looking/not looking at the TV screen and found several program attributes that were associated with increased attention levels: presence of women, children, puppets, peculiar voices, auditory changes, animation, movement, camera cuts, lively music, laughing, applause, rhyming, repetition, and alliteration. Attributes that tended to decrease attention are presence of men, extended zooms and pans, animals, inactivity, and still drawings. Huston-Stein and Wright (1979) aptly described the practical aims of pursuing this line of research:

> If one could identify the formal properties that are effective in attracting and holding child audiences, those features could be used to make educational and prosocial television maximally effective. Further, if such features could be separated from objectionable content, particularly violence, then they might be used by commercial producers to make less violent programs that could survive the ratings wars [p. 24].

Huston-Stein and her colleagues (Huston-Stein, Fox, Greer, Watkins, & Whitaker, 1978) argued that broadcasters use violence to attract children's attention, but that high action in the absence of violent content could perhaps do equally well. These researchers compared preschoolers' attention to programs that were (1) high in action and violence, (2) high in action but low in violence, and (3) low in both action and violence. They found that the form was more important than the content in affecting the children's attention; the youngsters were as attentive to the high action/low violent program as they were to the high action/high violence one. However, the high action/low violence program also stimulated as much aggressive behavior in a subsequent free play situation as the high action/high violence program. This supports an instigation-arousal theory of aggression (See Chapter 3), and unfortunately casts doubt on the value of developing high action/low violence fare.

Aside from program attributes, Anderson explored other aspects affecting children's attention to television. He and his colleagues (Anderson, 1977; Anderson, Alwitt, Lorch, & Levin, 1979) have discovered that children between one and five years of age tend to "lock-in" to what they are watching. Calculating the probability of a child's continued attending to the screen, Anderson has found that the longer the child had been looking at the screen, the greater the probability that he/she will continue to look. Similarly, the longer the child did not look at the TV screen, the less likely the child was to start looking. The term *attentional inertia* was coined by Anderson to describe this pattern of attention.

Research on children's comprehension of television

Much of the research on children's television comprehension has been conducted by Andrew Collins and his colleagues. The research is a series of studies examining how aspects of comprehension change with age. Collins has documented that young children retain surprisingly little information that is essential or central to the presented plot, and the amount retained increases with age (Collins, 1970; Collins, Wellman, Keniston, & Westby, 1978; Newcomb & Collins, 1979). Second and third graders remember only about 65% of the essential content (as judged by adults), whereas eighth graders recall 90% or more of the central content. Part of the younger child's difficulty seems to be an inability to discriminate between plot-important (central) and plot-irrelevant (peripheral) content for memory encoding. As children grow older, central content accounts for an increasing proportion of what they recall (Collins, 1970; Collins et al., 1978). There is also an age-related improvement in ability to correctly infer TV events and relationships that are implied. Rather than being due to the fact that younger children recall less, this relationship holds even when the younger subjects recall the explicit content necessary to make the inference (Collins et al., 1978; Newcomb & Collins, 1979).

A study by Newcomb and Collins (1979) suggests that part of the age differences in comprehension is due to the lesser social knowledge that the younger child brings to the viewing situation. Lower and middle socioeconomic status children in the second, fifth, and eighth grades were shown a program either with middle class or lower class characters. For the second graders, comprehension was significantly better when the program characters' class matched that of the subject, whereas both versions were equally well understood by the two older groups. The younger children's comprehension was hampered by limited social knowledge, whereas this was not the case for the older children.

The link between attention and comprehensibility

A study by Calvert, Watkins, Wright, and Huston-Stein (1979) illustrates the practical link between attention-getting formal features and comprehensibility. These researchers compared children's recall of program material that was presented with salient formal features (action, sound effects, or visual special effects) versus those low in salience (verbal dialogue). The essential (or central) content was better recalled when it was presented with highly salient formal features, especially for kindergarteners, the youngest subjects. The clear implication to the producers of children's programs containing cognitive or social lessons is that the valuable lessons should be highlighted using audio and visual techniques.

In another series of experiments, Anderson and his colleagues (Anderson, Lorch, Field, & Sanders, 1979) found that the comprehensibility of the TV content is an important determinant of children's visual attention to it. A *Sesame Street* program that contained auditory distortions was poorly attended to despite the presence of visual attributes that are associated with high attention levels. Anderson explains children's viewing process as follows. Through watching television, children learn that certain cues are present when they understand the program content, and when these cues are missing or distorted they are most likely not to attend to the screen. Anderson's is thus a more complex interpretation of children's attention to television than that described by social learning theory (Chapter 3). Rather than a simple process of capturing children's attention as a prerequisite to comprehension, Anderson's explanation is reciprocal so that comprehensibility becomes an important determinant of attention.

According to Salomon (1976), some of the age-related increases in the comprehension of television content are most likely attributable to learning the formal features or media "codes" of television. Salomon views media techniques as representing certain mental skills. For example, zooming in and out represents the skill of relating parts to a whole, and camera cuts of angles of an object represent the skill of taking different perspectives. Having mastery of such media codes enhances the viewer's comprehension of the actual content presented, and extensive exposure to these codes can improve the corresponding mental skills. In Salomon's words:

> It is the understanding of this code which requires particular cognitive skills for extracting and processing the message content. When the cognitive skills used to comprehend particular types of media messages gradually improve and can be *generalized* to other types of stimuli, it is possible to speak of "skill mastery" through exposure to the media [pp. 138–139].

Salomon's (1976, 1979) research on *Sesame Street* with Israeli and American children supports his theory that mastery of the media codes increases both with age and experience with the medium, that exposure to such codes can improve the corresponding mental skills, and that such mastery enhances the learning of the television content.

SOCIALIZATION THROUGH TELEVISION

We now come to the last and most difficult questions to be raised in this book. Can—and should—television be used purposely to cultivate and foster desirable or "prosocial" ways of thinking and acting? It is to these questions that the present section is devoted. Our discussion begins with a closer look at the term prosocial, which we have already used on several occasions.

Defining what is meant by prosocial

Wispé (1972) defined the behaviors encompassed by the term "prosocial":

> "Altruism" refers to a regard for the interest of others without concern for one's self interest. "Sympathy" refers to a concern with, or a sharing of, the pain or sadness of another person, or even an animal. . . . "Cooperation" is the willingness and ability to work with others, usually but not always for a common benefit. "Helping" refers to the giving of assistance or aid toward a definite object or end. "Aid" usually refers to providing what is needed to accomplish a definite end. And "donating" refers to the action of making a gift or giving a contribution, usually to a charity [p. 4].

Rushton (1979) defined prosocial as "that which is socially desirable and which in some way benefits another person or society at large" (p. 323). He included four categories of behavior: altruistic behaviors (including generosity, helping, and cooperation), friendly behavior, self-control behaviors (including delaying gratification and resisting temptation), and fear diminution.

Measuring prosocial television content. We saw in our discussion of the effects of TV violence that measurement of the amount and type of aggressive and antisocial content of television played an important role for both research and public policy discussions. Similarly, the new interest in prosocial effects created the need to identify and measure prosocial content.

The first step was accomplished in 1972 with the development of a coding and scoring system (Davidson & Neale, 1974; Rubinstein, Liebert, Neale, & Poulos, 1974). Drawing largely on the previous psychological investigations of prosocial behavior, the authors named and explicitly defined seven categories of behavior that are generally socially valued (altruism, control of aggressive impulses, delay of gratification, explaining the feelings of self and others, reparation for bad behavior, resistance to temptation, and sympathy). Each of these behaviors is defined in Table 8.3. The system has been used in several investigations of prosocial content in American programming.

In the most extensive analysis, 300 prime-time, afternoon, and cartoon programs were analyzed for prosocial content (Liebert & Poulos, 1975). The researchers found considerable variability in the frequency of the various prosocial categories. For instance, whereas there was an average of about eleven altruistic acts and six sympathetic behaviors per hour of programming, control of aggressive impulses and resistance to temptation appeared less than once an hour. These frequencies of prosocial behavior are

Table 8.3. Definitions of Prosocial Behaviors.

Altruism—consists of sharing, helping, and cooperation involving humans or animals.

Control of aggressive impulses—involves nonaggressive acts or statements which serve to eliminate or prevent aggression by self or others towards humans or animals.

Delay of gratification/task persistence—consists of the related acts of delay of gratification and task persistence, expressed either nonverbally or verbally.

Explaining feelings of self or others—consists of statements to another person(s) explaining the feelings, thinking, or action of self or others with the intent of effective positive outcome, including increasing the understanding of others, resolving strife, smoothing out difficulties, or reassuring someone.

Reparation for bad behavior—refers to behavior which is clearly intended as reparation for an act seen as a wrong-doing committed by the person himself.

Resistance to temptation—refers to withstanding the temptation to engage in behaviors generally prohibited by society (e.g., stealing), which may be prohibited in the program explicitly or implicitly.

Sympathy—is a verbal or behavioral expression of concern for others and their problems.

Source: Adapted from Rubinstein, Liebert, Neale, & Poulos, 1974.

similar to those obtained in a later analysis of children's Saturday morning programming. Here, Poulos, Harvey, and Liebert (1976) found about 13 altruistic acts and five sympathetic responses per hour, and almost a complete absence of control of aggressive impulses. Overall, it is clear that in both adult- and child-oriented programs, viewers are exposed to a fair number of prosocial interpersonal behaviors, but only infrequent displays of self-control behaviors.

Aside from knowing the amount of socially desirable behavior shown on TV, it is important to know where these behaviors are performed. Certainly context factors should influence the impact of prosocial actions on the viewer. In a study of 100 diverse entertainment programs, Sprafkin, Rubinstein, and Stone (1977) found that prosocial behaviors appeared most frequently in situation comedies and dramas and least often in crime adventures. Harvey, Sprafkin, and Rubinstein (1979) also found this pattern for prime-time programs.

Prosocial TV effects: Early simulation studies

Paralleling developments in research on antisocial TV effects, research on the prosocial effects of television has its roots in early modeling studies inspired by social learning theory. All these studies used "home made" videotapes shown to children on a television screen.

Sharing. The value placed by society on sharing is clearly shown in the adage that it is more blessed to give than to receive. But sharing is not innately built into the human organism, as any parent of a two year old can testify. It must be taught in the manner in which society attempts to teach all its values, by providing direct instruction and appropriate examples.

Bryan and Walbek (1970) investigated the effects of both these teaching techniques through simulated television programs on children's sharing. In one study, third and fourth grade youngsters were taken individually to a research trailer and permitted to play a bowling game for ten trials. The game was rigged so that all the children obtained high scores and thus "won" a gift certificate which could be exchanged for money or prizes. The children were informed that they could donate their winnings to the March of Dimes if they wished. After each child played the game for a while, he or she saw a TV program of another child of the same sex playing the game. The other child served as a model who was either generous, donating one-third of his/her winnings, or selfish, donating none. For two groups, the model also made statements about sharing, preaching either greed or generosity, while in the third no such statements were made. After viewing the program, each child played the game again and was given the opportunity to share in private. This test of prosocial behavior revealed that children who saw a charitable television model were significantly more likely to share than those who saw a greedy one, regardless of the nature of the preaching.

Resistance to temptation. In another early study using simulated television, Stein and Bryan (1972) demonstrated that a televised model also can influence children's resistance to temptation. Third and fourth grade girls viewed a sequence that showed a peer model playing a bowling game; half of the subjects saw a skilled model who won often, while the other half saw an unskilled model who won less frequently. In either case, the model was instructed to reward herself, according to a stringent rule, by taking a stack of nickels each time she obtained a certain high score.

The children were subdivided into four groups according to the model's preaching and practicing of the rule. Either she preached and practiced rule adherence, preached and practiced rule breaking, or was inconsistent in what she said and did. Then each child played the game herself. The measure of rule adherence was the number of nickels the child took on non-winning trials. Those who viewed a model who both preached and practiced rule adherence followed the stringent self-reward rule and thus successfully resisted temptation more than those who saw a model who preached and practiced transgression. Children who viewed an inconsistent model broke the rule the most.

Wolf (1972) also investigated the effects of televised models on resistance to temptation. He exposed five- seven-, and nine-year old boys to a television peer model who either said he was going to follow the rule not to play with certain toys or said he was going to break the rule. Boys who saw the deviant model played with the forbidden toys more than those exposed to a conforming model or no model. Boys who saw the obedient exemplar played with the toys less than subjects who saw no model. Thus the television model increased behavior like his own, regardless of what he did.

Demonstration of prosocial effects of existing shows

A major limitation of the early laboratory studies we have considered so far is that very few children would choose to watch any of the television sequences they employed, if given a choice between these sequences and "real television." So the next step was to determine whether existing shows had prosocial effects.

Stein and Friedrich studies. The first series tested was *Misterogers' Neighborhood*, a program that deliberately contains social lessons. In an investigation described in Chapter 4, Stein and Friedrich (1972) observed preschoolers' naturally occurring behavior during a four-week period in a nursery school setting both before and after exposing them to one of three conditions—*Misterogers' Neighborhood* which was the prosocial condition, *Batman* and *Superman* which was the aggressive condition, or neutral films. Children who watched the prosocial programs generally showed increases in self-control relative to those exposed to the aggressive or neutral fare. Further, lower socioeconomic children who saw *Misterogers' Neighborhood* also showed an increase in prosocial interpersonal behaviors.

In a later study, Friedrich and Stein (1975) examined the effect of providing verbal labeling and role-playing training after showing episodes from *Misterogers' Neighborhood* to kindergarten youngsters. They found that subsequent to viewing, children exposed to *Misterogers' Neighborhood* could correctly answer more questions about prosocial behavior, spontaneously verbalized more prosocial phrases, and were more likely to help another child than were children who saw neutral films. Furthermore, exposure to the prosocial program plus role playing resulted in the most helping.

Like *Sesame Street*, *Misterogers' Neighborhood* was designed for public television. Though millions of children may watch one or another public television show in a given week, public television reaches quite a small audience, composed mainly of the children of professional and upper managerial class parents.

So the next question was to ask whether *commercial* series, as broadcast, can have measurable prosocial effects. Several studies done over the past decade suggest that the answer is "yes."

Network efforts. A simple survey conducted by CBS (CBS, 1974) of over 700 children showed that about 90% were able to verbalize at least one prosocial message from specific episodes of the animated series *Fat Albert and the Cosby Kids*; widely cited messages were the importance of being kind to friends in trouble, being honest, and valuing property. Similar results were later reported for four other CBS Saturday morning programs: *The Harlem Globetrotters Popcorn Machine*, *U.S. of Archie*, *Shazam*, and *Isis* (CBS, 1977).

Squire D. Rushnell, vice-president of children's and early-morning programs for ABC, points out that since the early 1970s, each of the networks named vice-presidents in charge of children's programming exclusively and introduced inserts and programs with prosocial themes (Rushnell, 1981). For example, CBS consulted with educators and child psychologists to develop *Fat Albert and the Cosby Kids*. In addition, it created *Festival of Lively Arts for Young People* (specials on aspects of the arts), *In the News* (two-minute news stories written for children and inserted during program breaks), and *30 Minutes* (based on *60 Minutes*). ABC introduced high quality drama for children in *ABC Afterschool Specials* and educational messages in *Schoolhouse Rock*, *Grammar Rock*, *America Rock*, *Science Rock*, and *Body Rock*. NBC introduced *GO*, an informative live action Saturday morning program and *Special Treats*, after school dramas for children. Research has yet to determine how these programs affect children's behaviors and attitudes.

Sprafkin, Liebert, and Poulos (1975). In this study, we selected for our principal treatments two programs from the *Lassie* series that were similar in many ways (characters, setting, written for same audience). The critical difference was that one had a highly dramatic scene in which Jeff, the lead child character, risks his life to save a puppy. We also picked a noncanine family comedy episode from *The Brady Bunch*. We wanted to see whether children exposed to the prosocial *Lassie* program would be more willing to help than those shown either of two control programs. As a first assessment of prosocial influences from entertainment programs, we wanted to create the most sensitive or conservative assessment situation, and therefore employed a behavioral test which approximated that presented in the program. Since we couldn't have the children show their willingness to help a puppy in distress by risking their lives like Jeff did in the film, we constructed a situation in which they would have to make a choice between alerting adults that animals needed help or earning points toward prizes. We showed first grade children one of the three programs and then put them in the situation of having to choose between sacrifice and self-interest in the absence of any adults. As Figure 8.4 shows, children in the prosocial *Lassie* condition were more willing to help than those in either the neutral *Lassie* or *Brady Bunch* control conditions, which did not differ from each other. So, after seeing a boy sacrifice for an animal, the children were likely to do the same.

Collins and Getz (1976). Collins and Getz tested the effect of alternative versions of an action-adventure program. The half-hour program that had appeared on TV (*Mod Squad*) was edited for the study so that in one version the protagonist constructively coped with an interpersonal conflict, and in the other version he responded aggressively. Fourth, seventh, and tenth graders who saw one of these programs or a neutral program were subsequently faced with an adaptation of the "Help-Hurt game" which was previously used by Liebert and Baron (1972) and described in Chapter 4. It was found that the children who viewed the constructive coping model responded in a more helpful manner to a peer who was working on a task in another room than children in the other two conditions.

Baran, Chase, and Courtright (1979). Baran, Chase, and Courtright demonstrated prosocial effects with a *Waltons* episode which modeled a cooperative problem-solving solution to a conflict situation. Second and third grade children who viewed the cooperative program subsequently behaved more cooperatively in a game situation than those who saw either a control

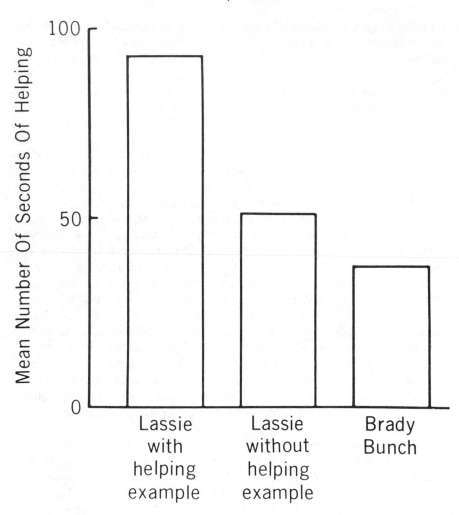

Fig. 8.4. Duration of children's helping in the Sprafkin, Liebert, & Poulos (1975) study.

"program" (a videotape which presented noncooperative behavior) or no program at all.

A field correlational study of the effects of prosocial TV. All prosocial television content appears in the larger context of programming which is characterized by violence and social stereotypes. Whether prosocial effects can be obtained in this "contaminated" experience of regular home viewing is unclear. Sprafkin and Rubinstein (1979) conducted a field correlational study to determine whether children who were exposed to a high concentration of prosocial programming behaved more "prosocially" in their school environment than children with lower exposure to such content. While having highly prosocial favorite TV programs tended to be associated with high levels of prosocial behavior in school, the strength of the relationship was significant but quite weak after controlling for sex, grade, socioeconomic status, and academic achievement ($r = +.12$).

Selective use of existing prosocial programs for specialized audiences. Once material has been created for television, it can be used selectively to reach specialized audiences for which it may be particularly appropriate or helpful. We will consider two examples.

Elias (1979) excerpted segments from the *Inside/Out* TV series (developed by the Agency for Instructional Television) dealing with such topics as peer pressure and expressing one's feelings. Fifty-two boys between seven and fifteen years old living in a residential treatment center for emotionally disturbed children were shown the *Inside/Out* segments twice weekly for five consecutive weeks. Each showing was followed by a group discussion which highlighted problem solving strategies and focused on aspects of the program content. A control group of fifty-seven boys did not see any special programs. Based on a sociometric measure and unobtrusive behavioral observations of boys in the two groups, it was found that the boys who saw the *Inside/Out* segments showed increased positive behaviors, decreased social isolation, and greater popularity relative to the control group.

A series of studies by Sprafkin, Rubinstein, and associates show the extent of TV use in institutional settings for emotionally disturbed children and the positive potential of using regularly broadcast prosocial programming to enhance the social functioning of this population. In an interview study of the staff of a state treatment facility for disturbed children, Rubinstein et al. (1977) found that the behaviorally disturbed children were reported to watch television about three and one-half hours per day, and overall the ward personnel believed that television viewing affected most of the children. Ninety-six percent of the respondents reported having observed various behaviors (both prosocial and antisocial) which appeared to be provoked by what the children had seen on television. Particularly noted was the children's frequent imitation of various super-heroes seen on TV. In a related study (Kochnower et al., 1978) in which the child residents were interviewed, the pervasive influence of television in this setting was corroborated, and it was further learned that the youngsters preferred violence-laden programs (such as cartoons and super-hero action shows) over other program types.

Clearly, the youngsters' normal TV viewing would not result in their being exposed to many prosocial themes. Accordingly, the researchers (Sprafkin & Rubinstein, 1982) designed a study which involved constructing a prosocial TV diet containing programs with frequent instances of prosocial behaviors and assessing its influence relative to a control TV diet composed of programs representative of the youngsters' typical viewing fare. The study also compared the effects of the two diets with and without a postviewing discussion which evaluated the pro- and anti-social behaviors contained in the programs, encouraging the former and discouraging the latter.

The four treatments (prosocial vs. control TV diet and with vs. without discussion) were rotated through four wards of the residential treatment center for disturbed children over a period of approximately one year. Each treatment phase involved (1) one week of observing the youngsters' social behavior, (2) two weeks of watching the ten programs (either prosocial or control) with or without the discussion, and (3) one week of follow-up behavioral observations. The ten programs in the prosocial diet were previously shown on television and were selected on the basis of their prosocial content and suitability for the age group studied (average age was 14 years). The kinds of themes dealt with in the final prosocial diet were: the benefits of helping others, compromising when there is a conflict, considering other peoples' feelings, cooperating with teachers, and problems with stealing and playing practical jokes. The half-hour series used included situation comedies (*Brady Bunch*), dramas (*Room 222*), and cartoons (*Fat Albert and the Cosby Kids*). The control diet was selected on the basis of a survey of the TV viewing habits and preferences of the youngsters on the four wards. The final diet was composed of the ten most popular series which included cartoons (*The Flintstones*) and situation comedies (*Sanford and Son*). Results showed that altruistic behaviors increased for the children exposed to the prosocial TV diet relative to those who saw the control TV diet. This facilitation of altruism was more pronounced for the youngsters who were above average on baseline physical aggression. Verbal aggression (e.g., threats, teases, name-calling) and aggression toward objects decreased for youngsters exposed to the prosocial TV diet without discussion, while both behaviors increased if the diet was followed by a discussion. Symbolic aggression (use of noncontact and nonverbal aggressive behaviors, including chasing and threatening gestures) decreased for the initially physically aggressive youngsters who were exposed to the prosocial TV diet relative to the other groups. For reasons perhaps unique to this population, the discussion following the prosocial program showings appeared to be at best ineffective and at worst detrimental in facilitating prosocial and reducing antisocial behavior. The researchers reasoned that the rather "tough" image youngsters reacted against the moralistic tone of the prosocial discussion. However, a promising first step has been taken in determining that a prosocial TV diet can be used as a therapeutic tool for shaping prosocial behavior in the institutionalized child.

Programs designed to have specific social effects

Shortly after the Surgeon General's Report there began an unprecedented effort to consciously and purposely develop TV programs for children that would have specific social effects.

Countering stereotypes and fostering intergroup goodwill. A major aim of many consciously "prosocial" programs for children is to counter stereotypes and foster intergroup goodwill. *Sesame Street* pioneered this type of social education in American television, especially by its systematic portrayal of Blacks and Hispanics in an almost exclusively positive light. Bogatz and Ball's (1972) findings suggest that exposure to *Sesame Street* makes children's attitudes toward these groups more favorable. Likewise exposure to the *Big Blue Marble*, which was designed to encourage international awareness, caused American youngsters in the fourth through sixth grades to perceive people around the world as being more similar to one another and children in other countries as happier, healthier, and better off than they had before viewing the program (Roberts et al., 1974). Finally, *Vegetable Soup*, which presents a favorable picture of many ethnic groups, was found to make child viewers between six and ten years of age more accepting of children of different races and to more strongly identify with their own racial/ethnic group (Mays, Henderson, Seidman, & Steiner, 1975).

An example of how television has been used to improve children's sex role attitudes is the *Freestyle* TV series. The program was funded in 1975 by the National Institute of Education ($4 million) in response to statistics indicating that only a small proportion of females were training for careers outside the home (Johnston, Ettema, & Davidson, 1980):

> The Career Awareness Division of NIE saw a partial remedy for this problem in a television intervention aimed at 9–12 year olds. Called the TV Career Awareness Project, the product would be a carefully articulated package designed to influence the attitudes and behaviors of this age group in a way that would reduce sex-role stereotypes and expand the "career awareness" of children, especially girls, in non-traditional ways. The task was to be accomplished by focusing on non-traditional possibilities in the 9–12 year old's own world, an approach that would distinguish it from more typical career education programs that focus on adult occupations. Its purpose would be to have children relate non-traditional childhood interests to educational, and ultimately to occupational choices [p. 159].

Based on attitude questionnaires administered before and after viewing the 13 episodes, *Freestyle* was shown to be successful in making boys more

accepting of girls engaging in mechanical activities, football, and basketball; girls increased their interest in mechanical activities, football, and
basketball (see Figure 8.5); boys and girls became more accepting of boys
doing traditional female activities (caring for younger children, helping
around the house, and assisting sick and old people); boys and girls became
more approving of men and women having non-traditional jobs (e.g.,
women as mechanics, truck drivers, or engineers; men as nurses or secre-
taries); and boys' and girls' perceptions of appropriate male and female
family roles (e.g., child care, cooking, home repair) became less traditional.

Selling cooperation to children. In 1975 we published an article entitled,
"Selling Cooperation to Children" which reported our involvement in an effort to use 30-second TV spot messages as "commercials" for cooperation.
The project was conceived by Ben Logan, who worked with an agency of
The United Methodist Church concerned with media. The agency was originally called the Television, Radio and Film Commission (TRAFCO) and
then became United Methodist Communications. Logan and his associates
had taken note of the Surgeon General's Report and specifically wanted to
direct their efforts and those of other church groups toward doing something positive about television.

The decision was made to capitalize on the availability of free air time on
the commercial networks through the vehicle of public service announcements (*PSA*'s). PSA's are typically 15 or 30 seconds long and are inter-
spersed with regular commercials. They are offered to networks or individual broadcasters on a gratis basis by nonprofit charitable, public service and
religious organizations. The broadcaster does not pay for the production

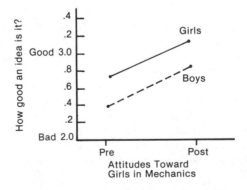

Fig. 8.5. *Freestyle's* effect on children's attitudes toward girls in mechanics.
    *Based on the responses to three questions: How do you feel about girls your age (1) fixing a
broken bike, (2) working with an adult on a car motor, and (3) building a radio or something
else that runs on electricity?
    Source: Adapted from Johnston, Ettema, & Davidson, 1980.

costs and receives a copy of the PSA free; the sponsoring agency does not pay for the air time.

Collaborating with our research team at the State University of New York at Stony Brook, Logan decided to build PSA's around the theme of cooperation, a type of prosocial behavior which commended itself for three reasons. First, cooperation is pragmatic as well as prosocial. Unlike sharing, in which one's own material resources are diminished, cooperation provides an opportunity for both parties to be nice *and* to benefit. Second, cooperation is often an alternative to aggression, as when a fight may break out over competition for resources. Third, cooperation can be taught and must be learned. Thus modeling of successful cooperation on TV might well influence children's cooperation with one another in real life.

The United Methodist Church and other church groups provided the money for developing, producing, and distributing three 30-second spots designed to make children more cooperative. Development involved ongoing consultation with our team on the application of psychological principles in writing the story lines. More important, the spots were subjected to an intensive formative research effort as they developed. Each spot was tested by positioning it next to regular commercials, which in turn were inserted into actual entertainment programming so that the format was identical to what would finally appear on the air. Children of the target age range (four to ten years) watched from a comfortable sofa in a relaxed, den-like atmosphere furnished with such natural distractors as toys, books, and wall decorations. As the children watched, video recordings of their facial expressions and reactions were made and later analyzed in detail. Tests of comprehension of the content and meaning of each element in the spots were also performed. As a final test, children were observed in an actual play situation after seeing either the cooperative spot or a commercial of the same length to obtain an actual behavioral measure of cooperation. This research procedure continued with each spot until a highly effective message, produced by a well-known Hollywood studio, was "in the can" and ready to go on the air.

As might be expected, the spots that ultimately emerged were simple and graphic. For example, the first and best known spot, *The Swing*, opens with a boy and girl, eight to ten years of age, running across a field to reach a swing on a playground. They begin to struggle over the swing, and each claims first rights. After a moment during which battle seems inevitable, with each youngster scowling at the other, one of them produces the insight that they should take turns and *suggests that the other child should go first*. Each of the children is finally shown taking a turn, joyfully swinging through the air with the help of the other. Over all of this, an announcer's voice concludes: "There are lots of things you can do when two people want the same thing. One of them is to take turns. And that is a good one." The spot ends with an upbeat musical flourish. (See Figure 8.6.)

Fig. 8.6. Scenes from *The Swing*.

Teaching prosocial behavior to retarded adults. The most ambitious effort to promote prosocial behaviors through specially prepared programs was reported by Gadberry (1980). Through a grant from the Bureau of Education for the Handicapped, Sharon Gadberry developed a ten-program series for retarded adults. Called "The Good Life," the programs followed a game show format and focused on themes such as helping others, controlling temper, dealing with frustrating situations, and various self-help skills. Prior to the actual program production, she conducted extensive research to determine the television viewing habits of mentally retarded adults in an institutional setting and the program features that maximized attention and learning. Evaluative research has demonstrated the effectiveness of the series. For example, research showed that compared to residents who saw nonhelping episodes, mentally retarded adults shown the helping episodes performed better in a role-playing task modeled on the helping sequences and helped more in contrived helping situations that were different from those depicted in the program (Borroni, 1980). The project is exemplary in demonstrating the effectiveness of a tailor made television-like series for a specialized audience.

LIMITATIONS AND RESERVATIONS

Evidence reviewed in this chapter shows quite clearly that television entertainment has great potential power to socialize in any direction in which carefully designed, systematic programming is offered. Despite this potential, there are some very important limitations and reservations that must be considered by anyone who would harness TV for the benefit of children.

Limits of current knowledge

Although most studies suggest that prosocial television can have desired effects, our ability to magnify these effects and minimize undesired ones is in its infancy. Also, it is evident that the entire process of socialization is highly complex. For example, there are a number of studies that indicate that *Misterogers' Neighborhood* and *Sesame Street's* prosocial episodes can have prosocial effects, but that the influence is limited to situations that are quite similar to those presented on the program (Coates, Pusser, & Goodman, 1976; Friedrich & Stein, 1975; Gorn, Goldberg, & Kanungo, 1976; Leifer, 1975; Paulson, McDonald, & Whittlemore, 1972). In addition, while a single exposure to a prosocial segment of *Sesame Street* apparently produces immediate effects, these do not even last for a day (Goldberg & Gorn, 1979).

Finally, two studies suggest that televised messages designed to teach children how to deal with interpersonal conflict may backfire with very young children. Silverman (1976) found that three-year-old children exposed to episodes from *Sesame Street* that contained conflict followed by a prosocial resolution became *less* cooperative in a subsequent task. In a follow-up study, Silverman and Sprafkin (1980a) examined the independent effects of the conflict and resolution portions of four of these problematic spots. It was found that while exposure to the resolution-only spots did not increase cooperation, the children who saw the conflict-only spots were actually less cooperative relative to a control group. This suggests that the decrement in cooperative behavior shown in the original study was due to the conflict portions of the *Sesame Street* spots. Clearly, even the best intentions for prosocial effects may be undermined, and extreme care should be used when attempting to teach very young children how to deal with interpersonal conflict through TV.

Should TV be used to socialize children?

In this final section we would like to relate an incident that effectively captures the significance of the question: "Should TV be used to socialize children?" The incident revolves around *The Swing*, which we have already described.

The Swing was first broadcast in May 1974 and soon had been shown by all three networks and numerous independent stations at favorable air times. It was also distributed internationally and had been seen within a few months by tens of millions of children all over the world. Then, on August 18, 1974, a new twist was introduced. Caryl Rivers, in a free-lance article for the *New York Times* based on a then recent conference on "Behavioral Control through the Media," pointed out that the entire effort could be seen as a highly objectionable form of psychological behavior control. Here is an excerpt from Rivers report of the conference:

> Dr. Liebert is so convinced of the harmful effects of televised violence on children that he is now making 30-second spots for TV to demonstrate to children that there are non-violent, non-aggressive alternatives for solving problems. For example, in one spot (distributed as a public service by the Broadcasting and Film Commission of the National Council of Churches and already shown on all three networks) two children are running toward the one empty swing in a playground. They arrive at the same time, and each child grabs an end of the swing. Impasse. The kids must either fight or find some other way to resolve the situation. Finally they decide to take turns. Both kids are winners, nobody loses.

The outburst that followed Liebert's presentation flashed around the conference table. Did he believe he had a right to deliberately try to impose values on children? Whose values were they? Should children indeed be taught cooperation? Did ghetto kids perhaps need to be taught to slug it out in order to survive in this society? Was it not, in fact, immoral to create a TV advertisement the prime function of which was to influence kids' behavior? Liebert was accused of hubris, manipulation and even brainwashing. One would have thought he had proposed setting up Hitler Youth Camps on Sesame Street. He was nonplussed. He had not expected that a 30-second spot about cooperativeness in sharing a swing would have raised such a furor.

However, I understood why the hackles had gone up around that conference table. I am one of those people who is terrified of manipulation. A Skinnerian world filled with conditioned people scares the daylights out of me—even if those people do hate war and do love their fellow man. I agree with Nobel Prize-winner George Wald that we reduce our unpredictability at our grave risk. "Our technology," he says, "has given us dependable machines and livestock. We shall now have to choose whether to turn it to giving us more reliable, convenient and efficient men, at the cost of our freedom." [© 1974 by The New York Times Company. Reprinted by permission.]

Rivers' concern reflects the basic dilemma that television has created. As we saw in Chapter 1, there is every indication that TV viewing will continue to rival school as the major pastime of children, and that this is becoming true all over the world. In addition, the accumulated evidence suggests that television's content does influence children's values, beliefs, attitudes, and actions to some extent, although in an unsystematic, willy-nilly fashion. Most important, perhaps, the accumulated evidence (as well as our own experience) also suggests that it would be possible to design TV entertainment for children on a conscious basis that, given their level of viewing (15 to 20 hours a week, week in week out, from infancy to adulthood) would exert great influence. This, apparently, is the strategy for socializing the young employed in some dictatorships. Such systematic use of television entertainment to influence children is undoubtedly a subtle but effective type of brainwashing. Now that we *can* harness the potential power of television to influence children, the question of whether we *will* remains.

Appendix A
ANSWERING QUESTIONS ABOUT TELEVISION

The experimental method

The experimental method involves the manipulation of some experience (called the *independent* variable) and then the measurement of some aspect of behavior (the *dependent* variable). The major purpose is to determine if the changes in the independent variable produce changes in the dependent variable; that is, to determine whether there is a causal relationship between the two. An additional goal is to insure that *only* the independent variable could have caused the differences—to eliminate alternative interpretations of the results. For example, an investigator may be interested in the effects of praise on children's friendliness. Suppose he asks a teacher to enthusiastically praise children in her class for a week, and finds that on the last day all are friendly. Can he now say that praise increases friendliness? No. Several so-called rival hypotheses can explain his data; for example, the weather may have been nicer on the day of testing, the class lessons may have been easier, or the weekend may have been nearer. Any of these factors might have put everyone in a good mood, thereby making them friendlier. The experimenter must try to eliminate these rival hypotheses, and usually does so by employing a *control group*.

The simplest kind of experiment, then, involves two groups: one, the experimental group, receives the experience (or "treatment") of interest while the other, the control group, does not. When the experiment is concluded, the investigator will have one or more scores for each participant—measures of the dependent variable. He will then compare the average scores of the two groups. If the children who received praise are friendlier than those who did not, nice weather presumably had nothing to do with it, since everyone benefited from the sunshine.

But the researcher wants to go yet a step further and ask: can I *infer* from the experiment that other children who did not actually participate in this research will also be similarly affected by praise? Or could my results have appeared, with the particular children who did participate, simply by chance? It is this pair of questions, regarding inference to the larger *population* of children who were not studied directly, that is critical.

213

Obtaining the answer involves performing an appropriate statistical test that tells us the probability that the difference between the experimental and control groups is due only to chance. If — and only if — the probability is low do we infer that the results hold in the larger population of untested individuals. In behavioral research, the probability level is acceptably low when the likelihood is 5 or less in 100 that the obtained results would have occurred by chance. This level is called the 0.05 level of significance and is commonly written, "$p < 0.05$" and read "probability less than five percent." All of the findings put forth as "significant" in this book have met this stringent criterion.

The correlational method

The correlational method is employed to determine if two (or more) variables are related; that is, to see if they change or co-vary together. Many social scientific research questions have been answered using this method. For example, "Is mental illness related to social class?" or, "Are grades related to IQ test scores?" The first step in applying the correlational method involves obtaining pairs of observations on a group of people. Next, the degree of relationship between the two sets of scores is assessed. A statistic called the *Pearson product moment correlation coefficient*, usually abbreviated *r*, is used for this purpose. This statistic may range in value from — 1.00 to + 1.00; the larger the absolute value of *r*, the stronger the relationship. An *r* of 1.00 (either plus or minus) indicates a perfect relationship. An *r* of 0.00 indicates no relationship. The sign of the correlation coefficient indicates the direction of the relationship. When the sign is positive, then the variables are *directly related*; as scores on one measure increase or decrease, the scores on the other tend to move in the same direction. When the sign is negative, the variables are *inversely related*; scores on one measure increase as scores on the other decrease.

Finally, the correlational study, like the experiment, usually requires an inference. When the investigator computes the correlation between two measures for some sample of individuals, this alone does not permit her to generalize the relationship and assume that it would hold for other people as well. To make such a determination, tests of statistical significance are employed in correlational studies just as they are employed in experiments (*see* pp. 38–39).

As with any type of research, there are problems accompanying the correlational method. The most serious one concerns establishing causality; usually we cannot infer, when *A* and *B* are related, whether *A* causes *B*, or *B* causes *A*. For example, the question of primary interest for our purpose is, "Is viewing television violence related to violent or aggressive behavior?"

The investigator collects data from many youngsters on the amount of viewing of violent TV and the amount of aggression they engage in at school, and then determines the degree of correlation. But in most instances — and without further special computation — it cannot be said that violence viewing *causes* violent behavior. For example, an equally plausible hypothesis is that children who are already aggressive *choose* to watch violence on TV.

Appendix B

The list that follows* describes each of the research reports and related publications of the NIMH Surgeon General's inquiry. The papers themselves are available in seven volumes:

Television and Social Behavior: Media Content and Control (Reports and Papers, Volume 1)

Television and Social Behavior: Television and Social Learning (Reports and Papers, Volume 2)

Television and Social Behavior: Television and Adolescent Aggressiveness (Reports and Papers, Volume 3)

Television and Social Behavior: Television in Day-to-Day Life: Patterns of Use (Reports and Papers, Volume 4)

Television and Social Behavior: Television's Effects: Further Explorations (Reports and Papers, Volume 5)

Television and Growing Up: The Impact of Televised Violence (Report of the Surgeon General's Scientific Advisory Committee on Television and Social Behavior)

Television and Social Behavior: An Annotated Bibliography of Research Focusing on Television's Impact on Children

*Reprinted, with minor modifications, from *Television and Growing Up: The Impact of Televised Violence.*

216

Any of these volumes can be purchased from the Superintendent of Documents, U.S. Government Printing Office, Washington, D.C. 20402

Author and Title	Subjects	Description
1. Baldwin & Lewis Violence in Television: The Industry Looks at Itself (Volume 1)	48 producers, writers, and directors	Interviews were conducted with the writers, producers, and directors of network action-adventure programming. The respondents were asked to describe the role of violence in such programs and how the industry handles this aspect (i.e., censorship activities). In addition, the subjects were asked to respond to the critics of television violence and to comment on their beliefs about the possible effects of viewing televised violence.
2. Bechtel, Achelpohl, & Akers Correlates between Observed Behavior and Questionnaire Responses on Television Viewing (Volume 4)	20 families Total $N = 82$	Video tape cameras were installed in the homes of participating families. Observations of viewing behavior were continuously recorded for five days. The video tape records were coded, in $2\frac{1}{2}$ minute intervals for attention to the set (e.g., watching/not watching), and types of simultaneous activity (e.g., eating, reading). These behavior records were compared with the viewer's responses to questionnaire measures of viewing behavior.
3. Blatt, Spencer, & Ward A Cognitive Developmental Study of Children's Reactions to Television Advertising (Volume 4)	20 children 5 kindergarten 5 second grade 5 fourth grade 5 sixth grade	Children were shown a one-hour videotape of "Saturday morning" television programming which included cartoons and other children's programs, plus 15 minutes of commercials. On the following day, the children were interviewed, in groups of five, concerning their reactions to the commercials (e.g., recall and understanding of the commercial message) and general attitudes toward advertising.
4. Cantor The Role of the Producer in Choosing	24 producers and writers	Twenty producers and four writers of children's programs were interviewed. Respondents were asked

Author and Title	Subjects	Description
Children's Television Content (Volume 1)		to describe the manner in which shows are selected by the networks and sponsors; the relationship between the producers and network; and the producer's conception of the audience for his program.
5. Chaffee Television and Adolescent Aggressiveness (Volume 3)		A summary of current research on the relationship between viewing televised violence and the aggressive behavior of adolescents.
6. Chaffee & McLeod Adolescent Television Use in the Family Context (Volume 3)	1292 junior and senior high school 641 eighth grade 651 tenth grade	This survey related adolescent's television viewing (e.g., viewing televised violence) to factors such as; IQ, parent's television use, SES, and family communication patterns. The latter factor was defined by the parent's relative emphasis on either socio—(i.e., maintaining interpersonal harmony/repression of conflicts) or concept—(i.e., free discussion and mutual understanding of conflicts) orientations.
7. Clark Race Identification, and Television Violence Experiment I (Volume 5)	71 teenagers 38 white 33 black	Adolescents were shown a videotape of a Dragnet episode which featured three main characters: "Black Militant," "Black Policeman," and "White Policeman." The subjects viewed the program in either racially "mixed" or "homogeneous" groups. Postviewing questionnaires assessed the viewer's identification with the various characters and the role of black consciousness in such identification.
Experiment II (Volume 5)	45 white, college students	Subjects viewed the Dragnet program in dyads composed of either a black or white confederate who either engaged in social communication (i.e., friendly conversation) or remained silent during the viewing period.

Author and Title	Subjects	Description
8. Clark & Blankenburg Trends in Violent Content in Selected Mass Media (Volume 1)		Several forms of mass media (e.g., front page newspaper stories, a weekly magazine, and television entertainment programming) were inspected for the presence of violent content and their treatment of violent themes. Comparisons were obtained between media violence and environmental or real violence (i.e., FBI Uniform Crime Reports).
9. Comstock Media Control and Content: An Overview (Volume 1)		A review of this program's research on decision-making in television production and violence in television content.
10. Dahlgren Television in the Sociali- zation Process: Structures and Programming of the Swedish Broadcasting Corporation (Volume 1)		A description of the broadcast policies of Sveriges Radio.
11. Dominick & Greenberg Attitudes Toward Vio- lence: The Interaction of TV Exposure, Family Attitudes, and Social Class (Volume 3)	838 children 434 fourth-, fifth-, and sixth-grade boys 404 fourth-, fifth-, and sixth-grade girls	Each child's prior exposure to televised violence, his perception of his parents' attitudes concerning the appropriateness of violence, and his family's socioeconomic level were related to various measures of the child's attitudes toward violence (e.g., willingness to use violence, perceived effectiveness of violence, and approval of aggression).
12. Ekman, Liebert, Friesen, Harrison, Zlatchin, Malmstrom, & Baron Facial Expressions of Emotion While Watching Televised Violence as Predictors of Subsequent Aggression (Volume 5)	65 5–6-year-old children (30 boys and 35 girls)	Children's facial expression while viewing televised violence were used as an index of the child's emotional reaction to such fare. This index was then used to assess the relationship between the child's emotional response to observing violent acts and his subsequent willingness to engage in interpersonal aggression.

Author and Title	Subjects	Description
13. Feshbach Reality and Fantasy in Filmed Violence Experiment I (Volume 2)	129, 9–11-year-old children	Children viewed either real (i.e., newsreel), fantasy (i.e., Hollywood movie), or control (e.g., circus movie) films and were then allowed to play a game in which they could engage in aggressive acts against an ostensible victim.
Experiment II (Volume 2)	40, 9–11-year-old children	In this study, each child was informed that the movie he was about to view was either real ("NBC news-reel") or fantasy ("Hollywood movie"). Measures of the child's subsequent aggressive behavior were identical to the first study.
Experiment III (Volume 2)	30, 9–11-year-old children	This study was similar to the second except that each child was informed that his aggressive behavior in the "guessing game" was only make believe. Results of this study were compared with the results of the previous experiment.
14. Feshbach & Singer Television and Aggression: Some Reactions to the Liebert, Sobol, and Davidson Review and Response (Volume 5)		A response to a comment on a reply to a critique of the catharsis thesis (see items 14, 35, and 36).
15. Feshbach & Singer Television and Aggression: A Reply to Liebert, Sobol, and Davidson. (Volume 5)		A reply to a critique of the catharsis thesis (see items 15, 35, and 36).
16. Foulkes, Belvedere, & Brubaker Televised Violence and Dream Content (Volume 5)	40, 10–12-year-old boys	This study was designed to assess the relationship between viewing televised violence and the subsequent content of the child's dreams. Children viewed either a violent or nonviolent program immediately prior to bedtime. Their dreams were monitored during the sleep period and scored on a variety of dimensions (e.g., hostility, vividness, and hedonic tone).

Author and Title	Subjects	Description
17. Friedman & Johnson Mass Media Use and Aggression: A Pilot Study (Volume 3)	80 preadolescent boys 40 "aggressive" 40 "nonaggres- sive"	Adolescent's attitudes toward aggression (e.g., tendency to engage in overt physical aggression) and his patterns of television use (e.g., amount of time spent viewing, program preferences) were studied in an attempt to assess the relationship between viewing televised violence and engaging in antisocial acts.
18. Gerbner The Structure and Process of Television Program Content Regulation in the United States (Volume 1)		A description of broadcast and content control structures operative in American television programming.
19. Gerbner Violence in Television Drama: Trends and Symbolic Functions (Volume 1)		This study provided an analysis of a one week sample of prime time entertainment programming. It described various factors relating to the frequency and symbolic characteristics of televised violence.
20. Greenberg Television's Effects: Further Explorations (Volume 5)		An overview of several current research projects that provide a diversity of theoretical and methodological approaches to research on the effects of television.
21. Greenberg, Ericson, & Vlahos Children's Television Behaviors as Perceived by Mother and Child (Volume 4)	85, fourth- and fifth- grade children and their mothers	Mothers, interviewed at home, were asked to describe their child's viewing patterns (e.g., program preferences, rules about viewing) while each child answered similar questions in the classroom. The child's self reported viewing behavior was compared with the mother's description.
22. Greenberg & Gordon Perceptions of Violence in Television Programs: Critics and the Public (Volume 1)	53 critics 303 men and women	A telephone survey (public) and mail questionnaires (critics) asked the respondents to rate the amount of violence contained in various television entertainment programs.

Author and Title	Subjects	Description
23. Greenberg & Gordon Social Class and Racial Differences in Children's Perception of Televised Violence (Volume 5)	325 fifth-grade boys 89 low SES white 89 low SES black 90 middle SES white 57 upper SES white	This study assessed boys' evaluation of violence portrayed on television in terms of the degree of perceived violence, acceptibility of violence, liking, degree of arousal, and perceived reality of the violent act.
24. Greenberg & Gordon Children's Perceptions of Television Violence: A Replication (Volume 5)	263 eighth-grade boys 66 low SES black 78 low SES white 37 middle SES white 82 upper-middle SES white.	A replication of the prior study conducted with younger boys (see item 23).
25. Gurevitch The Structure and Content of Television Broadcasting in Four Countries: An Overview (Volume 1)		An introduction to a review of the broadcasting policies of Great Britain, Israel, Sweden, and the United States.
26. Halloran & Croll Television Programmes in Great Britain: Content and Control (Volume 1)		A discussion of television broadcast- ing in Great Britain.
27. Israel & Robinson Demographic Charac- teristics of Viewers of Television Violence and News Programs (Volume 4)	6834 adults	Information on preferences and viewing patterns of a nationwide survey of adult television viewers were related to various demo- graphic characteristics (e.g., age, education, income, sex).
28. Johnson, Friedman, & Gross Four Masculine Styles in Television Program- ming: A Study of the Viewing Preferences of	80 eighth-grade boys 39 "aggressive" 41 "nonaggres- sive"	This study compared the program preference patterns of boys with a history of "social aggressiveness" with their nonaggressive peers in an attempt to construct a program classification scheme based on the

Author and Title	Subjects	Description
Adolescent Males (Volume 3)		masculine role concept portrayed in each program.
29. Katzman Violence and Color Television: What Children of Different Ages Learn (Volume 5)	240 fourth-, sixth-, and ninth-grade boys	Children viewed (in either color or black-and-white format) a color television program which had been edited into either "high-violence" or "low-violence" versions. Post-viewing measures tested the child's recall of central and peripheral details and related this recall to the color/violence variations.
30. Kenny Threats to the Internal Validity of Cross-Lagged Panel Inference, as re-lated to "Television Violence and Child Aggression: A Follow-up Study" (Volume 3)		A methodological note on the research design employed in a study by Lefkowitz, Eron, Walder, & Huesmann (*see* item 31).
31. Lefkowitz, Eron, Walder, & Huesmann Television Violence and Child Aggression: A Follow-up Study (Volume 3)	875 children— third-grade sample 382 adolescent eighth-grade sample 427, 19-year-olds	As part of a longitudinal study of childhood aggression, the investi-gators queried the child and/or his parents about his television view-ing patterns (e.g., program prefer-ences). Cross-lagged correlations between television viewing at age three and adolescent aggressive-ness at age 19 were obtained to provide causal inferences regarding television's role in the develop-ment of aggressive behavior.
32. Leifer & Roberts Children's Responses to Television Violence Experiment I (Volume 2)	271 children 40 kindergarten 54 third grade 56 sixth grade 51 ninth grade 70 twelfth grade	Subsequent to viewing a television program which contained a number of violent acts each child was asked to evaluate the motivations and consequences surrounding each depicted act of violence. The child's understanding of these characteristics of violent act was then assessed in terms of the child's willingness to engage in aggressive behavior.

Author and Title	Subjects	Description
Experiment II (Volume 2)	132 children 62 preschool 40 fifth grade 30 twelfth grade	Each child viewed a television program which was edited to provide one of four combinations of motivations/consequences for the portrayed violent acts: good-good, good-bad, bad-good, bad-bad. Post-viewing measures were similar to the prior study.
Experiment III (Volume 2)	160 children 51 fourth grade 56 seventh grade 53 tenth grade	Children viewed one of two versions of a movie in which the justifications for aggression had been edited to provide for an "aggression-less justified" version. Post-viewing measures of aggressive behavior were similar to those employed in the first experiment.
Experiment IV (Volume 2)	349 children 99 third grade 138 sixth grade 112 tenth grade	The temporal separation of the motivations for an aggressive act and consequences accruing to the aggressor on the child's post-viewing aggressive behavior, was explored in this present study. Measures of aggressive behavior were similar to previous studies.
33. Liebert Some Relationships Between Viewing Violence and Behaving Aggressively (Volume 2)		A review of current research on television's role in the imitation and/or disinhibition of aggressive behavior (with an additional report: Strauss & Poulos, "Television and Social Learning: A summary of the Experimental Effects of Observed Filmed Aggression").
34. Liebert & Baron Short-Term Effects of Televised Aggression on Children's Aggressive Behavior (Volume 2)	136 children (68 boys and 68 girls) (65, 5–6-year-olds) (71, 8–9-year-olds)	In this study the child-viewer's willingness to engage in interpersonal aggression was assessed subsequent to viewing either aggressive or neutral television programming.
35. Liebert, Davidson, & Sobol Catharsis of Aggression Among Institutionalized		A comment on a reply to a critique of the catharsis thesis (see item 14, 15, and 36).

Author and Title	Subjects	Description
Boys: Further Comments (Volume 5)		
36. Liebert, Sobol, & Davidson Catharsis of Aggression Among Institutionalized Boys: Fact or Artifact? (Volume 5)		A commentary on a study of the role of catharsis in evaluating the effects of viewing televised violence (*see* items 14, 15, and 35).
37. LoSciuto A National Inventory of Television Viewing Behavior (Volume 4)	252 families	A nationwide sample of American families were interviewed concerning various aspects of television viewing such as: why people watch television, what they learn from programs, extent of viewing, and program preferences
38. Lyle Television in Day-to-Day Life: Patterns of Use (Volume 4)		A review of current research on the role of television in some aspects of daily life.
39. Lyle & Hoffman Children's Use of Television and Other Media (Volume 4)	1682 children 300 first grade 793–877, sixth grade 469–505, tenth grade	Children were interviewed about the role television plays in their daily life (e.g., extent and duration of viewing, program preferences, attitudes toward television, use of other forms of mass media). In addition, the mothers of first-graders were also interviewed concerning their perceptions of the role of television viewing patterns and perceived extent of learning from television.
40. Lyle & Hoffman Explorations in patterns of television viewing by preschool children (Volume 4)	158 children 40 3-year-olds 82 4-year-olds 35 5-year-olds 1 6-year-old	A selected sample of Caucasian, Negro and Mexican–American preschool boys and girls were interviewed concerning their television viewing (e.g., program preferences, extent of viewing recognition of television characters). In addition, mothers were interviewed concerning their child's television viewing patterns and perceived extent of learning from television.

Author and Title	Subjects	Description
41. McIntyre & Teevan Television and Deviant Behavior (Volume 3)	2270 junior and senior high school students	Questionnaire responses were used to provide an estimate of the relationship between television viewing patterns (e.g., program preferences) and self reported aggressive and delinquent behavior.
42. McLeod, Atkin, & Chaffee Adolescents, Parents and Television Use: Self-Report and Other-Report Measures from the Wisconsin Sample (Volume 3)	648 students Maryland sample 229, seventh grade 244, tenth grade Wisconsin sample 68, seventh grade 83, tenth grade	Self-report, peer, and "other" rated indices of aggressive behavior were related to various aspects of the adolescent's pattern of television use (e.g., extent of viewing, program preferences, cognitive reactions to televised violence).
43. McLeod, Atkin, & Chaffee Adolescents, Parents and Television Use: Adolescent Self-Report and Other-Report Measures from the Maryland and Wisconsin Sample (Volume 3)		See item 42: A comparison between adolescent television viewing and self reported aggressive or delinquent behavior.
44. Murray Television in Inner-City Homes: Viewing Behavior of Young Boys (Volume 4)	27, 5–6-year-old boys	Observation of in-home television viewing, parent–child interviews, diary records of one week's television viewing and measures of cognitive and social development were used to provide a description of the role television plays in the daily lives of a selected sample of young boys (with an additional report: Furfey, "First Graders Watching Television").
45. Neale Comment on: Television Violence and Child Aggression: A Follow-up Study (Volume 3)		A methodological note on the Lefkowitz, Eron, Walder, & Huesmann study (see item 31).
46. Rabinovitch, MacLean, Markham, & Talbott Children's Violence	57 sixth-grade children 24 girls	This study was designed to assess changes in the child's perception of violence as a result of viewing

Author and Title	Subjects	Description
Perception as a Function of Television Violence (Volume 5)	33 boys	televised violence. Children viewed either an aggressive or nonaggressive television program and were then presented with a discrimination task (i.e., identifying a tachistoscopically presented slide as either "violent" or "nonviolent").
47. Robinson Television's Impact on Everyday Life: Some Cross-National Evidence (Volume 4)		This study was focused on the respondent's allocation of time ("time-budgets") to various activities (e.g., work, child care, leisure, mass media use) in his daily life. Time budgets were sampled in 15 cities in 11 counties.
48. Robinson Toward Defining the Functions of Television (Volume 4)		A review of current research on the role of television in relation to other daily activities.
49. Robinson & Bachman Television Viewing Habits and Aggression (Volume 3)	1559, 19-year-old males	As part of a nationwide survey of the changing characteristics of youth, respondents were asked to indicate the extent of their television viewing, program preferences, and the locus of "greatest-learning-about-life" — television vs. school. These findings were then related to the respondents' self-reported incidence of aggressive and delinquent behaviors.
50. Shinar Structure and Content of Television Broadcasting in Israel (Volume 1)		A review of television broadcasting policies in Israel.
51. Stein & Friedrich Television Content and Young Children's Behavior (Volume 2) (with Vondracek)	97, $3\frac{1}{2}$–$5\frac{1}{2}$-year-olds 52 boys 45 girls	Preschool children were exposed to either an "aggressive, neutral, or prosocial" television diet and then observed during the course of their daily interaction with other children in their classroom. The observations were conducted over a nine-week period including three-week baseline, four-week

Author and Title	Subjects	Description
		controlled viewing, and two-week follow-up periods. Changes (over baseline) in either aggressive or prosocial behaviors were used to provide a measure of the impact of television programming.
52. Stevenson 　　Television and the 　　Behavior of Preschool 　　Children 　　(Volume 2)		A discussion of research findings on the impact of television in early childhood and suggestions for future research.
53. Tannenbaum 　　Studies in Film- and 　　TV-Mediated Arousal 　　and Aggression 　　(Volume 5)		A review of research and theory on mediating factors (e.g., emotional arousal) in the relationships between viewing televised violence and subsequent aggressive behavior.
54. Wackman, Reale. & 　　Ward 　　　Racial Differences in 　　Responses to Advertising Among Adolescents 　　(Volume 4)	1149 eighth– 　twelfth-grade 1049 whites 100 blacks	This study was focused on a comparison of the responses of black-and-white adolescents to television advertising in terms of their favorite ads, extent of "learning consumer roles," and reasons offered for viewing commercials.
55. Ward 　　Effects of Television 　　Advertising on Children and Adolescents 　　(Volume 4)		A review and discussion of research, in the current program, on the impact of television advertising.
56. Ward, Levinson, & 　　Wackman 　　　Children's Attention to 　　Television Advertising 　　(Volume 4)	134 mothers of 5–12-year-old children	Interviews were conducted with the mothers of young children in order to determine the short-term consequences of watching television advertising.
57. Ward, Reale. & 　　Levinson 　　　Children's Perceptions, 　　Explanations, and 　　Judgments of Television Advertising: A 　　Further Exploration. 　　(Volume 4)		An elaboration of the Blatt, Spencer, & Ward study (*see* item 3).

Author and Title	Subjects	Description
58. Ward & Robertson Adolescent Attitudes Toward Television Advertising (Volume 4)	1094, eighth–twelfth-grade	This study was designed to relate adolescent's attitudes toward television advertising to demographic characteristics, family communication patterns, and television use.
59. Ward & Wackman Family and Media Influences on Adolescent Consumer Learning (Volume 4)	1094, eighth–twelfth-grade	This survey assessed the adolescent's "consumer skills" (i.e., recall of advertising content, attitudes toward commercials, materialistic attitudes, and buying behavior) and related these skills to various demographic characteristics.
60. Ward & Wackman Television Advertising and Intra-Family Influence: Children's Purchase Influence Attempts and Parental Yielding (Volume 4)	109 mothers of 5–12-year-old children	Interviewers asked the mothers of young children to describe the "effects of television advertising" in terms of the frequency and intensity of their child's "requests" for advertised products

References

Action for Children's Television. ACT petitions Federal Trade Commission. ACT NEWS-LETTER, Spring/Summer 1972.

Action for Children's Television. An international survey of children's television. *Phaedrus*, 1978, **5** (1), 4–5.

Action for Children's Television. FTC Children's Advertising Rulemaking Fact Sheet. ACT, Newtonville, Massachusetts, 1980.

Agostino, D. New technologies: Problem or solution? *Journal of Communication*, 1980, **30** (3), 198–206.

American Medical Association Policy, no, 38, Violence on TV: An Environmental Hazard, Reference Committee E, 367, 1976.

Anderson, D.R. Children's attention to television. Paper presented at the Biennial Meeting of the Society for Research in Child Development, New Orleans, March 1977.

Anderson, D.R., Alwitt, L.F., Lorch, E.P., & Levin, S.R. Watching children watch television. In G. Hale & M. Lewis (Eds.), *Attention and the development of cognitive skills*. New York: Plenum, 1979.

Anderson, D.R., & Levin, S.R. Young children's attention to "Sesame Street." *Child Development*, 1976, **47** (3), 806–811.

Anderson, D.R., Lorch, E.P., Field, D.E., & Sanders, J. The effects of TV program comprehensibility on preschool children's visual attention to television. Manuscript, University of Massachusetts, 1979.

Andison, F.S. TV violence and viewer aggression: A cumulation of study results 1956–1976. *Public Opinion Quarterly*, 1977, **41**, 314–331.

Atkin, C. "Effects of Television Advertising on Children — First Year Experimental Evidence," Report #1, Michigan State University, 1975.(a)

Atkin, C. "Effects of Television Advertising on Children — Second Year Experimental Evidence," Report #2, Michigan State University, 1975.(b)

Atkin, C. "Effects of Television Advertising on Children — Survey of Pre-Adolescent's Response to Television Commercials," Report #6, Michigan State University, 1975.(c)

Atkin, C. "Effects of Television Advertising on Children — Parent-Child Communication in Supermarket Breakfast Selection," Report #7, Michigan State University, 1975.(d)

Atkin, C. "Effects of Television Advertising on Children — Survey of Children's and Mother's Responses to Television Commercials," Report #8, Michigan State University, 1975.(e)

Atkin, C. Observation of parent-child interaction in supermarket decision making. *Journal of Marketing*, 1978, **42**, 41–45.

Atkin, C., & Gibson, W. Children's nutrition learning from television advertising. Unpublished manuscript, Michigan State University, 1978.

Atkin, C.K., & Heald, G. The content of children's toy and food commercials. *Journal of Communication*, 1977, **27** (1), 107–114.

Atkin, C.K., Murray, J.P., & Nayman, O.B. *Television and social behavior: An annotated bibliography of research focusing on television's impact on children*. Washington: U.S. Public Health Service, 1971.

Atkin, C., Reeves, B., & Gibson, W. Effects of television food advertising on children. Paper presented at the meeting of the Association for Education in Journalism, Houston, Texas, 1979.

Baker, R.K. The views, standards, and practices of the television industry. In R.K. Baker and S.J. Ball (Eds.), *Violence and the media*. Washington, D.C.: U.S. Government Printing Office, 1969, 593–614.

Baker, R.K., & Ball, S.J. *Mass Media and Violence. Staff Report to the National Commission on the Causes and Prevention of Violence*, Volume 9. Washington, D.C.: United States Government Printing Office, 1969.

Baldwin, T.F., & Lewis, C. Violence in television: The industry looks at itself. In G.A. Comstock & E.A. Rubinstein (Eds.), *Television and social behavior. Vol. 1. Media content and control*. Washington, D.C.: United States Government Printing Office, 1972.

Ball, S., & Bogatz, G. *The first year of Sesame Street: An evaluation*. Princeton, N.J.: Educational Testing Service, 1970.

Ball, S., & Bogatz, G. *Reading with television: An evaluation of the Electric Company*. Princeton, New Jersey: Educational Testing Service, 1973.

Bandura, A. "What TV Violence Can Do To Your Child." *Look*, October 22, 1963, 46–52.

Bandura, A. Influence of models' reinforcement contingencies on the acquisition of imitative responses. *Journal of Personality and Social Psychology*, 1965, **1**, 589–595.

Bandura, A., Ross, D., & Ross, S.A. Transmission of aggression through imitation of aggressive models. *Journal of Abnormal and Social Psychology*, 1961, **63**, 575–582.

Bandura, A., Ross, D., & Ross, S.A. Imitation of film-mediated aggressive models. *Journal of Abnormal and Social Psychology*, 1963, **66**, 3–11.

Bandura, A., & Walters, R.H *Social learning and personality development*. New York: Holt, Rinehart & Winston, 1963.

Baran, S.J., Chase, L.J., & Courtright, J.A. Television drama as a facilitator of prosocial behavior: "The Waltons." *Journal of Broadcasting*, 1979, **23** (3), 277–284.

Barcus, F.E. Television in the after-school hours. Newtonville, Massachusetts: Action for Children's Television, 1975.(a)

Barcus, F.E. Weekend children's television. Newtonville, Massachusetts: Action for Children's Television, 1975.(b)

Barcus, F.E. Commercial children's television on weekends and weekday afternoons. Newtonville, Massachusetts: Action for Children's Television, 1978.(a)

Barcus, F.E. Food advertising on children's television: An analysis of appeals and nutritional content. Newtonville, Massachusetts: Action for Children's Television, 1978.(b)

Barcus, F.E. The nature of television advertising to children. In E.L. Palmer & A. Dorr (Eds.), *Children and the faces of television: Teaching, violence, selling*. New York: Academic Press, 1980, 273–285.

Barcus, F.E. Weekday, daytime commercial television programming for children. Newtonville, Massachusetts: Action for Children's Television, 1981.

Barnouw, E. *A history of broadcasting in the United States. Vol. III—from 1953: The image empire*. New York: Oxford University Press, 1972.

Bechtel, R.B., Achelpohl, C., & Akers, R. Correlates between observed behavior and questionnaire responses on television viewing. In E.A. Rubinstein, G.A. Comstock, & J.P. Murray (Eds.), *Television and social behavior. Vol. 4, Television in day-to-day life: Patterns of use*. Washington, D.C.: Government Printing Office, 1972, 274–344.

Belson, W.A. *Television violence and the adolescent boy*. Hampshire, England: Saxon House, 1978.

Berkowitz, L. *Aggression: A social psychological analysis*. New York: McGraw-Hill, 1962.

Berkowitz, L. Some aspects of observed aggression. *Journal of Personality and Social Psychology*, 1965, **2**, 359–369.

Berkowitz, L. The frustration-aggression hypothesis revisited. In Berkowitz, L. (Ed.), *Roots of aggression: A re-examination of the frustration-aggression hypothesis*. New York: Atherton Press, 1969.

Berkowitz, L., & Geen, R.G. Film violence and the cue properties of available targets. *Journal of Personality and Social Psychology*, 1966, **3**, 525–530.

Berkowitz, L., & Geen, R.G. Stimulus qualities of the target of aggression: A further study. *Journal of Personality and Social Psychology*, 1967, **5**, 364–368.

Beuf, A. Doctor, lawyer, household drudge. *Journal of Communication*, 1974, **24** (2), 142–145.

Bever, T., Smith, M., Bengen, B., & Johnson, T. Young viewers' troubling responses to TV ads. *Harvard Business Review*, 1975, **53** (6), 109–120.

Blatt, J., Spencer, L., & Ward, S. A cognitive developmental study of children's reactions to television advertising. In E.A. Rubinstein, G.A. Comstock, & J.P. Murray (Eds.), *Television and social behavior. Vol. IV: Television in day-to-day life: Patterns of use.* Washington, D.C.: U.S. Government Printing Office, 1972, 452–467.

Boffey, P.M., & Walsh, J. Study of TV violence. Seven top researchers blackballed from panel. *Science*, May 22, 1970, **168**, 949–952.

Bogatz, G.A., & Ball, S. *The second year of Sesame Street: A continuing evaluation.* Princeton, N.J.: Educational Testing Service, 1972.

Borroni, A.V. Effects of content and media features on attention and learning of televised material. Presented at the 88th annual convention of the *American Psychological Association*, September 2, 1980, Montreal, Quebec, Canada.

Branscomb, A.W., & Savage, M. The broadcast reform movement: At the crossroads. *Journal of Communication*, 1978, **28** (4), 25–34.

Broadcasting. Wiley feels heat from TV's screen. October 21, 1974, 41.

Broadcasting. The matter of money and children's TV. October 29, 1979.

Broadcasting. $40 million each week for prime time. February 11, 1980.

Broadcasting. Revenues Up, Profits Down for TV in 1980. August 10, 1981, 38–55.

Broadcasting Yearbook. Washington, D.C.: Broadcasting Publications, Inc., 1980.

Brown, L. *Televi$ion: The Business behind the box.* New York: Harcourt Brace Jovanovich, 1971.

Brown, L. Study assails sponsors on TV violence. *New York Times*, July 30, 1976.

Brown, L. *The New York Times encyclopedia of television.* New York: Times Books, 1977.

Bryan, J.H., & Walbek, N.B. Preaching and practicing generosity: Children's actions and reactions. *Child Development*, 1970, **41**, 329–353.

Buchanan, J. "Zamora Didn't Mean to Shoot, Doctor Says." *Miami Herald*, October 6, 1977.(a)

Buchanan, J. "Zamora Guilty of Murder" *Miami Herald*, October 7, 1977.(b)

Busby, L. Defining the sex role standard in commercial network television programs directed toward children. *Journalism Quarterly*, 1974, **51**, 690–696.

Callum, M. "What Viewers Love/Hate About Television." *TV Guide*, May 12, 1979.

Calvert, S., Watkins, B., Wright, J.C., & Huston-Stein, A. Recall of television content as a function of content type and level of production feature use. Paper presented at the Biennial Meeting of the *Society for Research in Child Development*, San Francisco, March 1979.

Cantor, M.G. The role of the producer in choosing children's television content. In G.A. Comstock & E.A. Rubinstein (Eds.), *Television and social behavior. Vol. 1. Media content and control.* Washington, D.C.: United States Government Printing Office, 1972.

Cantor, M.G. *Prime-time television: Content and control.* Beverly Hills: Sage Publications, 1980.

Carnegie Commission. *Public television: A program for action.* New York: Harper & Row, 1967.

Cater, D., & Strickland, S. *TV violence and the child: The evolution and fate of the Surgeon General's Report.* New York: Russell Sage, 1975.

Chaffee, S.H., & McLeod, J.M. Adolescents, parents, and television violence. Paper presented at American Psychological Association meeting. Washington, D.C., September 1971.

Charren, P. The selling game. *Madison Avenue*, 1974, **17**, 4–5.

Children's Television Workshop, International Research Notes. New York: CTW, 1980.

Children's Television Workshop. The *Electric Company*: *Television and reading, 1971—80: A mid-experiment appraisal*. New York: CTW, 1976.

Choate, R.B. The politics of change. In E.L. Palmer and A. Dorr (Eds.), *Children and the faces of television*. New York: Academic Press, 1980, 323–338.

Cisin, I.H., Coffin, T.E., Janis, I.L., Klapper, J.T., Mendelsohn, H., Omwake, E., Pinder-hughes, C.A., Pool, I. de Sola, Siegel, A.E., Wallace, A.F.C., Watson, A.S., & Wiebe, G.D. *Television and growing up: The impact of televised violence*. Washington, D.C.: U.S. Government Printing Office, 1972.

Clancy-Hepburn, K., Hickey, A., & Nevill, G. Children's behavior responses to TV food advertisements. *Journal of Nutrition Education*, 1974, **6** (3), 93–96.

Clark, C.C. Race, identification, and television violence. In G.A. Comstock, E.A. Rubinstein & J.P. Murray (Eds.), *Television and social behavior. Vol. 5. Television's effects: Further explorations*. Washington, D.C.: United States Government Printing Office, 1972.

Cline, V.B. (Ed.) *Where do you draw the line? An exploration into media violence, pornography and censorship*. Provo, Utah: Brigham Young University Press, 1974.(a)

Cline, V.B. Another view: Pornography effects, the state of the art. In V.B. Cline (Ed.), *Where do you draw the line*? Provo, Utah: Brigham Young University Press, 1974, 203–244.(b)

Coates, B., Pusser, H.E. & Goodman, I. The influence of *Sesame Street* and *Mister Rogers' Neighborhood* on children's social behavior in the preschool. *Child Development*, 1976, **47**, 138–144.

Coffin, T.E., & Tuchman, S. Rating television programs for violence: Comparison of five surveys. *Journal of Broadcasting*, 1973, **17** (1), 3–20.

Cole, B., & Oettinger, M. *Reluctant regulators: The FCC and the broadcast audience*. Reading, Massachusetts: Addison-Wesley, 1978.

Collins, W.A. Learning of media content: A developmental study. *Child Development*, 1970, **41**, 1133–1142.

Collins, W.A., & Getz, S.K. Children's social responses following modeled reactions to provocation: Prosocial effects of a television drama. *Journal of Personality*, 1976, **44**, 488–500.

Collins, W.A., Wellman, H., Keniston, A.H., & Westby, S.D. Age-related aspects of comprehension and inference from a televised dramatic narrative. *Child Development*, 1978, **49** (2), 389–399.

Columbia Broadcasting System. A study of messages received by children who viewed an episode of *Fat Albert and the Cosby Kids*. New York: CBS Broadcast Group, 1974.

Columbia Broadcasting System. *Communicating with children through television*. New York: CBS, 1977.

Commission on Obscenity and Pornography. Report of the Commission on Obscenity and Pornography. New York: Bantam Books, 1970.

Comstock, G. *Review of television and antisocial behavior: Field experiments* (by S. Milgram and R.L. Shotland). *Journal of Communication*, Summer 1974, 155–158.

Comstock, G. *Television and human behavior: The key studies*. Santa Monica, California: The Rand Corporation, 1975.

Comstock, G., Chaffee, S., Katzman, N., McCombs, M., & Roberts, D. *Television and human behavior*. New York: Columbia University Press, 1978.

Comstock, G., & Fisher, M. *Television and human behavior: A guide to the pertinent scientific literature*. Santa Monica, California: The Rand Corporation, 1975.

Comstock, G., & Lindsey, G. *Television and human behavior: The research horizon, future and present*. Santa Monica, California: The Rand Corporation, 1975.

Cook, T.D., Appleton, H., Conner, R.F., Shaffer, A., Tabkin, G., & Weber, J.S. *Sesame Street revisited*. New York: Russell Sage, 1975.

Courtney, A.E., & T.W. Whipple. Women in TV commercials. *Journal of Communication*, 1974, **24**, 110–18.

Cowan, G. *See no evil: The backstage battle over sex and violence in television.* New York: Simon and Schuster, 1978.

Daily News. FTC gets off kiddie bandwagon. October 1, 1981, 40.

Daltry, L. "Television on trial: The tube made me do it." *New West*, March 3, 1978, 69–70.

Davidson, E.S., & Neale, J.M. Analyzing prosocial content on entertainment television. Paper presented at the 82nd Annual Convention of the *American Psychological Association*, New Orleans, September 1974.

Davidson, E.S., Yasuna, A., & Tower, A. The effects of television cartoons on sex-role stereotyping in young girls. *Child Development*, 1979, **50**, 597–600.

DeFleur, M.L. Occupational roles as portrayed on television. *Public Opinion Quarterly*, 1964, **28**, 57–74.

de Konig, T.L., Conradie, D.P., & Nell, E.M. The effect of different kinds of television programming on the youth. Pretoria, Republic of South Africa: Human Sciences Research Council, Report No. Comm-20, 1980.

Dominick, J.R., & Greenberg, B.S. Three seasons of blacks on television. *Journal of Advertising Research*, 1970, **10**, 21–27.

Dominick, J.R., & Greenberg, B.S. Attitudes toward violence: The interaction of television exposure, family attitudes, and social class. In G.A. Comstock & E.A. Rubinstein (Eds.), *Television and social behavior. Vol. III: Television and adolescent aggressiveness.* Washington, D.C.: U.S. Government Printing Office, 1972, 314–335.

Donagher, P.C., Poulos, R.W., Liebert, R.M., & Davidson, E.S. Race, sex, and social example: An analysis of character portrayals on interracial television entertainment. *Psychological Reports*, 1975, **37**, 1023–1034.

Dorr, A. Children's advertising rule making comment. Testimony to the Federal Trade Commission's Rulemaking Hearings on Television Advertising and Children, San Francisco, California, November, 1978.

Dorr, A., Graves, S.B., & Phelps, E. Television literacy for young children. *Journal of Communication*, 1980, **30** (3), 71–83.

Dorr, A., & Kovaric, P. Some of the people some of the time—But which people? Televised violence and its effects. In E.L. Palmer & A. Dorr (Eds.), *Children and the faces of television: Teaching, violence, selling.* New York: Academic Press, 1980.

Dougherty, P.H. "Thompson scores TV violence." *New York Times*, June 9, 1976.

Drabman, R.S., & Thomas, M.H. Does media violence increase children's toleration of real-life aggression? *Developmental Psychology*, 1974, **10**, 418–421.

Drabman, R.S., & Thomas, M.H. Does watching violence on television cause apathy? *Pediatrics*, 1976, **57**, 329–331.

Duffy, J., & Rossiter, J.R. The Hartford Experiment: Children's reactions to TV commercials in blocks at the beginning and the end of the program. Paper presented at the Conference on Culture and Communications, Temple University, Philadelphia, March 1975.

Dussere, S. The effects of television advertising on children's eating habits. Unpublished doctoral dissertation, University of Massachusetts at Amherst, 1976.

Elias, M.J. Helping emotionally disturbed children through prosocial television. *Exceptional Children*, 1979, November, 217–218.

Eron, L.D. Relationship of TV viewing habits and aggressive behavior in children. *Journal of Abnormal and Social Psychology*, 1963, **67**, 193–196.

Eron, L.D., & Huesmann, L.R. Adolescent aggression and television. *Annals of the New York Academy of Sciences*, 1980, **347**, 319–331.

Federal Communications Commission. Adding the Equal Employment Program Filing Requirement to Commission Rules, 1971, 709.

Federal Communications Commission. "Children's Television Programs—Report and Policy Statement." *Federal Register* **39**, November 6, 1974.

Fernandez-Collado, C., & Greenberg, B.S. Sexual intimacy and drug use in TV series. *Journal of Communication*, 1978, **28** (3), 30–37.

Feshbach, S. The drive-reducing function of fantasy behavior. *Journal of Abnormal and Social Psychology*, 1955, **50**, 3–11.

Feshbach, S., & Singer, R. *Television and aggression*. San Francisco: Jossey-Bass, 1971.

Federal Trade Commission. Staff report on television advertising to children. Washington, D.C.: U.S. Government Printing Office, 1978.

Federal Trade Commission. Presiding Officer's Order No. 78: Certification to the commission of recommended disputed issues of fact. Washington, D.C.: Federal Trade Commission, 1979.

Federal Trade Commission. *Citizen's guide to the Federal Trade Commission*. Washington, D.C.: Federal Trade Commission, February 1981.(a)

Federal Trade Commission. FTC final staff report and recommendation. Washington, D.C.: Federal Trade Commission, March 31, 1981.(b)

Federal Trade Commission. *1980 Annual report of the Federal Trade Commission*. Washington, D.C.: Federal Trade Commission, September 1981.(c)

Fowles, B. Building a curriculum for "The Electric Company." In *The Electric Company: An introduction to the new television program designed to help teach reading to children*. New York: Children's Television Workshop, 1971.

Franzblau, S., Sprafkin, J.N., & Rubinstein, E.A. Sex on TV: A content analysis. *Journal of Communication*, 1977, **27**, 164–170.

Friedrich, L.K., & Stein, A.H. Prosocial television and young children: The effects of verbal labeling and role playing on learning and behavior. *Child Development*, 1975, **46**, 27–38.

Frueh, T., & McGhee, P.E. Traditional sex role development and amount of time spent watching television. *Developmental Psychology*, 1975, **11**, (1), 109.

Gadberry, S. "'The Good Life': From formative research to production." Presented at the 88th annual convention of the *American Psychological Association*, September 2, 1980, Montreal, Quebec, Canada.

Galst, J., & White, M.A. The unhealthy persuader: The reinforcing value of television and children's purchase-influencing attempts at the supermarket, *Child Development*, 1976, **47**, 1089–1096.

Geen, R.G., & Berkowitz, L. Name-mediating aggressive cue properties. *Journal of Personality*, 1966, **34**, 456–465.

Geen, R.G., & Berkowitz, L. Some conditions facilitating the occurrence of aggression after the observation of violence. *Journal of Personality*, 1967, **35**, 666–676.

Gerbner, G. The television world of violence. In D.L. Lange, R.K. Baker, & S.J. Ball, *Mass media and violence* Vol. XI. Washington, D.C.: U.S. Government Printing Office, 1969, 311–339.

Gerbner, G. Violence in television drama: Trends in symbolic functions. In G.A. Comstock & E.A. Rubinstein (Eds.), *Television and social behavior (Vol. 1): Media content and control*. Washington, D.C.: United States Government Printing Office, 1972, 28–187.

Gerbner, G. Sex on television and what viewers learn from it. Paper presented at the annual conference of the *National Association of Television Program Executives*, San Francisco, California, February 19, 1980.

Gerbner, G., Gross, L., Morgan, M., & Signorielli, N. The 'mainstreaming' of America: Violence Profile No. 11. *Journal of Communication*, 1980, **30** (3), 10–29.

Gerbner, G., Gross, L., Signorielli, N., Morgan, M., & Jackson-Beeck, M. The demonstration of power: Violence Profile No. 10. *Journal of Communication*, 1979, **29** (3), 177–195.

Gertner R. (Ed.) International Television Almanac. New York: Quigley Publishing Company, 1981.

Goldberg, M.E., & Gorn, G.J. Children's reaction to television advertising: An experimental approach. *Journal of Consumer Research*, 1974, **1** (2), 69–75.

Goldberg, M.E., & Gorn, G.J. Material vs. social preferences, parent-child relations, and the child's emotional responses. Paper presented at the Telecommunications Policy Research Conference, Airlie House, Virginia, March, 1977.

Goldberg, M.E., & Gorn, G.J. Television's impact on preferences for non-white playmates: Canadian "Sesame Street" inserts. *Journal of Broadcasting*, 1979, **23** (1), 27–32.

Gorn, G.J., Goldberg, M.E., & Kanungo, R.N. The role of educational television in changing the intergroup attitudes of children. *Child Development*, 1976, **47** (1), 277–280.

Gould, J. TV violence held unharmful to youth. *The New York Times*, January 11, 1972.

Graves, S.B. *How to encourage positive racial attitudes.* Paper presented at the *Society for Research in Child Development*, 1975, Denver, Colorado.

Greenberg, B.S., Abelman, R., & Neuendorf, U. Sex on the soap operas: Afternoon intimacy. *Journal of Communication*, 1981, **31** (3).

Greenberg, B.S., & Gordon, T.F. Perceptions of violence in TV programs: Critics and the public. In G.A. Comstock & E.A. Rubinstein (Eds.), *Television and social behavior, Vol. I, Media content and control.* Washington, D.C.: Government Printing Office, 1972a, 244–258.

Greenberg, B.S., & Gordon, T.F. Children's perceptions of television violence: A replication. In G.A. Comstock. E.A. Rubinstein, & J.P. Murray (Eds.), *Television and social behavior. Vol. V: Television's effects: Further explorations.* Washington, D.C.: U.S. Government Printing Office, 1972b, 211–230.

Hanratty, M.A., Liebert, R.M., Morris, L.W., & Fernandez, L.E. Imitation of film-mediated aggression against live and inanimate victims. *Proceedings for the 77th Annual Convention of the American Psychological Association*, 1969, 457–458.

Hanratty, M.A., O'Neal, E., & Sulzer, J.L. The effect of frustration upon imitation of aggression. *Journal of Personality and Social Psychology*, 1972, **21**, 30–34.

Hartley, R.L. The impact of viewing "aggression": Studies and problems of extrapolation. New York: Columbia Broadcasting System, Office of Social Research, 1964.

Hartmann, D.P. Influence of symbolically modelled instrumental aggression and pain cues on aggressive behavior. *Journal of Personality and Social Psychology*, 1969, **11**, 280–288.

Hartmann, D.P., & Gelfand, D.M. Motivational variables affecting performance of vicariously learned responses. Paper presented at Western Psychological Association Meeting, Vancouver, British Columbia, June 1969.

Harvey, S.E., Sprafkin, J.N., & Rubinstein, E. Prime time television: A profile of aggressive and prosocial behaviors. *Journal of Broadcasting*, 1979, **23** (2), 179–189.

Head, S.W. Content analysis of television drama programs. *Quarterly of Film, Radio and Television*, 1954, **9**, 175–194.

Heller, M.S. *Broadcast standards editing.* New York: American Broadcasting Companies, 1978.

Heller, M.S., & Polsky, S. *Studies in violence and television.* New York: American Broadcasting Companies, 1975.

Hennessee, J.A., & Nicholson, J. "N.O.W. says: TV Commercials Insult Women," *New York Times Magazine*, May 28, 1972, 12–13.

Hickey, N. "Does America Want Family Viewing Time? *TV Guide*, December 6, 1975.

Hicks, D.J. Imitation and retention of film-mediated aggressive peer and adult models. *Journal of Personality and Social Psychology*, 1965, **2**, 97–100.

Hicks, D.J. Short- and long-term retention of affectively varied modeled behavior. *Psychonomic Science*, 1968, **11**, 369–370.

Himmelweit, H., Oppenheim, A.N., & Vince, P. *Television and the child: An empirical study of the effects of television on the young.* London: Oxford University Press, 1958.

Hinton, J., Seggar, J., Northcott, H., & Fontes, B. Tokenism and improving the imagery of blacks in TV drama and comedy. *Journal of Broadcasting*, 1973, **18**, 423–432.

Hoyt, J.L. Effect of media violence "justification" on aggression. *Journal of Broadcasting*, 1970, **14**, 455–465.

Huston-Stein, A., Fox, S., Greer, D., Watkins, B., & Whitaker, J. The effects of action and violence in television programs on the social behavior and imaginative play of preschool children. In Children's Television Project. *First Annual Report to the Spencer Foundation.* Research Report No. 3. University of Kansas, 1978.

Huston-Stein, A., & Wright, J.C. Children and television: Effects of the medium, its content and its form. *Journal of Research and Development in Education,* 1979, **13** (1), 20–31.

Ingelfinger, F.J. Violence on TV: "An unchecked environmental hazard." *The New England Journal of Medicine,* April 8, 1976, 837–838.

Iskoe, A. "Advertising via famous personalities and the effects on children," Unpublished manuscript, The Wharton School, University of Pennsylvania, 1976.

Jennings, R. *Programming and advertising practices in television directed to children.* Boston: Action for Children's Television, 1970.

Johnson, N. *How to talk back to your television set.* Boston: Little, Brown, & Co., 1967.

Johnston, J., Ettema, J., & Davidson, T. *An evaluation of "Freestyle": A television series designed to reduce sex role stereotypes.* Ann Arbor, MI: Institute for Social Research, 1980.

Kaplan, R.M., & Singer, R.D. Television violence and viewer aggression: A reexamination of the evidence. *Journal of Social Issues,* 1976, **32** (4), 35–70.

Katzman, N. Television soap operas: What's been going on anyway? *Public Opinion Quarterly,* 1972, **36**, 200–212.

Kochnower, J.M., Fracchia, J.F., Rubinstein, E.A., & Sprafkin, J.N. *Television viewing behaviors of emotionally disturbed children: An interview study.* New York: Brookdale International Institute, 1978.

Kumata, H. A decade of teaching by television. In W. Schramm (Ed.), *The impact of educational television.* Urbana: University of Illinois, 1960.

Lange, D.L., Baker, R.K., & Ball, S.J. *Mass media and violence, Vol. XI. A report to the National Commission on the Causes and Prevention of Violence.* Washington, D.C.: U.S. Government Printing Office, 1969.

Lee, S.Y. Status report of public broadcasting, 1980. Washington, D.C.: Corporation for Public Broadcasting, 1981.

Lefkowitz, M.M., Eron, L.D., Walder, L.O., & Huesmann, L.R. Television violence and child aggression: A followup study. In G.A. Comstock and E.A. Rubinstein (Eds.), *Television and social behavior. Vol. III: Television and adolescent aggressiveness.* Washington, D.C.: U.S. Government Printing Office, 1972, 35–135.

Leifer, A.D. Research on the socialization influence of television in the United States. In *Television and socialization processes in the family,* A documentation of the Prix Jeunesse Seminar, 1975.

Leifer, A.D., & Roberts, D.F. Children's response to television violence. In J.P. Murray, E.A. Rubinstein, & G.A. Comstock (Eds.), *Television and social behavior Vol. 2: Television and social learning.* Washington, D.C.: United States Government Printing Office, 1972.

LeRoy, D.J. Who watches public television? *Journal of Communication,* 1980, **30** (3), 157–163.

Lesser, G. *Children and television: Lessons from "Sesame Street."* New York: Vintage Books, 1974.

Levering, R. "TV on trial." *San Francisco Bay Guardian,* August 3, 1978, p. 5.

Levin, E. Censors in action. In B. Cole, (Ed.), *Television today: A close-up view,* New York: Oxford University Press, 1981, 322–329.

Levin, S.R., & Anderson, D.R. The development of attention. *Journal of Communication,* 1976, **26** (2), 126–135.

Levinson, R.M. From Olive Oyl to Sweet Polly Purebread: Sex role stereotypes and televised cartoons. *Journal of Popular Culture,* 1975, **9** (3), 561–572.

Liebert, D.E., Sprafkin, J.N., Liebert, R.M., & Rubinstein, E.A. Effects of television commercial disclaimers on the product expectations of children. *Journal of Communication,* 1977, **27** (1), 118–124.

Liebert, R.M., & Baron, R.A. Short-term effects of televised aggression on children's aggressive behavior. In J.P. Murray, E.A. Rubinstein, & G.A. Comstock (Eds.), *Television and social behavior (Vol. 2): Television and social learning.* Washington, D.C.: United States Government Printing Office, 1972.

Liebert, R.M., Cohen, L.A., Joyce, C., Murrel, S., Nisonoff, L., & Sonnenschein, S. Predisposition revisited. *Journal of Communication,* Summer 1977, 217–221.

Liebert, R.M., & Poulos, R.W. Television and personality development: The socializing effects of an entertainment medium. In A. Davids (Ed.), *Child personality and psychopathology: Current topics, Vol. 2.* New York: John Wiley & Sons, 1975, 61–97.

Liebert, R.M., & Schwartzberg, N.S. Effects of mass media. *Annual Review of Psychology,* 1977, **28,** 141–173.

Liebert, R.M., Sobol, M.P., & Davidson, E.S. Catharsis of aggression among institutionalized boys: Fact or artifact? In G.A. Comstock, E.A. Rubinstein, & J.P. Murray (Eds.), *Television and social behavior. Vol. V: Television's effects: Further explorations.* Washington, D.C.: U.S. Government Printing Office, 1972, 351–358.

Liebert, R.M., Sprafkin, J.N., & Poulos, R.W. Selling cooperation to children. *Proceedings of the 20th Annual Conference of the Advertising Research Foundation,* New York, 1975.

Locker, A. Testimony at the Hearings on Broadcast Advertising and Children before the Subcommittee on Communications of the Committee on Interstate and Foreign Commerce, House of Representatives, July 14, 15, 16, 17, 1975, Washington, D.C.: U.S. Government Printing Office, 345–362.

Logan, B., & Moody, K. (Eds.) *Television awareness training: The viewer's guide.* New York: Media Action Research Center, 1979.

Long, M.L., & Simon, R.J. The roles and statuses of women on children and family TV programs. *Journalism Quarterly,* 1974, **51** (1), 107–110.

Longley, L.D. The FCC's attempt to regulate commercial time. *Journal of Broadcasting,* 1967, **11,** 83–89.

Los Angeles Times, "FCC Delays Decision on Children's TV Programs," December 3, 1980.

Lovaas, O.I. Effect of exposure to symbolic aggression on aggressive behavior. *Child Development,* 1961, **32,** 37–44.

Lyle, J., & Hoffman, H.R. Children's use of television and other media. In E.A. Rubinstein, G.A. Comstock, and J.P. Murray (Eds.), *Television in day-to-day life: Patterns of use.* Washington, D.C.: Government Printing Office, 1972, 129–256.

Mandel, B. "Was TV born guilty?" *San Francisco Examiner,* August 10, 1978, 35.

Mannes, M. Television: The splitting image. *Saturday Review,* November 14, 1970.

Mark, N. Scientists say TV violence DOES influence children. *Birmingham News,* February 7, 1972.

Mayer, M. *About television.* New York: Harper & Row, 1972.

Mays, L., Henderson, E.H., Seidman, S.K., & Steiner, V.S. On meeting real people: An evaluation report on Vegetable Soup: The effects of a multiethnic children's television series on intergroup attitudes of children. Albany, NY: New York State Education Department, 1975. (ERIC Document Reproduction Service No. ED 123 319)

McIntyre, J.J., & Teevan, J.J., Jr. Television violence and deviant behavior. In G.A. Comstock & E.A. Rubinstein (Eds.), *Television and social behavior. Vol. III: Television and adolescent aggressiveness.* Washington, D.C.: U.S. Government Printing Office, 1972, 383–435.

McLeod, J.M., Atkin, C.K., & Chaffee, S.H. Adolescents, parents, and television use: Adolescent self-report measures from Maryland and Wisconsin samples. In G.A. Comstock and E.A. Rubinstein (Eds.), *Television and social behavior. Vol. III: Television and adolescent aggressiveness.* Washington, D.C.: U.S. Government Printing Office, 1972a, 173–238.

McLeod, J.M., Atkin, C.K., & Chaffee, S.H. Adolescents, parents and television use: Self-report and other-report measures from the Wisconsin sample. In G.A. Comstock and E.A. Rubinstein (Eds.), *Television and social behavior. Vol. III: Television and adolescent ag-*

gressiveness. Washington, D.C.: U.S. Government Printing Office, 1972b, 239–313.

McLuhan, M. *Understanding media: The extensions of man.* New York: McGraw-Hill, 1964.

McNeil, J.C. Feminism, femininity, and television series: A content analysis. *Journal of Broadcasting*, 1975, **19** (3), 259–271.

Melody, W.H. *Children's television: The economics of exploitation.* New Haven, Connecticut: Yale University Press, 1973.

Mendelson, G., & Young, M. *Network children's programming: A content analysis of black and minority treatment on children's television.* Newtonville, Ma.: Action for Children's Television, 1972.

Merriam, E. We're teaching our children that violence is fun. *Ladies Home Journal*, October 1964, 44, 49, 52. Reprinted in O. Larsen (Ed.), *Violence in the mass media.* New York: Harper & Row, 1968, 40–47.

Milavsky, J.R., Kessler, R., Stipp, H., Rubens, W.S. Television and aggression: Results of a panel study. Chapter in *Television and behavior: Ten years of scientific progress and implications for the 80's.* Washington, D.C.: U.S. Government Printing Office, 1982, in press.

Milavsky, J.R., Pekowsky, B., & Stipp. H. TV drug advertising and proprietary and illicit drug use among boys. *Public Opinion Quarterly*, 1975–1976, **39**, 457–481.

Milgram, S., & Shotland, R.L. *Television and antisocial behavior: Field experiments.* New York: Academic Press, 1973.

Miller, M.M., & Reeves, B. Linking dramatic TV content to children's occupational sex-role stereotypes. *Journal of Broadcasting*, 1976, **20**, 35–50.

Minow, N.N. *Equal time: The private broadcaster and the public interest.* New York: Atheneum, 1964.

Morgenstern, S. *Inside the TV business.* New York: Sterling Publishing Co., 1979.

Murray, J.P. *Television and youth: 25 years of research and controversy.* Boys Town, Nebraska: Boys Town Center for the Study of Youth Development, 1980.

Murray, J.P., & Kippax, S. From the early window to the late night show: International trends in the study of television's impact on children and adults. In L. Berkowitz (Ed.), *Advances in experimental social psychology.* New York: Academic Press, 1979.

Myrick, H.A., & Keegan, C. Review of 1980 CPB communication research findings. Washington, D.C.: Corporation for Public Broadcasting, 1981.

National Advertising Division. *Children's advertising guidelines*, New York, Council of Better Business Bureaus, 1975. Reprinted in National Science Foundation, *Research on the effects of television advertising on children.* Washington, D.C.: U.S. Government Printing Office, 1977, 201–206.

National Advertising Review Board. "Advertising and Women, A Report on Advertising Portraying or Directed to Women." New York, March 1975.

National Association of Broadcasters *Advertising guidelines: Children's TV advertising.* New York: NAB, January 1, 1976. *Reprinted in Research on the effects of television advertising on children.* Washington, D.C.: National Science Foundation, 1977, 193–201.

National Association of Broadcasters. *The Television Code.* New York: National Association of Broadcasters, July 1981.

National Commission on the Causes and Prevention of Violence, *Commission Statement on Violence in Television Entertainment Programs*, September 23, 1969.

National Educational Television and Radio Center. The content of educational television. In W. Schramm (Ed.), *The impact of educational television.* Urbana, Illinois: University of Illinois Press, 1960.

National Federation for Decency. *Sex on television.* Tupelo, Mississippi, 1977.

National PTA, Press Release. "National PTA Names Best and Worst TV Shows with New Program Guide." February 15, 1978.

National Science Foundation. *Research on the effects of television advertising on children: A review of the literature and recommendations for future research.* Washington, D.C.: National Science Foundation, 1977.

Nelson, J.P., Gelfand, D.M., & Hartmann, D.P. Children's aggression following competition and exposure to an aggressive model. *Child Development*, 1969, **40**, 1085–1097.

Newcomb, A.F., & Collins, W.A. Children's comprehension of family role portrayals in televised dramas: Effects of socioeconomic status, ethnicity, and age. *Developmental Psychology*, 1979, **15** (4), 417–423.

News from NAACP, July 19, 1951. Cited in *Window dressing on the set: Women and minorities in television*. U.S. Commission on Civil Rights, 1977.

Newsday. Pull plug on TV violence: AMA asks 10 big firms. February 7, 1977.

Newsweek. The last drag. January 4, 1971, 65.

Newsweek. Violence revisited. March 6, 1972, 55–56.

Newsweek. Sex and TV. February 20, 1978, 54–61.

Newsweek. P & G's Move in a 'Holy War.' June 29, 1981, 60.

O'Bryan, K.G. The teaching face: A historical perspective. Chapter in E.L. Palmer and A. Dorr (Eds.), *Children and the faces of television: Teaching, violence, selling*. New York: Academic Press, 1980.

Ormiston, L.H., & Williams, S. Saturday children's programming in San Francisco, California: An analysis of the presentation of racial and cultural groups. Prepared by the Committee on Children's Television, Inc., San Francisco, California, 1973.

Paisley, M.B. *Social policy research and the realities of the system: Violence done to TV research*. Institute of Communication Research: Stanford University, 1972.

Palmer, E.L., & McDowell, C.N. Program/commercial separators in children's television programming. *Journal of Communication*, 1979, **29** (3), 197–201.

Parke, R.D., Berkowitz, L., Leyens, J.P., West, S.G., & Sebastian, R.J. Some effects of violent and nonviolent movies on the behavior of juvenile delinquents. In *Advances in Experimental Social Psychology*, Vol. 10. New York: Academic Press, 1977.

Paulson, F.L., McDonald, D.L., & Whittlemore, S.L. "An evaluation of *Sesame Street* programming designed to teach cooperative behavior." Monmouth, Oregon: Teaching Research, 1972.

Pingree, S., & Hawkins, R. U.S. programs on Australian television: The cultivation effect. *Journal of Communication*, 1981, **31** (1), 97–105.

Poulos, R.W. Unintentional negative effects of good commercials on children: A case study. Hearings before the Subcommittee on Communications, Committee on Interstate and Foreign Commerce, U.S. House of Representatives, July 1975, 335–338.

Poulos, R.W., Harvey, S.E., & Liebert, R.M. Saturday morning television: A profile of the 1974–75 children's season. *Psychological Reports*, 1976, **39**, 1047–1057.

Rabinovitch, M.S., McLean, M.S., Jr., Markham, J.W., & Talbott, A.D. Children's violence perception as a function of television violence. In G.A. Comstock, E.A. Rubinstein, and J.P. Murray (Eds.), *Television and social behavior, Vol. 5. Television's effects: Further explorations*. Washington, D.C.: United States Government Printing Office, 1972.

Rivers, C. What sort of behavior control should TV impose on children: Violence or harmony? *New York Times*, August 18, 1974.

Roberts, C. The portrayal of blacks on network television. *Journal of Broadcasting*, 1970, **15**, 45–53.

Roberts, D.F., Christenson, P., Gibson, W.A., Mooser, L., & Goldberg, M.E. Developing discriminating consumers. *Journal of Communication*, 1980, **30** (3), 94–105.

Roberts, D.F., Herold, C., Hornby, M., King, S., Sterne, D., Whiteley, S., & Silverman, T. Earth's a big blue marble: A report on the impact of a children's television series on children's opinions. Manuscript, Stanford University, 1974.

Roberts, E.J., & Holt, S.A. TV's sexual lessons. In J. Fireman (Ed.), *The television book*. New York: Workman Publishing Company, 1977.

Roberts, E.J., Kline, D., & Gagnon, J. *Family life and sexual learning*. Cambridge, Mass. 1978.

Robertson, T.S., & Rossiter, J.R. Children and commercial persuasion: An attribution theory analysis. *Journal of Consumer Research*, 1974, **1** (1), 13–20.

Robinson, J.P. Television's impact on everyday life: Some cross-national evidence. In E.A. Rubinstein, G.A. Comstock, and J.P. Murray (Eds.), *Television and social behavior. Vol. IV: Television in day-to-day life: Patterns of use.* Washington, D.C.: U.S. Government Printing Office, 1972, 410–431.

Robinson, J.P., & Bachman, J.G. Television viewing habits and aggression. In G.A. Comstock and E.A. Rubinstein (Eds.), *Television and social behavior. Vol. III: Television and adolescent aggressiveness.* Washington, D.C.: U.S. Government Printing Office, 1972, 372–382.

Rosenkrans, M.A., & Hartup, W.W. Imitative influences of consistent and inconsistent response consequences to a model on aggressive behavior in children. *Journal of Personality and Social Psychology*, 1967, **7**, 429–434.

Rothenberg, M. Effect of television violence on children and youth. *Journal of the American Medical Association*, 1975, **234**, 1043–1046.

Rowland, W.D., Jr. The federal regulatory and policymaking process. *Journal of Communication*, 1980, **30** (3), 139–149.

Rubinstein, E.A., Fracchia, J.F., Kochnower, J.M., & Sprafkin, J.N. *Television viewing behaviors of mental patients: A survey of Psychiatric centers in New York State.* New York: Brookdale International Institute, 1977.

Rubinstein, E.A., Liebert, R.M., Neale, J.M., & Poulos, R.W. *Assessing television's influence on children's prosocial behavior.* New York: Brookdale International Institute, 1974.

Rushnell, S.D. Nonprime time programming. In Eastman, Head, Klein (Eds.), *Strategies for winning television and radio audiences.* Belmont, California: Wadsworth Publishing Company, 1981.

Rushton, J.P. Effects of television and film material on the prosocial behavior of children. In L. Berkowitz (Ed.), *Advances in experimental social psychology.* New York: Academic Press, 1979.

Ryan, M. "Family Viewing Time: Has it Passed the Test?" *TV Guide*, June 5, 1976.

Salomon, G. Cognitive skill learning across cultures. *Journal of Communication*, 1976, **26** (2), 138–144.

Salomon, G. *Interaction of media, cognition, and learning.* San Francisco: Jossey-Bass Publishers, 1979.

Sarasota Journal. "Actor Savalas Won't Testify," October 5, 1977.

Savitsky, J.C., Rogers, R.W., Izard, C.E., & Liebert, R.M. Role of frustration and anger in the imitation of filmed aggression against a human victim. *Psychological Reports*, 1971, **29**, 807–810.

Schramm, W. The audiences of educational television. In W. Schramm (Ed.), *The impact of educational television.* Urbana, Illinois: University of Illinois Press, 1960.

Schramm, W. What we know about learning from instructional television. In *Educational television: The next ten years.* Stanford, California: Institute for Communication Research, 1962.

Schramm, W., Lyle, J., & Parker, E.B. *Television in the lives of our children.* Stanford: Stanford University Press, 1961.

Schuetz, S., & Sprafkin, J.N. Spot messages appearing within Saturday morning television programs: A content analysis. Chapter in G. Tuchman, A.K. Daniels, & J. Benet (Eds.), *Home and hearth: Images of women in the mass media.* New York: Oxford University Press, 1978, 69–77.

Schuetz, S., & Sprafkin, J.N. Portrayal of prosocial and aggressive behaviors in children's TV commercials. *Journal of Broadcasting*, 1979, **23** (1), 33–40.

Seggar, J.F. Imagery of women in television drama: 1974. *Journal of Broadcasting*, 1975, **19** (3), 273–282.

Sharaga, S. The effect of television advertising on children's nutrition attitudes, nutrition knowledge, and eating habits. Unpublished doctoral dissertation, Cornell University, New York, 1974.

Sheikh, A.A., Prasad, V.K., & Rao, T.R. Children's TV commercials: A review of research. *Journal of Communication*, 1974, **24** (4), 126–136.

Siegel, A.E. Film-mediated fantasy aggression and strength of aggressive drive. *Child Development*, 1956, **27**, 365–378.

Signorielli, N., Gross, L., & Morgan, M. Violence in television programs: Ten years later. In *Television and behavior: Ten years of scientific progress and implications for the 80's*. Washington, D.C.: U.S. Government Printing Office, 1982, in press.

Silverman, L.T. *The effects of television programming on the prosocial behavior of preschool children*. Research report to the National Association of Broadcasters, 1976.

Silverman, L.T., & Sprafkin, J.N. The effects of *Sesame Street's* prosocial spots on cooperative play between young children. *Journal of Broadcasting*, 1980, **24**, 135–147.(a)

Silverman, L.T., and Sprafkin, J.N. Adolescents' reactions to televised sexual innuendos. Report prepared for the American Broadcasting Companies, Inc., April 1980.(b)

Silverman, L.T., Sprafkin, J.N., & Rubinstein, E.A. Physical contact and sexual behavior on prime-time TV. *Journal of Communication*, 1979, **29**, 33–43.

Singer, D.G., & Singer, J.L. Television viewing and aggressive behavior in preschool children: A field study. *Forensic Psychology & Psychiatry*, 1980, **347**, 289–303.

Singer, D.G., Zuckerman, D.M., & Singer, J.L. Helping elementary school children learn about TV. *Journal of Communication*, 1980, **30** (3), 84–93.

Smythe, D. Reality as presented by television. *Public Opinion Quarterly*, 1954, **18**, 143–156.

Somers, A. Violence, television and the health of American youth. *The New England Journal of Medicine*, 1976, **294**, 811–817.

Sprafkin, J.N., Liebert, R.M., & Poulos, R.W. Effects of a prosocial televised example on children's helping. *Journal of Experimental Child Psychology*, 1975, **20**, 119–126.

Sprafkin, J.N., & Rubinstein, E.A. A field correlational study of children's television viewing habits and prosocial behavior. *Journal of Broadcasting*, 1979, **23**, 265–276.

Sprafkin, J.N., & Rubinstein, E.A. Using television to improve the social behavior of institutionalized children. *Prevention in Human Services*, 1982, in press.

Sprafkin, J.N., Rubinstein, E.A., & Stone, A. *A Content analysis of four television diets*. New York: Brookdale International Institute, 1977.

Sprafkin, J.N., Silverman, L.T., & Rubinstein, E.A. *Public reactions to sex on television*. New York: Brookdale International Institute, 1979.

Sprafkin, J.N., & Silverman, L.T. Update: Physically intimate and sexual behavior on prime-time television: 1978–79. *Journal of Communication*, 1981, **31** (1), 34–40.

Sprafkin, J.N., Silverman, L.T., & Rubinstein, E.A. Reactions to sex on television: An exploratory study. *Public Opinion Quarterly*, 1980, **44**, 303–315.

Stein, A.H., & Friedrich, L.K., Television content and young children's behavior. In J.P. Murray, E.A. Rubinstein, & G.A. Comstock (Eds.), *Television and social behavior. Vol. II: Television and social learning*. Washington, D.C.: U.S. Government Printing Office, 1972, 202–317.

Stein, G.M., & Bryan, J.G. The effect of a television model upon rule adoption behavior of children. *Child Development*, 1972, **43**, 268–273.

Steinberg, C.S. *TV Facts*. New York: Facts on File, Inc., 1980.

Steiner, G.A. *The people look at television*. New York: Alfred A. Knopf, 1963.

Steinfeld, J.L. *TV violence is harmful. Readers Digest*, 1973, **4**, 37–45.

Sterling, C.H., & Haight, T.R. *The mass media: Aspen Institute guide to communication industry trends*. New York: Praeger Publishers, 1978.

Sternglanz, S.H., & Serbin, L.A. Sex role stereotyping in children's television programs. *Developmental Psychology*, 1974, **10** (5), 710–715.

Steuer, F.B., Applefield, J.M., & Smith, R. Televised aggression and the interpersonal aggression of preschool children. *Journal of Experimental Child Psychology*, 1971, **11**, 442–447.

Stookey, A., & Waz, J. The NAB: Not for all broadcasters. *Access*, April 7, 1980, 1.

Tan, A.S. TV beauty ads and role expectations of adolescent female viewers. *Journalism Quarterly*, 1979, **56**, 283–288.

Tannenbaum, P.H. Emotional arousal as a mediator of communication effects. *Technical reports of the Commission on Obscenity and Pornography*, Vol. 8. Washington, D.C.: U.S. Government Printing Office, 1971.

Tannenbaum, P.H. Entertainment as vicarious emotional experience. In P.H. Tannenbaum (Ed.), *The entertainment functions of television*. Hillside, New Jersey: Lawrence Erlbaum Associates, 1980.

Tedesco, N.S. Patterns in prime time. *Journal of Communications*, 1974, **24**, 118–124.

Television Information Office. *ABC's of radio and television*. New York: Television Information Office, 1981.

Thomas, M.H., & Drabman, R.S. Effects of television violence on expectations of others' aggression. Presented at the Annual Convention of the *American Psychological Association*, San Francisco, California, August, 1977.

Time. If the eye offend thee. September 26, 1977, 53.(a)

Time. Did TV make him do it? A young killer — and television — go on trial for murder. October 10, 1977, 87–88.(b)

Time. Striving to shake up Jell-o. December 15, 1980, 23–24.

Time. Another kind of ratings war: The campaign to take the sex and violence out of television. July 6, 1981, 17–19.(a)

Time. Fizzled boycott: Sponsors still face threat. July 31, 1981, 63.(b)

Turow, J. Advising and ordering: Day time, prime time. *Journal of Communication*, 1974, **24** (2), 138–141.

TV Bureau of Advertising. *TV Basics 24: Report on the scope and dimensions of TV today*. New York, 1980.

United Methodist Women's Television Monitoring Project. *Sex role stereotyping in prime time television*. Women's Division, Board of Global Ministries, United Methodist Church, March, 1976.

United States Commission on Civil Rights. *Window dressing on the set: Women and minorities in television*. Washington, D.C.: U.S. Government Printing Office, 1977.

United States Commission on Civil Rights. *Window dressing on the set: An update*. Washington, D.C.: U.S. Government Printing Office, 1979.

U.S. News & World Report, November 9, 1964, 49–50. Reprinted in O.N. Larsen (Ed.), *Violence and the mass media*. New York: Harper & Row, 1968, 210–214.

United States Senate, Committee on the Judiciary. Television and juvenile delinquency. *Investigation of Juvenile Delinquency in the United States*, 84th Congress, 2nd session, January 16, 1956, Report No. 1466.

United States Senate, *Effects on young people of violence and crime portrayals on television*. Part 10, Hearings before the Subcommittee to Investigate Juvenile Delinquency, Committee on the Judiciary, 87th Congress, 1961.

United States Senate, Subcommittee to Investigate Juvenile Delinquency. *Hearings on Juvenile Delinquency*. Part 16. *Effects on young people of violence and crime portrayed on television*. 88th Congress, 2nd session, July 30, 1964. Washington, D.C.: United States Government Printing Office, 1965.

United States Senate, Subcommittee on Communication. Federal Communications Commission policy matters and television programming (Part 2). Washington, D.C.: U.S. Government Printing Office, 1969.

United States Senate. Hearings before the subcommittee on Communications of the Committee on Commerce, March 1972.

Walters, R.H., & Thomas, E.L. Enhancement of punitiveness by visual and audiovisual displays. *Canadian Journal of Psychology*, 1963, **17**, 244–255.

Walters, R.H. & Willows, D.C. Imitative behavior of disturbed and nondisturbed children following exposure to aggressive and nonaggressive models. *Child Development*, 1968, **39**, 79–89.

Ward, S., Levinson, D., & Wackman, D. Children's attention to television advertising. In E.A. Rubinstein, G.A. Comstock, & J.P. Murray (Eds.), *Television and social behavior. Vol. IV: Television in day-to-day life: Patterns of use.* Washington, D.C.: U.S. Government Printing Office, 1972, 491–515.

Ward, S., Reale, G., & Levinson, D. Children's perceptions, explanations, and judgments of television advertising: A further exploration. In E.A. Rubinstein, G.A. Comstock, & J.P. Murray (Eds.), *Television and social behavior. Vol. IV: Television in day-to-day life: Patterns of use.* Washington, D.C.: U.S. Government Printing Office, 1972, 468–490.

Ward, S., & Wackman, D. Television advertising and intrafamily influence: Children's purchase influence attempts and parental yielding. In E.A. Rubinstein, G.A. Comstock, & J.P. Murray (Eds.), *Television and social behavior. Vol. IV: Television in day-to-day life: Patterns of use.* Washington, D.C.: U.S. Government Printing Office, 1972, 516–525.

Ward, S., Wackman, D., & Wartella, E. *How children learn to buy: The development of consumer information-processing skills.* Beverly Hills, CA: Sage, 1977.

Ward, S., & Wackman, D.B. Children's information processing of television advertising. In P. Clarke (Ed.), *New models for mass communication research.* Sage annual review of communication research. Beverly Hills, CA: Sage Publications, 1973.

Wells, W.D. Television and aggression: A replication of an experimental field study. University of Chicago, 1972. (Mimeographed abstract.)

White, M.E. Mom, Why's the TV Set Sweating? *New York Times*, March 29, 1978.

Whiteside, T. Annals of advertising. *The New Yorker*, December 19, 1970, 42–48ff.

Winick, M.P., & Winick, C. *The television experience: What children see.* Beverly Hills, CA: Sage Publications, 1979.

Wispé, L.G. Positive forms of social behavior: An overview. *Journal of Social Issues*, 1972, **28** (3), 1–19.

Wolf, T.M. A developmental investigation of televised modeled verbalizations of resistance to deviation. *Developmental Psychology*, 1972, **6**, 537.

Women on Words and Images. *Channeling children: Sex stereotyping on prime time TV.* Princeton, New Jersey: Women on Words and Images, 1975.

Zillmann, D. Emotional arousal as a factor in communication—mediated aggressive behavior. Unpublished doctoral dissertation, University of Pennsylvania, 1969.

Zuckerman, P., Ziegler, M., & Stevenson, H.W. Children's viewing of television and recognition memory of commercials. *Child Development*, 1978, **49**, 96–104.

Name Index

Subject Index

About the Authors

Robert M. Liebert (Ph.D., Stanford University) is Professor of Psychology and Psychiatry, State University of New York at Stony Brook, New York. A principal investigator and overview writer for the National Institute of Mental Health's program on Television and Social Behavior, Dr. Liebert has published widely on children's social development. He has coauthored other books. including *Personality*, *Science and Behavior*, and *Developmental Psychology*.

Joyce N. Sprafkin (Ph.D., State University of New York at Stony Brook) is the director of the Laboratory of Communication at Long Island Research Institute, State University of New York at Stony Brook, New York. Dr. Sprafkin has published numerous articles describing her research on television's effects on children. She has also coedited R_x *Television: Enhancing the Preventive Impact of TV*.

Emily S. Davidson (Ph.D., State University of New York at Stony Brook) is Associate Professor of Psychology at Texas A & M University. Her research is in the area of observational learning, particularly learning of stereotypes and achievement standards.

Pergamon General Psychology Series

Editors: Arnold P. Goldstein, Syracuse University
Leonard Krasner, SUNY at Stony Brook